T H E
NATIONAL SYMPHONY ORCHESTRA
AT THE KENNEDY CENTER

COOK BOOK

Приятного аппетита !

М. Ростропович

W A S H I N G T O N , D. C.

The National Symphony Orchestra travels throughout the United States and around the world. The selection of our recipes reflects the spirit of those journeys. It is with great pleasure that we invite you to share these culinary treats.

PATTY PERKINS ANDRINGA, GENERAL CHAIRMAN
LONIE LANDFIELD, FOOD EDITOR
ANNE B. KEISER, PUBLISHING EDITOR
BARRY E. HUBER, GRAPHIC DESIGNER

THE COMMITTEE

Kathryn C. Avery
Carol Becker
Pam Kloman
Jane Lehrman
Norma McCaig
David Messing
Beth Montgomery
Pamela Powers
Mary Ann & Stuart Scott

Jane Stein
Francine & Wayne Swift
Noelle Vitt
Maria Weiss
Carlene Weitzman
Dorothy Wheeler
Martha Wilson
Telle Zeiler
George Ziener

A SPECIAL THANK YOU

Jacqueline Anderson
Merithew H. Benington
Helene Berman
Albert Beveridge, III
Kate Burdick
Virginia Anne Delfosse
Fossy Fenwick
Laurie G. Firestone
Ike & Bea Friedlander
Linda Font
Mary Anne Goley
Donald Havas
Sally Hedrick
Gwen Holmes
Stephen J. Kelin

Carol Sue Lebbin
JoAnn Mason
Louise Millikan
Sheila O'Dell
Daphne O'Meara
Barbara Phillips
Adel Sanchez
Susan P. Schmalbach
Jean Searle
Theresa H. Shingler
Starr Sommer
Dorothy Stahl
Cathy Tennyson
Ruth Ann Wilson
The NSO Staff

Silhouette drawings of musicians by Carol Wisdom

1983 Printing, 10,000 copies.   1984 Revised Printing, 10,000 copies.

1987 Printing, 10,000 copies.

ISBN 0-9613672-0-2   Library of Congress Catalog Card Number 84-82184

C O N T E N T S

APPETIZERS

Liver and Prune Terrine

Makes 1 loaf

1 pound chicken or
 pork liver
¾ pound bacon
¼ pound (12–14) prunes,
 soaked and pitted
2 tablespoons rum or
 brandy
2 teaspoons each salt
 and freshly ground
 pepper, to taste
 A pinch of allspice,
 nutmeg, or thyme

Purée liver and rum together. Chop prunes and bacon. Prunes and bacon should stay coarse.

Pack in terrine, cover with foil and lid and set in another pan with 2 inches of water. Bake for 1¾ hours at 325°. Let cool in pan. Unmold.

Jane Stein

Chicken Liver Pâté in Aspic

Serves 12

ASPIC

2 teaspoons unflavored gelatin
1 cup sherry
2 tablespoons sugar
4 tablespoons water
½ teaspoon dried tarragon, crumbled

PÂTÉ

1 pound chicken livers
1 cup milk
¼ cup Cognac
1¼ cups (2½ sticks) butter at room temperature
2 cups sliced onion
¼ cup bourbon
¼ cup whipping cream
1¼ teaspoons salt
1 teaspoon fresh lemon juice

Butter an 8 × 4-inch loaf pan generously and set aside.

Dissolve gelatin in a small bowl with ¼ cup sherry. Combine sugar and water in a saucepan over medium-high heat and stir until sugar is dissolved. Continue cooking until mixture is a dark, caramel color (about 8 to 10 minutes). Whisk in remaining ¾ cup sherry and tarragon.

Reduce heat under saucepan and simmer for about 2 minutes. Add gelatin, stirring until dissolved.

Strain through a sieve or damp cheesecloth to remove tarragon crumbs into prepared loaf pan, covering bottom ⅛ inch to ¼ inch. Chill pan to set aspic.

Combine livers, milk, and Cognac in a bowl and let soak for 1 hour.

Melt ½ cup of butter in a large skillet over medium heat. Add sliced onions and sauté until browned. Using a slotted spoon, transfer onion mixture to a food processor (fitted with the steel blade) or blender.

Drain livers, discarding liquid. Return skillet to medium-high heat. Sauté livers until they are just pink (about 10 to 12 minutes). Add to onion mixture in processor or blender.

Reduce heat under skillet to medium; add bourbon and cook, scraping up any browned bits. Add bourbon and ¼ cup cream to liver mixture; purée until smooth. Let stand until it has cooled to lukewarm.

Beat remaining ¾ cup butter in a medium bowl until creamy. With food processor or blender running, add butter gradually to liver mixture, blending well. Add salt and lemon juice. Pour into pan over aspic, smoothing on top. Chill in refrigerator.

To serve, run a sharp knife around inside of pan, dip pan briefly into hot water, and invert pâté onto a serving platter. Garnish with parsley and serve with thinly sliced French bread or an assortment of crackers.

William J. Wooby

Easy Liver Pâté

Serves 24

1 pound liverwurst
½ stick butter, softened
3 ounces cream cheese
¼ cup parsley, minced
¼ cup onion, minced
¼ cup brandy
½ teaspoon curry powder

Beat liverwurst until fluffy; add butter and cream cheese. With beater, add remaining ingredients.
Store in refrigerator overnight before serving.

Ruth Thompson

Pork, Ham, and Pistachio Pâté

Serves approximately 10

6 slices bacon
¼ pound pistachios, shelled
1 pound pork sausage
2 teaspoons thyme
2 teaspoons salt
1 teaspoon freshly ground pepper
4 slices ham
¾ pound ground lean pork
2 laurel or bay leaves

"If you can make a meatloaf, then you can make a pâté!"

Line a terrine or 9 × 5-inch loaf pan with bacon. Blanch pistachios by pouring boiling, salted water over them, allowing them to sit in water briefly. Remove skins.
Start at bottom of pan and put in half the pork sausage, pressing down. Sprinkle half pistachios over sausage and ⅓ of thyme, salt, and pepper. Next add a slice of ham, then all ground, lean pork. Sprinkle with more thyme, salt, and pepper. Add another layer of ham, and rest of pistachios; finish with a layer of sausage. Sprinkle remaining thyme, salt, and pepper on top. Decorate with 2 laurel or bay leaves and cover pâté with strips of bacon.
Place terrine in hot water bath in large rectangular pan and bake, covered, in a 400° oven for 1 to 1½ hours. Remove from oven and take off lid or aluminum foil. Weight down with a heavy plate and can of tuna so that pâté will settle into fat in terrine. Allow to cool. Place in refrigerator for 24 to 48 hours before serving.

William J. Wooby

Ham Mousse with Cumberland Sauce

Serves 10 to 12 as an hors d'oeuvre and fewer as a main dish.
Doubles superbly.

A recipe that comes from the famous Goldener Hirsch in Salzburg, with modifications.

Mousse

2 cups diced ham
2 packages plain gelatin
½ cup cold chicken stock or broth
3 egg yolks
1½ cups heavy cream
¼ cup sherry
1 cup whipped cream
Black pepper, coarsely ground

Cumberland Sauce

6 ounces currant jelly
2 tablespoons confectioners sugar
1 teaspoon fresh horseradish
Juice and rind of 2 lemons
Juice and rind of 1 orange

Soften gelatin in cold stock. Dissolve in hot stock. Beat egg yolks, add heavy cream and beat until blended. Cook slowly, stirring faithfully until it begins to thicken a bit. Add gelatin mixture. Put some of chopped ham in blender with enough liquid so that it blends easily.

Do this until all ham is mixed with liquid. Add sherry and pepper. (If ham is not salty, you may want to add a little salt at this point.) Chill until mixture begins to firm but not set. Fold in whipped cream and pour into mold. (Rinse mold with cold water first).

Cumberland Sauce

Place ingredients in a blender and blend well. Start tasting. You may like more sugar, more horseradish, more jelly. Suit yourself. Cool it. Serve the mousse with the sauce in a side dish and let everyone pour his own.

Tastes best with a fine champagne.

Paul Hume

Caviar Mousse

Serves 20

6 ounces red caviar
¼ cup chopped parsley
1 tablespoon grated onion
1 teaspoon grated lemon rind
1 pint sour cream
1 cup heavy cream
1 envelope gelatin
¼ cup water
   Freshly ground pepper

The colors are beautiful. It is especially appropriate for Christmas.

In a large bowl combine caviar, parsley, onion and lemon peel. Stir sour cream into this mixture.

In a separate bowl whip heavy cream. Sprinkle gelatin over water in a saucepan over low heat until gelatin is dissolved (1 to 2 minutes). Stir gelatin into caviar mixture.

Fold into whipped cream and add pepper to taste. Pour mixture into a buttered 4-cup mold. Chill several hours. Unmold onto lettuce. Serve with melba rounds or pumpernickel bread.

Rita Meyer

Taramosalata
Red Caviar Sauce

Makes 4 cups

½ cup taramas (roe)
1½ cups bread, soaked in water and drained
1½ cups olive oil
1 cup lemon juice
1 small onion, finely chopped
   Parsley or black olives, for garnish

In food processor, add ingredients slowly and process until mixture forms a thick, smooth paste. Garnish with parsley or black olives. Serve with pita bread.

Mrs. Andrew Jacovides
Wife of the Ambassador of Cyprus

Crab Jeanne

Serves 20

1 pound crabmeat, backfin
16 ounces cream cheese
1½ tablespoons Worcestershire sauce
2 tablespoons mayonnaise
1½ teaspoons lemon juice
1 small onion, grated
10 ounces chili sauce
Parsley

With food processor or electric mixer, blend cream cheese, mayonnaise, Worcestershire sauce, lemon juice and onion. Put on a serving tray with a lip and chill for several hours.

Just before serving, pour chili sauce over cheese mixture and top with crabmeat and parsley. Serve with melba rounds or unflavored cheese crackers.

Jeanne Vander Myde

Ike's Chopped Herring

Serves 8 as hors d'oeuvre
Serves 4 as first course

12-ounce jar herring pieces with onion (in wine sauce)
2 slices jewish rye or pumpernickel bread
½ large onion
1 large stalk celery
½ medium carrot, scraped
½ green pepper
1 medium apple, peeled and cored
2 hard-boiled eggs
Sugar and freshly ground pepper to taste

Drain herring, reserving juice and onions. Soak bread in herring juice.

In a food processor with steel blade in place, chop onions from herring jar, ½ onion, celery, green pepper, carrot, and apple, *only until coarsely chopped.*

Add bread, herring, eggs, and continue processing until finely chopped. If too dry, add some herring juice; if too wet, add some crackers. Season with sugar and pepper to taste. Do not add salt.

Chill well and serve with crackers as an hors d'oeuvre or on lettuce, garnished with cherry tomatoes, black or green olives as a first course.

Ike Friedlander

Caviar Hors d'Oeuvre

Serves 8 to 10

8 hard-boiled eggs
1 stick melted sweet
   butter
1 pint sour cream
2 jars lumpfish caviar
1 small onion, minced

Chop hard-boiled eggs in food processor. Add melted butter and press mixture into 8½ or 9-inch pie plate. Freeze until hardened.

Remove from freezer and cover with sour cream. Return to freezer for about 2 hours or more.

Mix two jars of caviar with minced onion and spread over hardened egg and sour cream mixture.

Refrigerate until ready to serve. Can be served with slices of pumpernickel bread or matzoh or water biscuits.

Robert and Marion Merrill

Crab Bostwick

Serves 8 to 10

1 pound crabmeat
   (backfin or lump)
½ cup mayonnaise
2 tablespoons whipping
   cream
2 tablespoons chili
   sauce
½ teaspoon
   Worcestershire sauce
2 tablespoons chives
1 tablespoon lemon
   juice
2 tablespoons chopped
   green pepper
   Salt and freshly
   ground pepper to
   taste

Mix all dressing ingredients. Sort through crabmeat to remove any shell. Toss in crabmeat being careful to maintain lumps.

Serve with Bremer wafers or as a luncheon or supper dish with tomatoes or avocados.

Mrs. Phillip D. Bostwick

Swedish Herring Salad

Serves 6 to 8

13-ounce jar herring in
  wine sauce, Swedish
  style
½ yellow or green unpeeled
  apple, diced
½ red unpeeled apple,
  diced
2 small spring onions,
  minced
⅓ cup mayonnaise
⅓ cup sour cream

Drain herring and pat dry.
  Mix all ingredients together and chill to allow flavors
to blend. Serve with crackers.

Carlene Weitzman

Salmon Mousse with Dill Sauce

Serves 4 to 6

2 envelopes unflavored
  gelatin
⅓ cup water
2 tablespoons lemon
  juice
1 cup boiling water
2 7½-ounce cans pink
  salmon (drained,
  boned, and skinned)
½ cup half and half
½ cup mayonnaise
1 small onion,
  quartered

DILL SAUCE
1 cup sour cream
1 cup mayonnaise
2 tablespoons lemon
  juice
2 tablespoons chopped
  fresh dill
1 tablespoon chopped
  capers

In container of electric blender, sprinkle gelatin over
water and lemon juice and let stand 5 minutes. Add
boiling water and whirl about 30 seconds, until smooth.
  Add salmon, mayonnaise, half and half, and onion;
whirl again until smooth.
  Pour into an oiled mold, cover with plastic wrap, and
chill until set (about 3 hours or overnight).
  Combine ingredients for dill sauce and chill. Serve
with mousse.
  For a variation of the mousse, dill may be added
directly to the mousse and omitted from sauce. The same
is true of the capers.

Robert and Marion Merrill

Shrimp-Dill Mold

Serves 20 to 24

2 envelopes unflavored
  gelatin
1½ cups tomato juice
2 tablespoons lemon
  juice
1 cup chili sauce
½ teaspoon Tabasco
1 teaspoon Worcestershire
  sauce

1 tablespoon or more
  fresh dill
1 pint sour cream
2 cups (¾ pound)
  shrimp, cooked,
  shelled, and chopped

Sprinkle gelatin over tomato juice in saucepan. Place over moderate heat and stir constantly until dissolved, 2 to 3 minutes. Remove from heat and stir in next 5 ingredients. When mixture is cool, add sour cream and beat until smooth. Stir in shrimp and turn into 5-cup mold.

Chill until firm. Unmold. If desired, a garnish of whole shrimp and sprigs of dill may be added.

Mrs. Lloyd W. Swift

Oeufs en Gelée

Serves 6

6 eggs
3 packages gelatin
3 cups chicken broth
¼ cup tarragon vinegar
¼ cup water
  Chives
  Parsley
  Salt
  Freshly ground
  pepper

Poach 6 eggs. Chill in refrigerator.

Soak 3 packages of gelatin in ¼ cup cold water plus ¼ cup tarragon vinegar. Mix into gelatin 3 cups boiling chicken broth, canned or homemade, until gelatin is dissolved. Add salt and pepper to taste.

Fill baking dish (casserole, pyrex, etc.) with ½ of broth mixture and sprinkle with chopped chives and chill. When moderately firm (1 hour or so), arrange eggs on top of jellied broth, and pour remaining cool broth on top. Sprinkle chopped parsley on top and chill until firm.

Serve with any dressing, such as Russian, caper, hollandaise, or sour cream and caviar.

Mrs. Marvin Braverman

Turtle Creek Avocado Cocktail

Serves 2 to 4 per avocado

Avocados, scooped into
  balls
Lemon juice
Thousand Island dressing
Bacon
Lettuce, for garnish

Make desired size balls with melon scoop.
   On lettuce, shredded or leaf, place avocado balls. Squeeze a few drops of lemon juice on them. Cover with Thousand Island dressing and top with crisp, crumbled bacon.

Cecilia DeGolyer McGhee

Mom's Italian Appetizer

Serves 8 to 10

½ cup olive or salad oil
2 cloves garlic, peeled
   and cut in half
4–5 stalks celery
2 carrots
3 pickled peppers
½ pound fresh green
   beans or a 9-ounce
   package of frozen
   green beans
1 small jar capers
3 crisp dill pickles
5 large ripe olives

¼ pound green Sicilian
   olives, pitted
¼ cup white vinegar
   Salt and freshly
   ground pepper to
   taste
1 tablespoon oregano
   Anchovies, pimentos,
   one jar marinated
   artichoke hearts
½ jar pickled eggplant

Marinate garlic in oil overnight. Before using, remove garlic. Cook green beans; do not overcook. They should be crisp.
   Cut all vegetables in chunks except for carrots which should be shaved or sliced very thin. With paper towels, remove moisture from vegetables. Place all vegetables in large mixing bowl *except* pimentos, artichokes, and ripe olives. Add salt, pepper, and oregano; also oil and vinegar. Mix well. Before serving, decorate with anchovies, pimentos, artichokes, and black olives. Serve on lettuce leaves.

You can add or subtract ingredients, depending on how many people you wish to serve. This appetizer keeps well when refrigerated in a covered container.

Frank J. Sinatra
Former NSO Member

Layered Nacho Dip

Makes about 8 cups

16-ounce can refried
  beans
package Taco
  seasoning mix
6-ounce frozen
  avocado dip thawed
8-ounce carton sour
  cream
4½ ounce can ripe
  olives, chopped
2 large tomatoes, diced
1 small onion,
  chopped
4-ounce can green
  chiles, chopped
1½ cups Monterey Jack
  cheese, grated

Combine beans and Taco mix; spread into $12 \times 8 \times 2$-inch dish.

Layer remaining ingredients as follows: avocado dip, sour cream, olives, tomatoes, onion, green chiles, and cheese on top.

Serve with tostitos.

Bernice Feinstein

Linda's Curry Dip

Makes 1 pint

1 pint mayonnaise
3 tablespoons chili
  sauce
1 tablespoon curry
  powder
1 tablespoon
  Worcestershire sauce
¼ teaspoon each salt and
  freshly ground pepper

Blend all ingredients and allow to stand in refrigerator for 1 hour.

Serve with raw carrots, cauliflower, mushrooms, celery, etc.

Suzanne J. Rucker

Walnut Brie Wheel

Serves 18 to 20

2-pound wheel of Brie
½ cup walnuts, chopped
1 pound whipped
   butter, softened

Mix walnuts with softened butter. While Brie is still hard, slice in 2 layers and fill with walnut filling. Serve Brie "sandwiches" at room temperature with crackers.

Mrs. A. A. Sommer, Jr.

Strawberry and Cheese Ring

Serves 15

16 ounces sharp
    Cheddar cheese,
    shredded
16 ounces mild
    Cheddar cheese,
    shredded
1 small onion, grated
1 cup mayonnaise
½–1 teaspoon red pepper
1 cup chopped pecans
   Strawberry
   preserves

Mix together cheeses, onion, mayonnaise and red pepper.

Line a 7-cup oiled mold with ¼ cup chopped pecans. Put in cheese mixture and let firm up in refrigerator. Unmold on plate and add remaining pecans around it. In center put strawberry preserves. Serve with crackers.

Maria Weiss

Cheese Cookies

Makes 75 to 100 cookies

¼ pound butter
8 ounces sharp Cheddar
   cheese, grated
1 cup flour
¾ cup chopped pecans
   or walnuts

Blend all ingredients. Shape into log, 2 inches in diameter and wrap in wax paper. Chill.

Cut slices ¼ to ⅛ inch thick, as desired. Bake 10 minutes at 400° or until crisp and golden.

Gloria Hamilton

Cocktail Salt Sticks

Makes 4 dozen

½ pound Farmer's
   cheese
½ pound all-purpose
   flour
½ pound unsalted butter
   Egg wash of 1 egg yolk
   and 1 tablespoon water
   Salt, to sprinkle on
   top, optional
   Caraway seeds,
   optional

Mix ingredients together in a food processor or by hand.

Roll out ¾ inch thick and cut in lengths (any size desired). Brush with egg wash. Sprinkle with salt and caraway seeds, if desired.

Bake in preheated 400° oven for 15 minutes or until browned on top.

Keep in tin; can be frozen and reheated in 350° oven.

Ingrid Monaghan

Tiropita

Serves 6

BATTER

1½ cups all-purpose flour
2 egg yolks, beaten
¾ cup flat beer
1 tablespoon oil
1 teaspoon salt
¼ teaspoon freshly ground pepper

16 ounces feta cheese

Prepare batter, and cut cheese into triangles ¼ inch thick.

Dip cheese in batter and drop in very hot (400°) cooking oil. Cook until batter is light gold, and cheese inside has melted.

Serve immediately!

Delicious served with deep-fried eggplant slices and yogurt.

Sir Michael Tippett CH

Pirozhki

Makes 75 turnovers

DOUGH

10 ounces evaporated milk
½ cup warm water
4 eggs
½ pound butter
½ pound margarine
2 packets dry yeast plus 2 teaspoons sugar
1 teaspoon salt
6½ cups all-purpose flour

FILLING

¾ pound lean ground beef
2 large onions, chopped
4 hard-boiled eggs, chopped
2 tablespoons finely chopped dill, fresh or 1 tablespoon dry dill weed
Salt, freshly ground pepper to taste

DOUGH

Proof yeast: in large glass measuring cup or pan, mix sugar and yeast. Add warm water and stir to dissolve. Put in a warm place to rise. Mix well with hands, in a large bowl, butter and margarine (softened), 3 eggs, and evaporated milk. Add yeast mixture. Add flour and salt. Mix thoroughly until smooth and elastic (about 5 minutes). Wrap in floured foil, and place on a large bread board or platter and refrigerate overnight or at least 8 hours.

FILLING

Sauté beef in small quantities until just brown. Put in a large bowl and tilt bowl to side to drain off fat. Remove fat. Sauté chopped onion in one stick of butter until transparent. Add to beef. Add finely chopped eggs, dill, salt and pepper. Mix well. Chill.

ASSEMBLY

Divide dough into four quarters. Roll dough ¼ inch thick one quarter of dough at a time. Cut in 2½ inch squares. Place a heaping teaspoonful of filling in center and bring corners together to make a square pillow shape. Crimp seams tightly. Place one inch apart on ungreased cookie sheets. Chill for 30 minutes. Brush with egg wash made by beating 1 egg with 1 teaspoon of water. Bake in a 425° oven for 20 to 25 minutes.

Can be made ahead and frozen. Will keep up to six months in freezer. To freeze: cool thoroughly; freeze in heavy duty freezer bags. Reheat in foil-lined baking pan in one layer for 25 minutes in a 375° oven.

Serve warm with cocktails, or as an accompaniment to soup or consommé.

Galina Vishnevskaya

Dolmadakia Avgolemono
Stuffed Grape Leaves With Egg and Lemon Sauce

Makes 35 to 40 pieces

1	pound ground beef	¼	bunch parsley
½	pound ground pork	¼	bunch dill
¼	cup rice	½	cup butter
1	whole egg	2	ounces flour
3	egg yolks		Salt and freshly
½	cup peeled tomatoes		ground pepper
8	ounces grape leaves	1	ounce chicken
1	medium onion, grated		bouillon
		3	lemons

To prepare the stuffed grape leaves, boil water in a large saucepan and add leaves (unrolled). Allow water to come to a second boil, then place under cold running water. Remove leaves when they are cold and stack them by hand, one by one, into a loose pile.

Put both ground meats in a large bowl; add whole egg, rice, onion, tomatoes (cut into small pieces), liquid from chopped tomato, finely chopped parsley and dill, salt and pepper to taste, and a cup of water (or, if available, a cup of beef or chicken broth instead of water).

Knead all ingredients in bowl together. Spread leaves, one by one, on a flat surface and wrap each one around meat mixture, allowing a heaping tablespoonful or more for each. (Note: before wrapping, stalk of each leaf should be cut off. The leaf should be wrapped around stuffing so that shiny side of leaf is on outside.)

Place stuffed vine leaves one by one into a large saucepan, cover with ½ lemon cut into thin slices, and weight them down with a plate placed over top of contents. In another saucepan, boil enough water to cover leaves. Pour over leaves, together with chicken bouillon.

Cover saucepan and simmer slowly for 2 hours, adding more liquid if necessary.

Remove saucepan from heat and drain remaining liquid (to be used in making egg and lemon sauce).

EGG AND LEMON SAUCE

Melt butter in a saucepan, add flour and stir for a few minutes with a wooden spoon. Add liquid from vine leaves, after it has cooled to lukewarm. Stir with a wire whisk until it forms a smooth paste and allow to boil slowly over low heat, stirring from time to time for about 5 minutes. (Care must be taken not to cook mixture at too high heat.)

Remove from heat and allow to cool. Beat juice of remaining lemons with 3 egg yolks and add sauce little by little. Strain sauce and cover it, leaving in a warm place.

To serve, place hot stuffed leaves on a platter and pour warm sauce over. Dolmadakia are eaten hot and may be served either as a first or main course. They are also often served as cocktail snacks. Sauce may be adjusted, if too thick, with broth and water or a little milk or, if too runny, with a little corn starch.

The Embassy of Greece

Mousseline St. Jacques

Makes 12 appetizers

1 pound scallops
1 pint heavy cream, whipped
   Salt and freshly ground pepper
12 large leaves of Boston lettuce
½ cup julienne of carrots
½ cup julienne of celery
½ cup fresh, diced tomatoes

2 tablespoons julienne of truffles
½ pound sweet butter
2 egg yolks
2 tablespoons chopped shallots
½ cup white wine
½ cup fish stock

Purée scallops in food processor. Add cream and mix. Season mousseline with salt and pepper.

Blanch lettuce leaves. Cool and drain on napkin. Stuff lettuce leaves with mousseline and wrap.

Cook julienne of carrots and celery. Peel and seed tomatoes. Then dice. Prepare julienne of truffles.

To prepare hollandaise, clarify butter. Whip egg yolks on top of double boiler. Then add clarified butter.

Combine shallots, white wine and fish stock in saucepan. Bring to a boil and add mousseline. Cook for 5 minutes. Remove mousseline from cooking juice. Reduce juice to half. Add carrots and celery juilienne, tomatoes, and truffles. Cook for 2 more minutes. Add hollandaise and mix together. Season to taste.

To serve, pour sauce on bottom of platter and place mousseline on top.

Chef Jean-Pierre Goyenvalle
Le Lion d'Or Restaurant

Crabmeat Remick

Serves 6

1 pound of fresh lump
    crabmeat
½ cup mayonnaise
½ cup ketchup
    Bacon, partially
      cooked as it should
      be crisp
    Salt and freshly
      ground pepper to
      taste

*This is an adaptation of
Crabmeat Ponchartrain.*

Mix all ingredients except bacon which is sprinkled on top and bake 20 minutes at 350°.

Mrs. David Treen

Crab in Chafing Dish

Makes 2 to 3 pounds

1 pound crab meat
16 ounces cream cheese
1 stick butter
1 teaspoon seafood
    seasoning

Mix all ingredients together. To serve, heat over double boiler.

Jack Blanton

Fried Shrimp Hors d'Oeuvres

Serves 16 to 20

2 pounds fresh, raw shrimp, cleaned and chopped
2 small cans water chestnuts, chopped
2 tablespoons, chopped scallions
1 teaspoon powdered ginger
2 teaspoons salt
4 eggs
2 tablespoons corn starch
Peanut oil, for cooking
Thinly-sliced white bread

Chop shrimp and water chestnuts together. Add scallions, ginger, salt, eggs, and corn starch.

Heat oil in electric skillet to about 350°. Cut crusts from bread. Pile on shrimp and cut into 4 triangles.

Just before serving, fry in peanut oil starting with shrimp side down and turning over when honey brown in color. Drain on paper towel and serve.

David Messing

Hot Asparagus Rolls

Makes 60 pieces

8 ounces cream cheese
3 ounces blue cheese
1 egg
1 or more boxes frozen asparagus spears (or fresh cooked asparagus in season)
20 slices of melba thin bread, crusts trimmed
1 cup butter, melted

Have cheese at room temperature and then mix well with egg. Cook asparagus spears and cool. Do not overcook! Roll out each slice of bread lightly with a rolling pin and then spread cheese mixture on each slice. Put one spear in center and roll up bread lengthwise. Working quickly, dip rolls in melted butter and put in freezer to set butter. (Wrap for permanent freezing.) Before baking, cut in thirds.

Bake at 450° for 10 to 15 minutes and serve hot. Canapés should be nice and crisp and rosy in color.

Cookbook Committee

Puffed Cheese Hors d'Oeuvres

Makes 36

8-ounce package
  cream cheese
1 egg yolk
½ teaspoon grated onion
¼ teaspoon salt
9 slices firm white bread
6 tablespoons butter,
  approximately

Blend cheese thoroughly with egg yolk, onion, and salt. Chill.

Cut 4 rounds from each slice of bread with round cookie cutter. Brush both sides of bread with melted butter. Place on a cookie sheet. Bake 5 to 7 minutes until bottoms are very light brown. Turn and do same to other side.

Cover entire top of bread with cheese mixture, rounding a little on top. (At this point, rounds can be frozen individually on a cookie sheet and when well frozen placed in a plastic bag).

Bake at 325° for 5 minutes and then place under broiler for 2 to 3 minutes until light brown. Serve hot.

Barbara Phillips

Curry Canapés

Makes 2 to 2½ dozen

1½ cups grated Cheddar
  cheese
1 cup chopped black
  olives
½ cup mayonnaise
1 teaspoon curry
  powder
  A little salt
1 package party rye or
  party pumpernickel
  bread

Mix all ingredients; spread on party rye bread and broil for 4 to 5 minutes or until browned on top.

Cookbook Committee

Ham Balls
with Sauce

Serves 8 as an appetizer
Serves 4 as a main course

1 pound ham
1½ pounds pork
2 eggs
1 cup cracker crumbs
  (salted or unsalted)
1 cup milk
½ teaspoon pepper,
  freshly ground

SAUCE
½ cup vinegar
1½ cups water
1½ cups brown sugar
1 teaspoon dry
  mustard

Grind ham and pork; mix together. Add other ingredients. Form mixture into balls, ¾ inch for buffet or 1½ inches for main course.

SAUCE

Combine sauce ingredients and mix well. Pour over meatballs in a roasting pan. Bake uncovered 1½ to 2 hours in a 350° oven. Baste and turn occasionally.
  Can be frozen.

Laurel Bennert Ohlson
NSO Member

Sausage-
Cheese Balls

Serves 15

1 pound hot country
  sausage
2 cups shredded
  Cheddar cheese
1 cup Bisquick
2 tablespoons prepared
  horseradish

With hands, mix all ingredients thoroughly. Shape into ½-inch balls and bake on an ungreased cookie sheet until browned, but still spongy to touch, about 15 minutes at 375°.
  The amount of Bisquick may be increased to as much as 2 cups for a drier consistency. These may also be undercooked by as much as 5 minutes and cooking completed at a later time. Freezing is best when done after shaping mixture into balls but before any cooking. Thawing is not necessary; however, cooking time may increase if mixture is frozen.

I suggest that these be served with hot mustard. The recipe is in the Sauces and Relishes Section.

Mark Conrad

Hot Mexican Cheese Dip

Serves 10 to 15

1 can Jalapeño bean dip
8 ounces cream cheese
8 ounces sour cream
1¼ ounces taco seasoning mix
Tabasco sauce, 5–6 dashes
½ pound Monterey Jack cheese, grated
½ pound yellow Cheddar cheese, grated
2 bags tortilla chips

Combine and blend first 5 ingredients until creamy. Pour into ovenproof serving dish. Sprinkle combined cheeses on top.

Heat in 325° oven until dip becomes warm and cheese is melted. Do not let dip bubble. This takes approximately 20 minutes.

Serve with tortilla chips.

Mrs. Stephen Burkes

Chili Dip

Serves 25 to 50

3 pounds lean ground beef
2 tablespoons bacon or beef fat
½ cup flour
3 chopped onions
1 can beef consommé
3 ounces chili powder
1 teaspoon powdered cumin
½ teaspoon oregano
1 teaspoon salt or less
2 pounds Cheddar cheese, grated

Sauté ground beef, just covering bottom of skillet with bacon or beef fat (suet). When cooked, add 1 tablespoon of fat to skillet and blend in ½ cup flour. Add ½ can beef consommé and stir until mixture is smooth.

Put mixture in large pot and add 3 chopped onions, ½ can beef consommé, chili, cumin, oregano, and salt. Simmer for 30 minutes, stirring often. Turn up heat and stir constantly until mixture thickens. If desired, this can be divided and frozen.

When ready to serve, heat half of mixture with one pound Cheddar cheese. It takes 15 to 20 minutes for cheese to melt. Stir well and serve with corn chips. The second half can be prepared as your guests devour the first half.

Mrs. Dale Miller

S O U P S

Apple and Butternut-Squash Soup

Serves 6

1 pound butternut squash, peeled, seeded, and coarsely chopped

3 tart apples, peeled, cored and coarsely chopped

1 medium onion, chopped

¼ teaspoon rosemary

¼ teaspoon marjoram

6–7 cups chicken broth

1 teaspoon salt

¼ teaspoon pepper, freshly ground

¼–½ cup heavy cream
Parsley (optional)

Combine all ingredients except cream in heavy saucepan. Bring to boil and simmer uncovered for 45 minutes. Cool to lukewarm.

Purée in blender. Return mixture to saucepan and bring to boil. Remove from heat, and stir in cream. Serve sprinkled with finely chopped parsley, if desired.

The contrast of apples and squash is heavenly! Perfect with roast pork or for a winter lunch with crusty bread.

Pamela Wojtowicz

Australian Leek and Carrot Soup

Serves 4

½ cup chopped celery
1 cup thinly-sliced carrots
   Butter or margarine
3 cups milk
2 tablespoons chopped parsley
5 leeks, washed well and sliced
1 teaspoon salt

¼ teaspoon pepper, freshly ground
1½ teaspoons flour

In 2 tablespoons hot butter, sauté celery and leeks until tender. Add carrots; sauté a few minutes longer. Add salt, pepper and milk; simmer covered for 25 minutes, stirring occasionally.

Purée vegetables in blender or food processor. Melt 2 tablespoons butter, stir in flour, and gradually add vegetables. Simmer until well blended and thickened, stirring occasionally. If too thick, add more milk.

Before serving, sprinkle with parsley.

Sheldon Lampert
NSO Member

Avgolemono Chicken with Rice Soup

Serves 8

7 cups chicken broth
½ cup long grain rice
   Salt and freshly ground pepper, to taste
6 large eggs, beaten
½ cup strained lemon juice
   Chopped fresh parsley leaves for decoration, optional

Heat chicken broth almost to rolling state and slowly pour in rice, stirring to prevent sticking. Lower heat to slow roll. Caution: continue stirring and watch carefully until certain that soup will not overflow.

When rice is almost cooked, beat eggs well. Slowly add lemon juice to eggs and blend well. Continue beating egg and lemon mixture while adding about 1½ cups of hot soup to it. Pour this mixture back into soup kettle, stirring constantly to prevent curdling. Serve immediately.

Garnish with parsley, if desired.

Mrs. Tas Coroneos

Chervil Soup

Serves 6

8 cups bouillon
½ pound carrots
3 tablespoons butter
2 ounces wheat flour
¾ pound fresh chervil, chopped

GARNISH
6 hard-boiled eggs
½ pound very small meatballs
Bread croutons

Scrape carrots and boil them whole in bouillon.

Cream together butter and flour. Add this roux to bouillon to thicken. Stir well and bring to a boil.

Remove from heat and add chopped chervil. Season to taste with salt. Garnish with sliced carrots, chopped hard-boiled eggs, cooked meatballs and croutons.

Mrs. Astrid Borch
Wife of the Ambassador of Denmark

Cep Soup

Serves 6

⅔ cup dried cep, or any dried mushroom
3 pints beef or chicken broth (including liquid in which mushrooms are soaked)
¼ cup rice or ⅓ cup barley
2 large onions

3–4 tablespoons oil
Salt and white pepper to taste
1 tablespoon all-purpose flour
Parsley, chopped
Sour cream

Rinse mushrooms and let them soak in about 2 cups water for 2 to 3 hours.

Chop onions and sauté them in oil in a saucepan. Chop mushrooms; add them to onions and brown. Add mushroom liquid and broth. Add rice, salt, and pepper; allow to simmer until rice is cooked.

For a thicker soup, mix flour in a little water, add to soup and cook for 5 minutes or so. Sprinkle soup with chopped parsley and serve sour cream separately.

If you use barley, boil it before adding to soup, since cooking time for barley is longer than for rice.

Kaarina Kaurinkoski
Embassy of Finland

Onion Soup

Serves 6 to 8

1½ pounds yellow
   onions
2 cloves garlic, crushed
4 tablespoons butter
2 quarts beef stock or 4
   10-ounce cans plus 1
   cup water
1 teaspoon salt (omit if
   using canned stock)

Pinch sugar
1 teaspoon dried
   mustard
1 bay leaf
1½ teaspoons sage
1 cup dry red wine
   Salt and freshly
   ground pepper to
   taste

Peel onions; slice very thin. Melt oil and butter together in a very heavy 3-quart saucepan. Toss onions and garlic in melted fat to coat thoroughly; cook covered over medium heat until very tender. Uncover, add sugar, and raise heat. Stir frequently to prevent sticking or burning; cook until onions are a deep caramel color.

Heat 2 cups of stock or stock and water to boiling; add slowly to onions, stirring vigorously. When this mixture is well blended, add rest of liquids and seasonings except salt and pepper. Bring to a boil, reduce heat, and simmer covered for 35 to 40 minutes, stirring occasionally. Correct seasoning, but do not oversalt if serving soup with a strong cheese.

GRATINÉE

   Slightly dry
   French bread
   Oil or butter
1½ cups grated cheese—
   Swiss, Gruyère,
   Parmesan

Slice bread about 1 inch thick, enough to cover surface of an ovenproof baking disk or casserole, or to fit snugly in individual ovenproof bowls. Lightly butter or oil both sides and toast to a light brown on both sides. Bring soup to a simmer and ladle it into serving vessel or bowls. Top with toasted bread, covering as much of surface as possible; then spead cheese on top. Sprinkle a little oil over cheese and place in middle of a 350° oven for 30 minutes. The cheese should be slowly bubbling.

Francine Morris Swift

Crème Constance

Serves 4

10 ounces chicken or
    light vegetable
    stock
10 ounces milk
2 tablespoons butter
1 teaspoon curry
    powder
2–3 tablespoons flour

Salt and white pepper
    to taste
Yolk of one egg
3 ounces heavy cream

Melt butter. Add flour and curry powder. Cook for a few minutes; gradually add stock and milk. Simmer for 5 minutes. Prepare and add liaison—yolk of 1 egg and 3 ounces cream. Season to taste and cook for few minutes longer but do not boil.

Liaison—a thickening and enriching agent. Mix together in a small bowl, add a little of hot mixture to it and return to main mixture.

Ann Woollatt

Antonia's Minestrone Soup

Serves 4 to 6

1 quart homemade meat
    stock
½ cup chopped onion
1 cup diced celery
1 cup cooked kidney
    beans
2 cups peeled and
    mashed tomatoes
2 cups shredded
    cabbage
2 tablespoons cooking
    oil
1 clove garlic

1 cup tubellini (available
    in Italian stores)
Grated Parmesan
    cheese

Brown garlic in oil, remove and toss away. Brown onion very lightly. Add meat stock (chicken soup can be used), celery, beans, cabbage and tomatoes. Cook for 20 minutes in covered pot.

Cook tubellini separately in boiling water, drain and add to minestrone. Add more meat stock if needed. Let sit for 20 minutes before serving. Pass grated parmesan cheese.

Serve with garlic bread and red wine.

Armand Sarro
Former NSO Member

Minestra Di Fagioli Con La Pasta

Bean Soup With Macaroni

Serves 6

¾ pound dried white beans
1½ pound ham bone with meat on it
3 quarts cold water
¼ teaspoon freshly ground pepper
1 teaspoon salt
¼ pound ham fat, chopped
½ onion, chopped
1 clove garlic, chopped
2 stalks celery, chopped
3 sprigs parsley, chopped
3 tomatoes, peeled, seeded, and chopped
½ pound elbow macaroni (or other spaghetti)

Soak white beans overnight; drain.

Parboil ham bone for 10 minutes; drain. Wash beans under running water and put into an earthenware or enamel pot with ham bone. Cover with cold water and season with salt and pepper. Bring to a boil and reduce heat to moderate; cook covered for 1½ hours or until beans are tender.

In a separate saucepan, brown onion, garlic, celery and parsley in ham fat over medium heat; add tomatoes; blend well and cook gently for about 10 minutes.

When beans are tender, remove ham bone and cut meat from it into slivers. Add slivered ham to soup along with tomato mixture.

Bring soup back to a boil. Drop in pasta and cook until pasta is al dente, 10 to 12 minutes. Correct seasoning and let soup rest a few minutes.

Serve with grated Parmesan cheese on the side.

Frank C. C. Gasparro
Former NSO Member

Minestra Genovese di Fagiolini al Pesto

Bean Soup with Pesto

Serves 8

SOUP

- 2 cups dried navy beans
- 2½ quarts water
- 1½ cups peeled, diced potatoes
- 1 stalk celery, diced
- 1 large leek, sliced
- 1 cup grated carrots
- 1½ teaspoons salt
- ½ teaspoon freshly ground pepper
- 2 slices bacon, chopped small
- 1 cup uncooked noodles

PESTO

- 1 cup *fresh* basil leaves (fresh basil is a must for pesto)
- ½ cup pine nuts or almonds
- 2 garlic cloves, peeled
- ¾ cup fresh grated Parmesan cheese
- ½ cup good quality olive oil
- ½ bunch parsley without stems

SOUP

Soak beans in cold water for 1 hour. Drain. Cook beans in 2½ quarts water for 2½ hours.

Add vegetables, salt, and pepper; continue simmering for 30 minutes. Add pesto and cook for 10 minutes more. Add noodles and cook until al dente. While soup is cooking make pesto sauce.

Blend all pesto ingredients in a blender or food processor, adding olive oil last. Dribble olive oil.

Combine pesto with soup and serve immediately.

Joan C-C Oppenheimer

Potpourri of Lentils

Austrian Lentil Soup

Serves 4

½ pound lentils
1 pound smoked ham or ham bone, with ham on it
½ pound carrots, diced
2–3 celery stalks, diced
2–3 potatoes, diced
2–3 parsnips, diced

Salt and freshly ground pepper to taste
2 tablespoons butter
2–3 onions, minced
Parsley, chopped fine
Tomato paste, amount according to taste

Soak lentils overnight. Drain and cover with about 1 quart water. Simmer with ham bone about 20 to 30 minutes.

Add vegetables and continue simmering for 30 minutes more. Remove ham bone, chop up meat and return to pot. Mince onions and sauté in butter.

Add parsley and stir in tomato paste. Simmer soup for 10 minutes and serve.

Ingrid Monaghan

Beef Vegetable Chowder

Serves 6

1 pound ground beef
1 cup tomatoes, or 12-ounce can of V-8 juice
½ cup carrots, sliced
½ cup celery, sliced
1 medium onion or 2 leeks, chopped
1 teaspoon salt
¼ cup barley
½ teaspoon pepper, freshly ground
2 cups water
1 cup potato cubes

Brown meat. To a 4-quart soup pot, add tomatoes (or V-8 juice), carrots, celery, onion, salt, barley, pepper, water and potatoes. Cover pot and cook for 1 hour.

Julie Schreder

Vegetable Chowder

Serves 4

3 cups chicken broth
1 cup chopped potatoes
½ cup diced carrots
½ cup diced celery
½ cup diced onion
¼ green pepper, diced
¼ cup butter
½ cup butter
½ cup flour
2 cups milk
3 cups Cheddar cheese,
  grated
Dash of freshly
  ground pepper

To make roux, melt ½ cup butter. Add flour to it and blend. Cook for 2 minutes.

Add first 7 ingredients and cook 15 minutes or until done. Add roux, milk and cheese. Stir until thick and serve.

Brendon G. Bowers

Southern Vegetable Soup

Serves 6 to 8

1 large soup bone, piece
  of beef shank 3–4
  pounds with meat on
  it
8 large ripe tomatoes,
  peeled and cut
½ green pepper, minced
4 large, or 6 medium,
  onions, minced
2 cups lima beans
2 cups fresh corn, cut
  but not scraped from
  cob
2 cups fresh okra, sliced

Fresh parsley
Sprig of thyme, tied
  together to be removed
  later
Salt to taste
Black pepper, freshly
  ground to taste
Piece of hot pepper, or
  pinch of cayenne

Start soup bone in pot of cold water to cover and let cook very slowly for 1 hour. Skim and add about 2 quarts of water, tomatoes, green pepper, onions, lima beans, corn, okra, parsley, thyme and seasonings.

This soup must be thick and has to be stirred regularly after corn is added. Cook slowly several hours. Skim off fat and remove bone, parsley and thyme. Cut off meat from bone and return to soup after cutting in small pieces. Do not add any other vegetables. This soup is a meal in itself and better the second day.

Milly Dent

Tomato Consommé

Serves 6

4 cups chicken or
  beef broth
16-ounce can Italian
  plum tomatoes with
  their juice
2 teaspoons tomato paste
½ teaspoon thyme
1 teaspoon basil
2 teaspoons lemon juice
½ cup dry sherry or
  Madeira
2 tablespoons finely
  chopped, fresh
  chives or parsley

Place first 6 ingredients in a saucepan. Simmer for 15 minutes. Add wine and garnish with chives or parsley.
Wonderful to serve in punch cups before sitting down for dinner.

Cookbook Committee

Cod Fish Bouillabaise

Serves 2

2 tablespoons olive oil
1 stalk celery, chopped
1 clove garlic, chopped
1 small onion, sliced
1 large leek, sliced
1 pinch thyme
1 bay leaf
1 cup finely chopped
  tomatoes
⅔ cup bottled clam juice
½ cup dry white wine
½ teaspoon crushed
  fennel seeds

Pinch saffron
1 ounce Pernod
  Chopped fresh parsley
1 pound cod

Sauté first 6 ingredients in olive oil for 5 to 10 minutes.
Add next 6 ingredients and boil about 5 minutes. Then simmer for about another 40 minutes.
Add cod and simmer for another 10 minutes.
Serve in soup bowls sprinkled with parsley.
Broth can be made first and frozen. Broth is better if made in advance and used a day or 2 later.

Jack DeSipio

Scallop Soup

Serves 8

1½ pounds scallops,
    washed, diced and
    drained
¼ pound bacon
6 tablespoons butter
2 cups light cream
1 stalk celery, diced
1½ cups chopped onions
1 leek (white part
    only), diced
3 cups clam juice and 3
    cups water or 6 cups
    fish stock
1½ cups sliced fresh
    mushrooms
½ teaspoon thyme
1 teaspoon salt
½ teaspoon white
    pepper
6 sprigs parsley
1½ pounds potatoes,
    peeled and diced
1 pound tomatoes,
    peeled and chopped

Dice bacon, brown in saucepan and pour off fat. Add butter, onions, leek, celery, mushrooms, and tomatoes. Cook over low heat, covered, for 5 minutes.

Add clam juice, water, salt, pepper, thyme, and parsley. Cook over low heat for 30 minutes. Add potatoes and cook for 20 minutes. Add scallops, cook 10 minutes. Discard parsley. Stir in cream. Season to taste and heat.

Janice Sanchez

Quick, Cold Beet Borscht

Serves 4

1 jar sweet and spiced or
   sweet and sour
   Harvard beets
1 egg, raw
1 can consommé
1 cup sour cream

Put all ingredients in a blender or food processor and blend until smooth. Serve icy cold.

An extra dollop of sour cream may be floated on top.

Elizabeth H. Bernbaum

Consommé d'Ouest

Serves 4

1 can consommé
   (10½ ounces)
6 ounces cream cheese
½ teaspoon curry
   powder
1 small clove garlic,
   crushed
1 teaspoon lemon juice

GARNISH
   Chopped chives,
      chopped cucumber or
      chopped hardboiled
      egg

Put two-thirds of consommé, cheese, and garlic in a blender and blend until smooth. Add curry powder and lemon juice. Blend again and pour into individual pots or glasses. Put into refrigerator until set. Soup will almost be pudding-like.

Sprinkle garnish over surface. Spoon rest of consommé over garnish to form a glaze about ¼ inch thick. Chill and serve.

Ann Woollatt

Chilled Cucumber Soup

Serves 4

3 large cucumbers,
   peeled, seeded, and
   chopped
1 cup plain yogurt
1 clove garlic
⅔ cup sour cream
2 tablespoons fresh dill
   Salt and freshly
      ground pepper, to
      taste
   Paprika, for garnish

Place all ingredients except paprika into a food processor; beat until smooth.

Chill. Serve with additional, minced dill and paprika for garnish. Soup can be made in advance.

Mrs. Harry E. Gould, Jr.

Gazpacho

Serves 6

2 large tomatoes, peeled
1 large cucumber, peeled
1 medium onion
1 medium green pepper
24 ounces Sacramento tomato juice
¼ cup olive oil
⅓ cup red wine vinegar
¼ teaspoon Tabasco
⅛ teaspoon black pepper, coarsely ground
1½ teaspoons salt

Use blender or food processor to combine all solid ingredients and blend with some of tomato juice until puréed. Add remaining ingredients and rest of tomato juice. Chill for 2 hours. You can reserve some of vegetables, chop them up and use them to garnish soup along with freshly toasted croutons.

This is easy to take to a picnic and serve in plastic cups.

Mrs. Edison W. Dick

Cold Spinach Soup

Serves 6

1 package frozen, chopped spinach, cooked
4 cups light cream
4 chicken bouillon cubes
¼ cup dry vermouth
½ teaspoon ground mace
2 hard-boiled eggs (chopped)
1 tablespoons grated lemon rind

Put cooked spinach into blender and reduce to pulp.

Put bouillon cubes into cream and scald, stirring until cubes are dissolved. (I put cream in top of double-boiler; it is easier and keeps from burning!!) Remove from heat. Stir in spinach, vermouth, lemon rind and mace. Chill. Top with eggs or serve piping hot with croutons.

Mrs. Barbara Bush

Cold Zucchini Soup

Serves 4

2 tablespoons butter
2 tablespoons finely
      chopped shallots
1 clove garlic, minced
1 pound zucchini,
      cleaned and sliced
      thin (do not peel)
1 teaspoon curry, or to
      taste
1 teaspoon salt
1 cup cream (light or
      heavy)
1¾ cups chicken broth,
      preferably home-
      made

In a skillet heat butter and add shallots, garlic and zucchini. Cover pan and simmer ingredients for about 10 minutes. Stir every few minutes. Do not let brown. Cool.

Place mixture in blender and add curry, salt, cream, and broth. Blend mixture 1 minute and chill.

Laurie G. Firestone

Cantaloupe Soup

Serves 4 to 6

1 cantaloupe, diced
5 tablespoons butter
1 teaspoon sugar
¼ teaspoon ginger
      Grated lemon rind
      Pinch of salt
2½ cups milk
      Fresh mint leaves

OPTIONAL
      White wine or lemon
      juice to taste

Sauté cantaloupe (reserving part for garnish) in butter with sugar, ginger, lemon rind, and salt. When melon is soft, add milk. Bring to a boil. Turn heat to low and simmer for 10 minutes. Cool.

When cool, blend in blender or food processor. Chill. Serve cold with a garnish of remaining cantaloupe and mint leaves.

Milt & Betty Stevens
NSO Members

Cold Sour Cherry Soup

Serves 6

2 cups cold water
1 cup sugar
1 cinnamon stick
4 cups sour cherries,
    pitted and drained, if
    canned
1 tablespoon arrowroot
¼ cup heavy cream,
    chilled
¾ cup dry red wine,
    chilled

In a 2-quart saucepan, combine water, sugar and cinnamon stick. Bring to boil and add cherries. Simmer over low heat for 35 to 40 minutes if cherries are fresh, or 10 minutes if they are canned. Remove cinnamon stick.

Mix arrowroot and 2 tablespoons of cold water to make a paste, then beat into cherry soup. Stirring constantly, bring soup almost to a boil. Reduce heat and simmer for about 2 minutes, or until clear and slightly thickened. Pour into shallow glass bowl, and refrigerate until chilled. Before serving, preferably in chilled soup bowls, stir in heavy cream and wine.

Bèla Màrtay
Former NSO Member

EGG

&

CHEESE

DISHES

Dutch Fondue

Serves 4

4 tablespoons butter
1 small onion, chopped
6-ounce can tomato
   paste
¼ cup flour
14 ounces beef broth
7 ounces Gouda cheese,
   grated

4 ounces sour cream
   Salt, freshly ground
   pepper, to taste
   Fresh parsley, chopped
   Chopped ham, green
   pepper, and
   mushrooms, optional

Chop onion finely and sauté until golden.

Mix in tomato paste and flour. Add stock, continually stirring until mixture is smooth.

Add cheese, salt, pepper, and sour cream; blend well. To make this dish even more exciting, add finely chopped, optional ingredients and fresh parsley.

Serve with chunks of fresh bread for dipping.

Royal Netherlands Embassy

Geneva Fondue

Serves 4

2 loaves French bread
1 pound Gruyère
¼ pound Emmenthal
¼ pound Appenzeller
1½ cups dry white wine

2 teaspoons cornstarch
3 cloves garlic
2 ounces kirsch
   Dash pepper and
   nutmeg

Break bread into bite-size morsels and dry in warm oven (do not toast). Peel clove of garlic and vigorously rub it over interior surface of cooking pot. Pare rind from cheeses and medium grate.

Peel and mince 2 remaining cloves of garlic. Make a paste with cornstarch, garlic, and kirsch.

Place wine in cooking pot. Heat for 3 minutes over medium heat. Do not allow it to come to a boil. When wine is warm, begin to add grated cheese, handful by handful, stirring constantly with a wooden spoon. After cheese is melted completely, add paste mixture and bring to a boil, continuing to stir constantly. Boil for no more than 2 minutes. Sprinkle with nutmeg and pepper.

Remove cooking pot from stove and place on burner at dining table. Burner should be set to keep cheese bubbling slowly throughout the meal. Spear bread on fork and swirl in cheese. The cheese crust left at the bottom of the pot is one of the tastiest parts of the meal.

Serve with chilled white wine, gherkins, boiled new potatoes (optional), and kirsch. Do not drink anything cold for some time after the meal as this causes the cheese to congeal in a lump.

William & Teresa Manning

Spanish Omelet

Serves 1 to 2

FILLING
½ Spanish onion, chopped
1 green onion, chopped
2 mushrooms, sliced (optional)
½ medium potato, peeled and diced
1 rib celery, chopped
¼ bell pepper, chopped
1 tablespoon parsley, chopped
¼ teaspoon garlic powder
¼ teaspoon chili powder
Salt and freshly ground pepper to taste
1 small tomato, chopped
2 tablespoons ketchup
3 dashes Tabasco sauce
1 teaspoon Worcestershire sauce
1 tablespoon olive oil
2 tablespoons butter

OMELET
2 whole eggs
1 tablespoon water
2 tablespoons butter

In a medium-size skillet, melt butter with olive oil over medium heat. Add mushrooms and sauté them for 2 minutes.

Add onions, potatoes, celery, bell pepper, and parsley. Cook until all ingredients are softened. Add garlic powder, chili powder, salt and pepper. Stir.

Add tomato and cook for 1 or 2 more minutes. Add ketchup, Tabasco, Worcestershire, olive oil, and butter. Heat, mixing well. Keep this mixture warm while preparing eggs.

To make eggs, place an 8-inch omelet pan over medium-high heat and add butter. While butter is melting, whisk eggs into a bowl and add water.

When butter is melted, lift pan; tilt to swirl butter, coating sides and bottom. After butter is very hot, give eggs another whisk and pour into pan (they will almost immediately begin to curl around edges). Tilt pan slightly; with spatula, draw some of partially set egg toward center, allowing runny top to pour into pan bottom. Do this several times around omelet as it cooks (ridges will form near center and give omelet a thickness).

As top loses its runny appearance, pour some of hot filling in a line across center of omelet, perpendicular to handle. Lift side of omelet nearest handle with spatula and fold over filling.

Omelet can be kept warm in an oven while another is prepared. Pour some of hot filling over omelet and garnish with parsley before serving.

Filling can be prepared in advance, refrigerated, and reheated when needed.

Parker C. Folse, Jr.

Squash-Tropovich Frittata

Serves 4

2 zucchini, thinly sliced
2 leeks, thinly sliced
2 tablespoons butter
6 eggs
2 tablespoons chopped parsley
2 tablespoons water
⅛ teaspoon rosemary
½ teaspoon salt
⅛ teaspoon freshly ground pepper
½ cup grated cheese (or sharp cheese slices)

In small saucepan, cook zucchini and leeks in a small amount of boiling salted water for about 5 minutes; drain.

Butter bottom of a 10-inch skillet with an ovenproof handle.

Mix eggs, parsley, water, rosemary, salt, and pepper in a bowl. Place zucchini and leeks in skillet, pouring egg mixture over vegetables.

Cook over low heat, without stirring, until set about ¼ inch from edge of skillet. Lift some egg from sides to allow runny eggs to flow to bottom. Continue cooking until almost set.

Add cheese slices on top. Place pan in a 400° oven and bake uncovered for 4 or 5 minutes until eggs are set and cheese is melted.

James Kraft
NSO Member

Roulade Josephine

Serves 6

BATTER
2 tablespoons butter
4 tablespoons flour
1 cup milk
4 eggs, separated
Salt and freshly ground
   pepper to taste

SAUCE
Mayonnaise
Sour cream
Ketchup
Parmesan cheese

FILLING
1 pound mushrooms
2 tablespoons butter
1 onion
   Salt and freshly
      ground pepper to
      taste
   Sherry to taste
4 ounces cream cheese
   Dill or parsley
⅓ cup bread crumbs

Prepare filling first. Slice mushrooms and chop onion. Sauté mushrooms and onion in butter; add salt, pepper, and dill or parsley. Add cream cheese, sherry, and bread crumbs. Set aside.

Make batter with butter, flour, and milk warmed in a saucepan. Let cool; add egg yolks and mix well. Whip egg whites and fold into mixture. Add salt and pepper to taste.

Line a jelly roll pan with lightly greased and floured foil. Pour mixture in pan to evenly fill ¾ full. Bake for 15 to 20 minutes at 350°.

When done, turn out cake onto slightly floured towel. Peel off foil and roll carefully. Let cool.

Spread roll out flat and fill with mushroom mixture. Roll up again. Put in an ovenproof dish.

Prepare sauce with one part mayonnaise, one part sour cream, and a little ketchup to make about 1 cup.

Pour sauce over filled roll. Sprinkle with Parmesan and reheat for about 20 minutes.

Roulade Josephine makes a very good luncheon dish; it can also be filled with ham or crabmeat. Serve with a salad.

Franziska Mayer

Spinach Roll With Ham

Serves 4 to 6

1 pound fresh spinach
6 eggs, separated
¼ pound butter
3 tablespoons flour
1 tablespoon grated
   cheese

½ tablespoon salt
1 pound ham, finely
   chopped
1 egg yolk
2 tablespoons sour
   cream

Rinse spinach well; cook, drain, chop fine, and let cool.

Melt butter; add flour to make a light roux and cool.

Beat egg yolks well; add cheese, roux, and spinach. Beat egg whites until stiff and add slowly to spinach mixture.

Grease and flour well a jelly roll pan. Pour in mixture and bake at 350° for 20 minutes.

To make filling, mix together finely chopped ham, egg yolk, and sour cream.

When spinach mixture is baked, turn out on a damp cloth; fill and roll up. Serve hot.

Mrs. Janja Loncar
Wife of the Ambassador of Yugoslavia

Hot Brown

Serves 4

4 slices toast
4 slices cooked turkey
   or chicken (white
   meat)
4 slices ham
½ cup grated sharp
   American cheese
2 tablespoons flour
2 tablespoons butter
8 strips crisp bacon
¼ teaspoon salt

Dash nutmeg
Dash cayenne pepper
8 slices tomato
About 1 cup warm
   milk
Parmesan cheese,
   grated

Melt butter and blend in flour; cook, stirring but do not brown. Add milk gradually, stirring until smooth. Add salt, pepper and nutmeg. Blend cheese into sauce until melted.

In individual ramekins, preferably, place chicken and ham on toast, cover with ¼ sauce. Top with 2 strips of crisp bacon and sprinkle with Parmesan. Put in shallow pan under broiler and flame until cheese melts to a golden brown. Serve at once, topped with slice of tomato.

Popular dish from the old Brown Hotel in Louisville, Kentucky.

Cecilia DeGolyer McGhee

Cheese Grits Soufflé

Serves 4 to 6

1 cup quick cooking grits
4½ cups water
1 teaspoon salt
¾ stick butter
1 stick Kraft Garlic Cheese, (garlic optional)
2 eggs
¼ cup milk
Salt and freshly ground pepper
1 cup corn flakes, crushed
¼ stick butter, melted

Cook grits in water with salt. When done, stir in ¾ stick butter and garlic cheese. Allow to cool.

Add beaten eggs into milk. Combine with grits-cheese mixture and season with salt and pepper. Pour into buttered casserole dish and cover with corn flakes mixed with ¼ stick butter.

Cover and bake in 350° oven for 40 to 45 minutes. Serve hot.

Willard Scott

Camembert Tart

Serves 4

4 slices ham (or enough cooked bacon to cover bottom of pastry shell)
3 tablespoons butter
8 small scallions, chopped
1 cup soft Camembert cheese
½ cup Parmesan cheese
4 eggs, beaten
2 cups whipping cream
Dash nutmeg and white pepper
1 baked 9-inch pastry shell

Cut ham in strips and sauté in butter. Add onions. Spread mixture over bottom of baked pastry shell.

Spread Camembert on top of ham mixture and sprinkle with Parmesan.

Beat eggs and cream; add nutmeg and pepper. Pour over cheese.

Bake at 325° for 30 minutes or until custard is set. Make holes in the Camembert to let heat cook through the pie.

Constance Berkley

S A L A D S

Avocados With Hot Sauce

Serves 4 to 6

¾ cup salad oil
¼ cup tarragon vinegar
2 teaspoons sugar
½ teaspoon salt
  Dash of Tabasco
2 hard-boiled eggs, sieved
1 tablespoon chives, chopped
1 tablespoon parsley, chopped

1 teaspoon dry mustard
½ teaspoon Worcestershire sauce
2–3 avocados, halved

In saucepan combine oil, vinegar, sugar, salt, and Tabasco. Bring mixture to boil, remove from heat, and stir in eggs, chives, parsley, mustard, and Worcestershire sauce.

Spoon hot sauce into cavities of unpeeled avocado halves and serve as first course.

Marjorie Benton

Broccoli Scavelli

Serves 4 to 6

1 large head fresh broccoli
  Juice of 1 fresh lime
2–3 cloves fresh garlic, or to taste
½ cup fresh Italian parsley, chopped
1 small red onion (optional)
1–2 jars marinated artichoke hearts

1–2 fresh tomatoes (optional)
  Salt and freshly ground pepper (optional)

Clean and cut fresh broccoli into medium to small pieces, being sure to peel and cut lower portion of stalk and add it as well. Steam in small amount of water until just tender. Drain and spread out onto a large platter.

Add fresh garlic, finely chopped parsley, onion, and tomatoes. Add lime juice. Open artichoke hearts and toss with other ingredients. No additional oil is needed.

Add salt and pepper if desired, or grated Romano cheese. Serve warm or cold. Makes a good accompaniment to pasta.

Mrs. Ramon Scavelli

California Salad with Lemon Dressing

Serves 8 to 10

1 head Boston lettuce
1 pint cherry tomatoes, halved
1 medium cantaloupe
2 11-ounce cans mandarin orange sections. drained
½ cup pitted black olives
2 avocados, peeled, sliced, sprinkled with lemon
1 sweet Italian onion, sliced very thin
3 heads Belgian endive, leaves separated

LEMON DRESSING
3 tablespoons fresh lemon juice
⅛ teaspoon salt
Freshly ground pepper, to taste
¼ cup salad oil
¼ cup olive oil
1 teaspoon dried basil
or
2 tablespoons fresh chopped basil

This is my favorite summer salad, beautiful to behold and wonderful to eat.

Chill lettuce, tomatoes, cantaloupe, orange sections, olives, avocados, onion, and endives.

Using a large, wide salad bowl, line sides and bottom with lettuce leaves. Arrange chilled ingredients inside, using your artistic abilities.

To make dressings, combine lemon juice, salt, pepper, salad oil, olive oil, and basil; mix well with a wire whip or shake together in a bottle.

Drizzle dressing over salad after your guests have seen your work of art, and toss lightly until ingredients are well coated. Serve immediately.

Note: Leave avocado pit in avocado until you are ready to toss salad with dressing. The pit will keep avocado from turning dark. Also, stand endive leaves straight up behind lettuce, like flower petals.

Lonie Landfield

Chinese Vegetable Salad

Serves 10

1 can water chestnuts, sliced
½ green pepper, chopped
½ cup sliced celery
½ cup sliced scallions
1½ cups bean sprouts
1½ cups shredded Chinese cabbage
½ cup toasted slivered almonds
⅓ cup toasted sesame seeds

DRESSING
⅓ cup sesame oil
2 tablesoons soy sauce
1 teaspoon mustard
Juice of ½ lemon
Black pepper, freshly ground
2 teaspoons Worcestershire sauce

Wonderful, crunchy, salad!

Toss all ingredients together. Make up salad dressing and pour over salad.

Allow to mellow 10 minutes before serving. Add almonds last.

Susan Koehler

Colorful Marinated Salad

Serves 6 to 8

2 medium onions
2 red or green bell peppers
½ pound broccoli
½ pound cauliflower
2 large carrots, peeled
4 large mushrooms, sliced
½ pint cherry tomatoes
6 tablespoons olive oil

2 tablespoons wine vinegar
Salt and freshly ground pepper to taste
1 tablespoon oregano
8 black oil-cured olives
8 pimento-stuffed green olives

Place unskinned onions and peppers in oven at 450°, checking every 15 minutes and turning them until all sides are blistered and brown (not to exceed 1 hour). When done remove from oven. Place peppers in plastic bag. Onions can remain in pan until cooled.

Clean broccoli, cauliflower, and carrots and cut into bite-size pieces. Steam until slightly tender to touch of a fork. Do not overcook.

Slip onions out of their skins and quarter them. Peel skins off peppers and sliver.

Combine all ingredients in salad bowl, toss and let marinate for at least 2 hours in refrigerator.

Before serving, let stand at room temperature for at least 15 minutes.

Denise Wilkinson
NSO Member

Eggplant Salad Rabat Style

Serves 4

1 eggplant (about 1 pound)
1 clove garlic, peeled and slivered
2 tablespoons chopped parsley
2 sprigs fresh coriander, chopped (optional)
½ teaspoon ground cumin
½ teaspoon paprika
2 tablespoons olive oil
1–2 tablespoons lemon juice
Salt

Eggplant is traditionally grilled over a charcoal brazier; for convenience in this recipe it is baked in the oven.

Stud eggplant with garlic slivers, using paring knife to "drill" holes. Bake eggplant in a 400° oven until very soft. Remove from oven to cool.

When cool enough to handle, rub skin off eggplant and squeeze pulp to release bitter juices or scoop out pulp with a wooden spoon and let drain in a sieve.

Mash or push eggplant pulp and garlic slivers through a food mill. (Avoid temptation to use a blender or food processor; it destroys the character of the dish).

Add chopped herbs and spices; mix well. Fry in oil over moderate heat, turning eggplant often with perforated spatula until all liquid has evaporated and eggplant has been reduced to a thick black jam. This takes about 15 to 20 minutes. Sprinkle with lemon juice, taste for salt, and readjust seasonings to taste. Serve warm or slightly cooled. Dish can be decorated with baby tomatoes.

Mrs. Ali Bengelloun
Wife of the Ambassador of Morocco

Fatoosh

Serves 4 to 6

2 loaves Syrian bread (stale or toasted bread is excellent)
1 small bunch fresh mint, minced
1 bunch scallions, minced
Juice of 2 lemons
⅓ cup olive oil
1 head Romaine lettuce
1 large cucumber, peeled
1 small bunch parsley, minced
Salt and freshly ground pepper to taste
1 clove garlic (optional)

In a large bowl break Syrian bread into bite-size pieces. Cut vegetables into small pieces and add to bread.

Add other ingredients and mix well. This is extra special when served cold on a hot summer day.

Embassy of Lebanon

Hearts of Palm Salad

Serves 6

SALAD
- 2 heads Bibb lettuce
- 2 14-ounce cans palm hearts, chilled
- 12 thin slices pimento
- 6 large sprigs parsley

DRESSING
- 1 shallot
- ½ cup garlic vinegar
- 1 tablespoon lemon juice
- 1 teaspoon dry mustard
- 1 whole egg
- 1 egg yolk
- ⅔ teaspoon anchovy paste
- 1½ cups virgin olive oil

Carefully separate Bibb lettuce leaves and wash well in cold water. Drain and spin dry and set aside. Drain palm hearts and refresh under cold water.

Arrange lettuce leaves on 6 chilled salad plates. Center palm hearts on beds of lettuce.

Pour dressing over salads and garnish with pimento slices and parsley sprigs. The dressing, a great favorite, is also wonderful for a chef's salad.

DRESSING

Place shallot, garlic vinegar, lemon juice, dry mustard, egg, egg yolk, and anchovy paste in an electric blender or food processor; blend well. Continue processing while adding olive oil in a thin stream until well blended.

Chef George Gianakos
The Prime Rib Restaurant

Les Crudités Obernoises

Serves 6 to 8

2 teaspoons finely
   minced onion
1 tablespoon peanut oil
1 teaspoon white wine
   vinegar
½ teaspoon salt
   Freshly ground white
   pepper
1 pound Gruyère cheese
6 large, fresh beets
   Salt to taste
6 large carrots
4 medium-size celery
   roots
   Fresh chopped parsley

REMOULADE SAUCE
1 cup mayonnaise
1½ teaspoons dry
   mustard
⅛ teaspoon sugar
½ teaspoon lemon juice

*With pâté, french bread
and wine, this is a meal in
itself.*

Combine onion, oil, salt, and white pepper to form dressing. Set aside.

Remove rind from Gruyère cheese and cut into julienne strips the size of matchsticks. Place in a bowl and gently toss with half dressing.

Cook beets in lightly salted, boiling water about 35 to 45 minutes, or until done. Drain. When cool enough to handle, peel and slice into julienne strips. Place in a bowl and toss with remaining dressing.

Peel carrots and grate on a medium-size grater. Place in a bowl and season lightly with salt.

Peel celery roots, cut into julienne strips, and place in a bowl.

REMOULADE SAUCE

Combine all ingredients of Remoulade Sauce and mix gently with celery root until well coated.

Arrange Gruyère, beets, carrots, and celery root on a large platter in separate, carefully formed piles.

Garnish with generous portions of chopped parsley and serve.

Chef François Haeringer
L'Auberge Chez François

Make Ahead Caesar Salad

Serves 6

1 large head romaine lettuce
¼ cup salad oil
1 raw egg yolk
1½ teaspoons Worcestershire sauce
2 tablespoons lemon juice
¼ teaspoon freshly ground pepper
¼ cup grated Parmesan or Romano cheese

1 clove mashed garlic
2-ounce can flat anchovy filets
Garlic croutons (optional)
Marinated artichoke hearts, (optional)
Diced avocado (optional)

Wash lettuce, dry, and place in plastic bag. Refrigerate several hours.

Into jar with tight lid or a blender, mix all ingredients except anchovies. Shake until well mixed or blend a few seconds in blender. Drain and chop half of anchovies; then stir into mixture. Add more to taste.

Just before serving, break up Romaine into a bowl and toss. Add crisp, garlic croutons, marinated artichoke hearts, and/or diced avocado for an extra touch.

Sandy Wheeler

Mushroom Salad

Serves 6

½ pound medium-size mushrooms
½ cup packed parsley sprigs
1 clove garlic
⅓ cup salad oil
2 tablespoons white wine vinegar
1 tablespoon mayonnaise

½ teaspoon salt
⅛ teaspoon dry mustard
⅛ teaspoon freshly ground pepper
12–18 Boston lettuce leaves, washed and chilled

Wash and drain mushrooms. Slice evenly. Mince parsley and add to mushrooms. Cover and chill until ready to serve.

Cut garlic in half and chop fine (food processor may be used). Add oil, vinegar, mayonnaise, salt, mustard, and pepper. Blend well.

Just before serving, pour dressing over mushrooms and toss until well mixed. Arrange 2 or 3 lettuce leaves on each individual serving plate and spoon salad onto center of leaves.

Kathy Murphey

Salad Mélange

Serves 10

½ head lettuce, shredded
3 hard-boiled eggs, chopped
½ cup sliced spring onions
8 slices bacon, cooked crisp and crumbled
1 cup shredded Swiss cheese
½ cup grated carrots
½ cup diced celery

1 cup mayonnaise, homemade is better
10-ounce package frozen petite peas, thawed and blanched
Salt, freshly ground pepper, and sugar to taste

In a $8 \times 12 \times 2$-inch rectangular dish, place a layer of lettuce. Sprinkle with salt, pepper, and sugar. Place a layer of eggs and sprinkle with salt.

Layer, in order, onions, celery, peas, carrots, bacon, and cheese.

Spread mayonnaise over all, sealing to the edges. Cover and refrigerate for 24 hours.

Stasch Zimmerman

Pea Salad Vinaigrette

Serves 8

This salad is colorful, tasty, easy, and refreshingly different!

2 10-ounce packages frozen peas (tiny or regular size)
½ cup salad oil
3 tablespoons red wine vinegar
2 tablespoons scallions, finely chopped
1 tablespoon parsley, minced

1 tablespoon diced pimento
2 tablespoons sweet pickles, finely chopped
Freshly ground pepper, to taste
1 teaspoon salt

Cook frozen peas by pouring boiling water over them to cover. Let stand for approximately 3 minutes and drain.

Combine salad oil, wine vinegar, scallions, pickles, parsley, pimento, salt, and pepper in a jar. Cover and shake well to make dressing.

Pour dressing over peas and refrigerate at least 2 hours; make a day ahead if possible. Toss lightly before serving.

Marnie Nicholson

Spinach and Mushroom Salad

Serves 6

10 ounces fresh spinach	¾ teaspoon salt
6 slices lean bacon, broiled until crisp	⅛ teaspoon pepper, freshly ground
1 bunch scallions, sliced	1 finely minced garlic clove
¼ pound mushrooms, sliced	⅛ teaspoon dry mustard
2 tablespoons lemon juice	¼ teaspoon sugar
6 tablespoons olive oil	1 egg yolk

Trim, thoroughly wash and dry spinach. Place in a salad bowl.

Crumble bacon over spinach; add scallions and mushrooms. Chill.

Combine remaining ingredients and blend well. Chill. Use to dress salad.

Loren Kitt
NSO Member

Spring Salad

Serves 2

	DRESSING
⅓ head Romaine lettuce	½ cup light salad or olive oil
1 cup fresh strawberries	¼ cup tarragon vinegar
1 large grapefruit	2 teaspoons dry or prepared mustard
4–5 sprigs fresh dill	Salad herbs, to taste
	Tarragon leaves, to taste
	Fresh dill, to taste
	Diced pieces of cream cheese, optional

Tear bite-size pieces of lettuce. Clean and slice strawberries in half. Cut grapefruit in half and cut out sections.

Put grapefruit and strawberries on lettuce and squeeze remainder of grapefruit juice over them.

DRESSING

Mix dressing ingredients together and shake well. Pour over fruit and lettuce.

Add diced pieces of cream cheese over all, if desired.

Elizabeth H. Bernbaum

Spring Salad Bowl

Serves 6 for a lovely
luncheon main course

1½ pounds fresh
     spinach, washed
     and torn up
6   hard-boiled eggs,
     quartered
2   pounds tomato
     wedges
     1-pound can hearts of
     palm, sliced in
     strips, lengthwise
     1-pound can beets,
     cut in julienne
     strips
¾   pound fresh
     mushrooms, sliced

DRESSING
¼   cup mayonnaise
2   tablespoons red wine
     vinegar
1   tablespoon Dijon
     mustard
½   cup oil
1   teaspoon salt
     Sugar to taste (1–3
     teaspoons)

On individual plates, arrange beds of spinach. Place vegetables and eggs either in individual sections or randomly scattered.

DRESSING

Make dressing by mixing mayonnaise, vinegar, mustard, oil, salt, and sugar together in a blender or food processor. Drizzle over salad or pass at the table.

Mrs. Robert J. Garrison

Vegetable Salad With Pesto

Serves 4

2 pounds green beans, cooked briefly (crisp)
2 fresh tomatoes, diced
1 large green pepper, diced
½ pound Fontina cheese, diced same size as vegetables

1 leaf fresh basil, chopped *or*
3 tablespoons pesto*
¼ cup olive oil
¼ cup wine vinegar
Salt and freshly ground pepper to taste
Zucchini (optional)

Cook beans and cool. Cut up other vegetables. Cut up cheese. Chop basil.

Dilute pesto with oil and vinegar. Toss all vegetables and cheese together with pesto. Season to taste.

Leftover beans or other vegetables such as zucchini can be used. Other cheeses may be substituted for Fontina.

*See Pesto Recipe in Sauces and Relishes Section.

Cookbook Committee

Watercress, Endive, and Orange Salad

Serves 6 to 8

3 endives
1 bunch watercress
2–3 oranges

MUSTARD DRESSING
½ cup vegetable oil
2 tablespoons olive oil
2 tablespoons cider vinegar
1 teaspoon honey
1 tablespoon Dijon mustard
2–3 peeled and chopped shallots

Wash endives and cut lengthwise into thin strips. Wash, dry, and trim watercress. Peel and slice oranges.

On a large platter, arrange watercress in a circle. Place endive strips around watercress, and put oranges in middle.

MUSTARD DRESSING

To make dressing, place all ingredients in a blender or food processor and blend well. Pour over salad.

Jane Lehrman

Potatoes with Sauce Huancaina

Serves 6 to 8

8–10 medium-size potatoes
1 teaspoon finely grated onion
1 teaspoon ground chili (hot red peppers) without seeds, or to taste
1 tablespoon oil
½ cup cottage cheese
6 ounces feta cheese

Milk, enough for mixing following ingredients:
1 teaspoon salt
½ teaspoon turmeric
1 teaspoon lemon juice
½ cup mayonnaise
Olives, hard-boiled eggs, and lettuce for garnish

Fry onion and ground chili in oil.

Blend cheeses and milk to make a thick cream and season with salt and turmeric. Add onion and chili mixture, then lemon juice and mayonnaise.

Boil potatoes in their jackets and let cool. Peel and slice or quarter them.

Serve sauce over potatoes and garnish with olives and hard-boiled eggs on lettuce.

Embassy of Peru

Warm Potato Salad

Serves 4

2 pounds new potatoes, cleaned and cut into bite-size pieces
4–5 slices bacon
½ red pepper, cut into ½-inch cubes
3 green onions, sliced
1 clove garlic, minced

1 tablespoon white wine vinegar
1 tablespoon red wine vinegar
1½ tablespoons Dijon mustard
2 tablespoons fresh herbs, chopped (parsley, chives, and/or rosemary)
Salt and freshly ground pepper

Place potatoes in a 2-quart pan and cover with cold water. Add 2 teaspoons salt, bring to a rapid boil, then decrease heat and continue cooking until tender. Drain well.

Meanwhile cook bacon, reserving ¼ cup of bacon fat in pan in which bacon was cooked. Crumble bacon and return to pan. Add red pepper, onions, garlic, vinegars, mustard, herbs, salt, and pepper. Mix well.

Place potatoes in a heat-proof bowl, add bacon dressing, and mix well. Correct seasonings. Keep warm in a 200° oven until ready to serve.

Cookbook Committee

Wild Rice Salad

Serves 8

1 cup wild rice, cooked, drained, and chilled
1 jar marinated artichoke hearts, drained and sliced
10-ounce box frozen peas, blanched
1 pint cherry tomatoes, halved
1 bunch green onions, chopped
½ green pepper, chopped
1 package Good Seasons Old Fashioned French dressing mix
1 ripe avocado

To cook wild rice, wash; cover with 3 inches salted water. Cook 30 minutes until tender, not mushy. Rice will open and expose white interior.

Chill all ingredients and toss together.

Mix dressing according to directions and blend all avocado into it. Use food processor or blender to do this.

Toss dressing with vegetable mixture. Good as a summer main course with muffins and a carrot salad.

Mrs. Robert J. Garrison

Chicken-Fruit Salad

Serves 6

3–4 whole chicken breasts or 1 whole chicken
1 can pineapple chunks or mandarin oranges, drained and cut in halves
1½ cups seedless grapes
½ ounce can water chestnuts, sliced
1 cup celery, sliced diagonally
⅔ cup mayonnaise
1 tablespoon soy sauce, or to taste
½ teaspoon curry powder
1 cup slivered, toasted almonds (optional)
Lettuce
Fresh diced apples, (optional)

Poach chicken in broth, cool, and cube to make about 3 cups chicken.

Combine chicken, fruit, water chestnuts, and celery. Mix mayonnaise, soy sauce, and curry (taste to adjust seasonings to personal liking).

Toss chicken and mayonnaise mixture together. Chill and serve on lettuce. Garnish with toasted almonds or mandarin oranges.

This is wonderful preceeded by a good soup, and served with whole wheat muffins.

Virginia MacLaury

Jane's Chicken Bombay

Serves 6

4 cups cooked chicken
   pieces (4 whole
   chicken breasts)
1 cup green seedless
   grapes
½ cup blanched almonds
6 ounces chutney
½ cup mayonnaise
1 banana, sliced
   Salt and freshly
   ground pepper, to
   taste

Cook chicken and cut into bite-size pieces. Add salt and pepper. Add grapes and blanched almonds.

Mix together chutney and mayonnaise. Pour over chicken mixture. Stir. Chill several hours or overnight.

Just before serving, add sliced banana.

Doris Curtis

Warm Chicken Salad

Serves 8

4 cups cold, cut up
   chicken chunks
   (cooked)
2 tablespoons lemon
   juice
¾ cup mayonnaise
1 teaspoon salt
2 cups chopped celery
4 hard-boiled eggs,
   sliced
¾ cup cream of chicken
   soup
1 teaspoon finely
   minced onion
2 pimentos, cut fine
1½ cups crushed potato
   chips
1 cup grated cheese
⅔ cup finely chopped,
   toasted almonds

Combine all ingredients except cheese, potato chips and almonds. Place in a large rectangular dish. Top with remaining 3 ingredients.

Let stand overnight in refrigerator. Bake in 400° oven for 20 to 25 minutes.

Mrs. Richard M. Nixon

Joanne's Smoked Chicken Salad With Curry

Serves 6 to 8

4 cups shredded,
   smoked chicken meat
2 cups diced celery
½ cup chopped parsley
1 cup chopped pecans
1 cup white raisins
1 cup shredded coconut
1 cup heavy cream,
   whipped
½ cup mayonnaise
2 tablespoons mild
   curry
   Salt and freshly
   ground pepper, to
   taste

Prepare chicken in a smoker or covered kettle-type charcoal grill, following manufacturer's directions for indirect cooking of poultry. Let chicken stand to cool and pour out any liquid which has collected in cavity.

Pull meat from chicken and shred. Do not use skin.

Combine chicken, celery, parsley, pecans, and raisins. Toss gently to mix.

Add half of whipped cream and all of mayonnaise, coconut and curry. Toss gently to mix ingredients.

Add remaining whipped cream for desired moistness. Additional curry may be added and salt and freshly ground pepper to taste.

Salad should stand overnight. Before serving pile into crisp lettuce cups.

VARIATION

Smoked turkey is a good substitute for chicken. Increase amounts of other ingredients relative to amount of meat.

Barry E. Huber

Salat Olivier

Serves 6

2 large whole chicken breasts, halved
1 large onion, peeled and quartered
1 teaspoon salt
4 new potatoes, boiled, peeled, and thinly sliced
3 hard-boiled eggs, peeled and thinly sliced
3 spring onions, chopped
½ cup celery, chopped
1 teaspoon salt
⅛ teaspoon white pepper
½ cup mayonnaise
1 cup sour cream
1 tablespoon fresh dill, minced

1 medium tomato, peeled and cut lengthwise into eighths
Lettuce leaves

In a heavy 2 to 3 quart pot, combine chicken, onion quarters, and salt. Cover with about 1½ quarts cold water and bring to a boil, uncovered, over high heat, skimming off fat and scum as it rises to surface. Partially cover pan, reduce heat to low, and simmer 15 to 20 minutes, or until chicken is tender.

Chill cooked chicken breasts, if desired. With a sharp knife, remove and discard skin and cut meat away from bones. Cut meat into strips about ½ inch wide and combine them in a large mixing bowl with potatoes, eggs, celery, and spring onions. Sprinkle with salt and white pepper.

In a small bowl, combine mayonnaise and sour cream, and stir half of it into salad. Taste for seasoning.

To serve, place salad on lettuce leaves and garnish with sliced tomato. Top with dressing and sprinkle dill over all.

Cathy Tennyson

Springtime Roast Beef Salad

Serves 2

SALAD
- ¼ pound cooked roast beef, cut in julienne strips
- 14 asparagus stalks, peeled and cooked
- 4 medium mushroom caps, cut in julienne strips
- 3 tablespoons blue cheese, crumbled
- 3 scallions, minced
- 1 tablespoon parsley, chopped
- 1 tablespoon chives, chopped
- 6 leaves Romaine lettuce, washed, dried, and left whole

DRESSING
- 1 teaspoon mustard
- 2 tablespoons red wine vinegar
- ¼ cup olive oil
  Salt and freshly ground pepper to taste
- ½ clove garlic, minced

SALAD

Wonderful luncheon dish!

Place 3 Romaine leaves on each of 2 salad plates. Place asparagus on plates as in spokes of a bike.

In a 1-quart mixing bowl, toss together mushrooms, roast beef, scallions and parsley. Place half roast beef mixture on center of each plate. Pour some dressing over roast beef (recipe below). Sprinkle salad with blue cheese and chives. Pass remaining dressing on side.

DRESSING

Mix mustard, vinegar, salt, pepper, and garlic well. Slowly add olive oil. Set aside.

Salad can be made several hours in advance, covered with plastic and stored in refrigerator. Bring to room temperature ½ hour before serving.

Julia M. Logue-Riordan

Raspberry Vinaigrette Dressing

RASPBERRY VINEGAR

1 bottle raspberry syrup and
1 bottle red wine vinegar
   both in equal quantity
2 tablespoons raspberry
   vinegar
4 tablespoons walnut oil
1 teaspoon Dijon
   mustard
   Sea salt and freshly
   ground pepper to
   taste

To make raspberry vinegar, mix raspberry syrup and vinegar together well. Allow to set for one week before using.

TO MAKE DRESSING

Put raspberry vinegar in a mixing bowl. Add mustard, sea salt, and pepper.
Add walnut oil, slowly mixing well with a whisk. Mix or shake well before serving. Serve over mildly favored lettuce.

Store in a dark, cool place tightly covered or in a dark glass container tightly covered. Keeps practically forever.

Cookbook Committee

B R E A D S

General Comments about Bread Baking

Baking bread is simple and fun. Too often, people consider a recipe an inflexible rule, one that cannot be changed. The truth is, a recipe should be used as a guide, a guide that only indicates direction, not one to be followed unswervingly. If you worry too much about details, you'll miss the pleasure of baking bread. Bread being prepared needs to be touched. Baked bread needs to be tasted. If you simply bake by the numbers, you will miscount. Only when you enjoy both the touch and the taste of bread—both the process and the product—will you become a real bread baker.

Here are some thoughts about bread baking. Use them as a guide, especially when trying something new.

INGREDIENTS

Have all ingredients out before you start. There is nothing more frustrating than having your hands covered with dough and discovering that you need sugar which is on the top shelf of the cupboard.

Have all the ingredients at room temperature. Milk and other liquids should not be used directly from the refrigerator because cold ingredients do not permit the yeast to do its work properly. If ingredients are cold, your large loaf of dough might never rise or might take all morning and part of the afternoon to rise properly.

If the recipe calls for heating ingredients or melting butter, let everything cool before using. But how cool is cool? The answer is simple if you've ever prepared a baby's bottle. If not, cool is warm, but not hot, to the touch. You can use a thermometer, but it takes away all the fun.

Substitute unbleached, enriched flour for white flour. It's better for you, and it tastes better, too. For variety, add wheat or rye flour instead of using all white flour. However, if you use only wheat or rye flour, the result will be a coarse, heavy bread that will not rise as far or as fast as one made with white flour.

Nuts make a fun addition in almost any bread. About ¼ cup coarsely chopped nuts per loaf is about the right amount.

If you are making oatmeal breads, try using steel-cut oats. Use them as you would rolled oats. They'll give a very different texture to the finished bread.

PREPARING YEAST

Yeast is the life of your bread. If you do a lot of baking, buy yeast in bulk from a food co-op. This will not only save you money, but the yeast also tends to be fresher. Yeast will keep for months in the refrigerator in a sealed jar.

Make it a habit to "proof" your yeast, a simple test to be sure the yeast is still active. To proof, simply take warm water or some of the liquid used in the recipe, sprinkle the yeast on top, and add a little sugar. The mixture should start to foam within five minutes or less, little bubbles should appear at least. Proofing also assures that the yeast will dissolve and gives it a head start on the work it has to do.

KNEADING AND RISING Many people think of kneading bread dough as hard work. Actually, it is a pleasure second only to eating the finished product. Kneading stretches the dough and gives the bread its texture. You know the dough has been kneaded sufficiently when you push down and the dough pushes back. For most breads, this should take from six to ten minutes.

Letting the bread rise scares people. Just how much is double? Don't worry, it's easy to tell. To tell if the dough has risen sufficiently, stick your finger in it. If the dough springs back, let it rise a little longer. If your finger's imprint stays there, the dough has risen enough. Don't test bread this way on the second rising when it is in the baking pans or your bread will have finger holes in it.

If you have a gas oven, it is the best place to let the dough rise, but be sure to have both the pilot light and the inside light on. This gives an ideal warm, draft-free place for dough to rise.

BAKING Any kind of baking pan is fine. However, if you use a glass pan, lower the recommended temperature 25 degrees. Try not to mix metal and glass pans when baking the same recipe.

Bread is done when you tap the bottom of the loaf and it sounds hollow, like a drum. Take the loaf out of the pan first, of course!

Cool bread completely on wire racks before storing. Most breads freeze well and will keep for weeks. Be sure to wrap them air tight before storing.

One final suggestion. Make more than one loaf of bread at a time. If your oven holds six baking tins, then make six loaves of bread. Preparation time is exactly the same, and the extra bread can be stored. For the same amount of effort, you'll get six times the pleasure.

Bohemian Rye Bread

Makes 2 loaves

2 packages dry yeast
2 cups warm water
¼ cup brown sugar or molasses
3 cups all-purpose flour
2 cups rye flour
2 teaspoons salt

3 tablespoons melted shortening
1 tablespoon caraway seeds
1 teaspoon cornstarch
½ cup water

Combine warm water and brown sugar or molasses. Sprinkle in dry yeast. Stir in 1 cup of each of the flours. Beat until smooth. Let stand 20 minutes until spongy.

Stir in cooled, melted shortening, salt, and caraway seeds. Add remaining flour to make soft dough. Knead on floured board until smooth and elastic, about 10 minutes, adding flour if necessary.

Let rise in covered, greased bowl in warm place until double in bulk. Punch down, knead several times, and allow to rest 20 to 30 minutes. Divide into 2 pieces and knead each into a smooth, round shape. Place in pie tins sprinkled with rye flour. Let bread rise until double in bulk.

Preheat oven to 375°. Place pan of water in bottom of oven. Carefully spray loaves with water and bake about 40 to 50 minutes, spraying occasionally.

Mix cornstarch in water, boil, and cook for 1 minute. Brush on baked loaves. Return loaves to oven for about 3 minutes.

C. Z. Serpan

Simply Simple Supper Bread

Makes 4 loaves

3 packages yeast
1 cup warm water
2 teaspoons sugar
3 cups warm water
½ cup oil (olive or corn)

2 teaspoons salt
6 cups white flour (approximately)
6 cups wheat flour (approximately)
Sesame seeds

Proof yeast by sprinkling yeast over 1 cup water, add sugar and let yeast dissolve. After about 5 minutes, it should start foaming.

Mix yeast, 3 cups water, oil, and salt in a large bowl. Add flour alternating white and wheat. Mix as you add. When the dough is firm enough to knead, take it out of bowl and knead using additional white flour if necessary to keep from sticking. Knead for about 10 minutes.

Place dough in a buttered bowl and butter it all over. Cover and let rise for about 2 hours.

Divide dough into 4 parts. Shape into French style loaves. Place on oiled cookie sheets. Wet tops and sprinkle sesame seeds on top. Slash tops diagonally and place loaves in oven.

Turn oven to 400°. Bake for 35 minutes or until done. Test by tapping bottom of loaf. If it sounds hollow, bread is done.

This bread can be started from scratch 3 hours before dinner. It produces an Italian type loaf that goes well with almost any meal. If you make more than you need, put the remaining loaves in the freezer.

George Ziener

Cornell Bread

**Makes 2 large or
3 medium loaves**

3 cups warm water (95°
   to 110°)
2 packages dry yeast
2 tablespoons honey
7–8 cups unbleached
   flour
⅓ cup full fat soy flour
½ cup skim milk
   powder
4 teaspoons salt
2 tablespoons
   vegetable oil
¼ cup wheat germ

"This bread was originated at Cornell University to produce a nutritionally improved bread so far superior to the commercial product that life could be sustained on bread and butter alone."

Put water, yeast, and honey in bowl of electric mixer and let stand for 5 minutes while yeast dissolves. Sift flour, wheat germ, soy flour, and milk powder together in a separate bowl. Begin stirring yeast mixture in electric mixer. Add salt and 3 cups of flour mixture. Beat for 2 minutes. Add oil and 3 more cups of flour mixture. Blend well and knead, either on floured board or using a dough hook, until smooth and elastic.

Turn dough into a greased bowl, brush top with soft butter, cover, and let rise until double in bulk, about 1½ hours. Punch down, fold edges over, and let rise another 20 minutes.

Turn dough onto board and shape into 2 loaves. Place in greased or buttered loaf pans. Cover and let rise until doubled.

Bake loaves at 350° for 50 to 60 minutes.

If in doubt, tap loaves with your finger after 50 minutes. If they sound hollow, they are done.

Frances Fogel

Danish Buttermilk Bread

Makes 2 loaves

2 cups buttermilk,
  scalded
4 tablespoons butter
1 tablespoon sugar
1 tablespoon salt
1 tablespoon yeast
¼ cup warm water
6 cups all–purpose
  flour, approximately

Melt butter in warm buttermilk. Cool. Soften yeast in warm water.

Add cooled buttermilk mixture to softened yeast. Add sugar and salt. Gradually mix in flour. Knead for 5 to 10 minutes. The dough should be soft but not sticky. Place in a bowl and let rise until double in bulk (approximately 1½ hours). Punch dough down. Repeat process if time permits.

Form into 2 loaves and place in 5 × 9-inch bread pans. Let rise until double in bulk (approximately 1½ hours).

Bake at 375° for 35 minutes. Remove from pans and cool on rack. For extra touch, brush tops of warm loaves with butter.

VARIATIONS

For up to 2 cups of the white flour, substitute equal quantities of whole wheat flour, wheat germ, oatmeal, etc.

For cinnamon bread, before forming into loaves, roll each half of dough into a 9–inch wide rectangle. Rub surface of dough with soft butter and sprinkle with cinnamon, ground cloves, or nutmeg, and raisins and nuts. Roll up, beginning with 9-inch edge. Pinch edges together to seal. Place in bread pan, sealed edge down.

Ann Leonard

Danish Rye Bread

Makes 1 loaf

SPONGE
1 cup rye flour
½ cup buttermilk
½ teaspoon salt

BREAD
2 cups water
1 tablespoon salt
3 packages dry yeast
3–4 cups rye flour

SPONGE

Mix rye flour with buttermilk and salt. Cover with plastic wrap and keep in cool place for at least 2 days but no longer than 3.

BREAD

Stir sponge with water and salt. Add yeast. Add rye flour gradually until dough holds together. Dough will feel somewhat greasy. Knead for 8 to 10 minutes.

Let rise for 1 hour, shape dough into loaf, and let rise again for 45 minutes. Dough will not double as wheat flour dough does. Punch bread with fork. Brush with water and melted butter.

Bake at 425° in lower portion of oven for 1¼ to 1½ hours.

Susanne Misner

Granola Bread

Makes 2 or 3 loaves

2 packages dry yeast
2 teaspoons sugar
1 cup warm water
⅓ cup butter
1 cup boiling water
1 cup plain granola
½ cup dark molasses
1 tablespoon salt
5½ cups flour
1 egg

Mix yeast and sugar in 1 cup warm water and let stand 10 minutes.

Mix butter and boiling water until butter is melted. Combine granola, molasses, and salt with butter and boiling water. Add yeast mixture and stir. Add egg. Stir in flour. Mix until sticky.

Refrigerate overnight or at least 2 to 4 hours.

Knead well. Shape into 2 or 3 loaves. Let rise until double in bulk. Bake in 350° oven, 1 hour for 2 loaves, 45 minutes for 3 loaves.

Ruth Thompson

Easy Oatmeal Bread

Makes 2 loaves

2 cups boiling water
1 cup quick oats
½ cup whole wheat flour
3 tablespoons butter
1 teaspoon salt
½ cup brown sugar
2 packages dry yeast
½ cup warm water
5 cups all-purpose flour

Pour 2 cups boiling water over first 5 ingredients. Dissolve yeast in ½ cup warm water. Cool wheat flour mixture, then add yeast. Mix together. Add white flour until mixture gathers into a ball (you may not need all 5 cups). Knead on a floured board until smooth.

Put in greased bowl. Let rise until double in bulk (1½ to 2 hours). Punch down. Let rise again until double. Punch down.

Shape into 2 loaves. Let rise about 15 minutes. Bake at 350° for 30 minutes.

Wynne B. Beaman

Oatmeal Sunflower Gluten Bread

Makes 2 loaves

2 cups rolled oats
½ teaspoon salt
2 cups boiling water
2 packages dry yeast
¼ cup lukewarm water
½ cup molasses
1 tablespoon oil
1 cup raisins
¾ cup hulled raw sunflower seeds
½ cup gluten flour
5 cups unbleached flour, approximately

Mix rolled oats and salt, cover with boiling water and let stand for about 1 hour, stirring at least once.

Dissolve yeast in lukewarm water and add to oats. Add remaining ingredients (be sure oats have cooled sufficiently before mixing) and knead in enough flour to make a smooth, elastic dough (10 minutes).

Let rise until double in bulk, about 2 hours. Knead down for 1 minute and let rise again until double, about 1 hour.

Knead down for 1 minute and shape into 2 loaves. Place in greased bread pans. Cover with damp cloth and let rise until cloth begins to lift.

Bake at 350° for about 1 hour. Remove from pans immediately and cool on wire racks.

William Foster, NSO Member &
Viola Foster

Tomato Bread

Makes 4 loaves

1 package yeast
½ cup warm water
2 tablespoons sugar
2½ cups tomato juice
2 tablespoons butter
2 teaspoons salt
7–8 cups flour
Sesame seeds
1 egg, slightly beaten

Heat tomato juice, butter, and salt in a saucepan until butter melts. Let cool until just warm. Let yeast soften in warm water. Add sugar.

Stir tomato juice mixture and yeast mixture together in large bowl. Add 2 to 3 cups flour and beat 200 strokes (4 minutes with electric mixer). Add remaining flour one cup at a time, stirring until each cup is completely mixed in.

When dough is firm enough to knead (sticky but not gooey) place on floured surface and knead for 8 minutes, adding flour until dough is smooth and springs back to shape when poked with finger.

Place in covered bowl and let rise until double in bulk (1 hour). Shape into 4 long rectangles and roll into long loaves. Place on cookie sheet, brush with egg and sprinkle with sesame seeds. Slash tops. Place in cold oven to rise until double in bulk (45 minutes).

Bake at 375° for approximately 30 minutes. Bread is done when light brown and hollow sounding when tapped on bottom.

George H. Ziener

Lithuanian Christmas Bread

Makes 1 loaf

1 cake yeast or 1
    package dry yeast
¼ cup butter
¼ cup sugar
1½ teaspoons salt
½ cup scalded milk
¼ cup cold water
1 egg

1½ cups white raisins
¼ cup poppy seeds
3 cups all–purpose
    flour, sifted
Honey

Dissolve yeast in ¼ cup lukewarm water. Combine butter, sugar, salt, milk, and cold water. Add the egg, raisins, poppy seeds, and yeast mixture. Add sifted flour and mix well until blended thoroughly.

Grease a 9 × 5 × 3-inch pan and pour mixture into it. Cover with towel and let rise in warm place (85°) for about 1½ hours, or until light.

Bake in moderate 350° oven for about 50 to 60 minutes. The last 5 minutes of baking, remove from oven, brush with warmed honey, and sprinkle with poppy seeds. Return to oven. Make sure honey does not get too dark.

Mrs. Ona Backis
Embassy of Lithuania

Sue's Rolls

Makes about 48 rolls

1 cup shortening
1 cup boiling water
½ cup sugar
1 teaspoon salt
2 packages dry yeast
2 eggs

1 cup lukewarm water
6–7 cups all purpose
    flour
2 tablespoons butter

Combine first 4 ingredients and set aside. Add yeast to warm water and add to first mixture. Add eggs. Begin to add flour to form a soft dough.

Put in warm place and let rise for 1 hour.

Punch down and roll out on floured board. Cut into rounds. Fold over and place on lightly greased baking sheet. Brush with melted butter. Cover, and let rise, 1 hour.

Bake at 450° for 20 to 25 minutes, or until browned

VARIATION

Shape dough into 2 loaves and bake in loaf pans at 300° for approximately 45 minutes.

Mrs. Charles G. Rose

Quick Icebox Rolls

Makes 18 to 24 rolls

¾ cup milk
¼ cup sugar
3 tablespoons shortening
1 teaspoon salt
1 package yeast
¼ cup lukewarm water
1 egg, beaten
3½ cups flour

Scald milk. Add sugar, shortening, salt and cool to lukewarm. Soften yeast in warm water. Add yeast and beaten egg to milk mixture. Add flour, ½ cup at a time and knead.

Put dough in a greased bowl and grease top half of dough. Place in refrigerator. When ready to bake, take dough out of refrigerator, roll on floured board to about ½-inch thickness and cut out circles with biscuit cutter. Place small chunk of butter in middle of circle and fold over. Let rise until double in bulk. Bake at 425° for 20 minutes.

Loren Kitt
NSO Member

Alice's Fluffy Biscuits

Number of biscuits will depend on the size of the cutter

2 cups flour, sifted
4 teaspoons baking powder
1 teaspoon salt
2 teaspoons sugar
½ teaspoon cream of tartar
½ cup shortening
⅔ cup milk

Mix dry ingredients. Cut in shortening with 2 knives. Add milk and mix well.

Knead dough lightly; roll to desired thickness. Bake in 400° oven until brown.

Patrick Hayes

Mrs. Lyndon B. Johnson's Popovers

Makes 6 to 8 popovers

"This is one of our favorite 'house dishes.' Our friends know they're sure to have popovers for one meal during a house-party."

1 cup sifted flour
1 cup milk
2 eggs, beaten
¼ teaspoon salt
2 tablespoons shortening, melted

Mix and sift flour and salt. Combine eggs, milk, and shortening. Add gradually to flour mixture, beating about 1 minute or until batter is smooth. Fill greased, sizzling-hot pans three-quarters full and bake in very hot oven (450°) for about 20 minutes. Reduce heat to 350° and continue baking for 15 to 20 minutes.

Lady Bird Johnson

Bran Muffins

Makes 2 to 3 dozen

1 cup boiling water
1 cup 100% Bran cereal
1 cup sugar
¼ cup butter
¼ cup oil or shortening
2 eggs
1 cup flour
1½ cups whole wheat flour
2½ teaspoons baking soda
½ teaspoon salt
1¾ cups buttermilk
2 cups All-Bran cereal
¾ cup sunflower seeds
⅓ cup wheat germ
⅓ cup chopped dates

Mix all ingredients and refrigerate overnight. Do not stir again. Pour batter into muffin tins and bake at 400° for 20 minutes.

VARIATION

Sunflower seeds, wheat germ, and dates are optional.

Batter will keep in refrigerator for a few days.

Susan Koehler

Marmalade Brunch Brans

Makes 18 to 24 muffins

1 cup marmalade
2 cups All-Bran cereal
½ cup honey
2½ cups all-purpose flour
2½ teaspoons baking soda
½ cup safflower oil
1 teaspoon salt
2 eggs, beaten
2 cups low-fat
   buttermilk
½ cup sugar

Mix marmalade, honey, sugar, flour, cereal, baking soda, and salt. Add oil, eggs, and buttermilk and combine well. Place batter in greased or paper-lined muffin tins. Bake at 375° for 20 minutes.

For stronger honey taste, use raw honey instead of processed honey.

Helen P. Panarites

Coffee Cake

Serves 8 to 12

½ pound butter
1 cup sugar
2 eggs
2 cups flour
1 teaspoon baking
   powder
1 teaspoon baking soda
1 cup sour cream
¼ teaspoon salt
1 teaspoon vanilla
½ cup sugar
1 tablespoon cinnamon
½ cup chopped nuts

Mix together sugar, cinnamon, and nuts. Set aside. Mix together baking soda and sour cream. Set aside.
Cream butter with sugar. Add eggs and mix well. Add all dry ingredients and mix well. Add vanilla and sour cream mixture.
Spoon half of batter into greased tube or bundt pan and sprinkle with one-third of cinnamon-nut mixture. Add remainder of batter and sprinkle with cinnamon-nut mixture. Swirl with knife to marbelize. Sprinkle remaining cinnamon-nut mixture on top. Bake at 350° for 35 to 45 minutes.

Cookbook Committee

Ruth Tozar's Favorite Coffee Cake

Serves 8 to 12

2½ cups flour
¾ cup white sugar
1 cup brown sugar
1 teaspoon nutmeg
½ teaspoon salt
¾ cup salad oil
1 cup sour milk
1 teaspoon baking soda
1 beaten egg
½ cup nuts
2 teaspoons cinnamon

Mix flour, brown and white sugar, nutmeg, salt, and oil well. Remove ¾ cup of mixture and to it add nuts and cinnamon.

To rest of mixture add sour milk with baking soda and beaten egg. Mix well and put in a greased 8½ × 11-inch pan. Sprinkle nuts and cinnamon mixture on top.

Bake at 350° for 1 hour.

Ruth Strickland Tozar

Sticky Buns

Makes 24 to 36 buns

1 cup milk
1 scant tablespoon
    salt
2 tablespoons sugar
3 walnut-sized blobs
    shortening
1 cake yeast
¼ cup warm water
3–3½ cups flour
    Brown sugar-
      cinnamon mixture
    Raisins, optional

Combine milk, salt, sugar, and shortening. Scald. Set aside to cool. Soak yeast in warm water. Combine yeast with cooled milk mixture and mix. Stir in flour by hand. Dough will be very sticky.

Let rise. Turn onto board and knead just a little. Cut dough in half.

Roll out one half of dough into 8 × 14-inch rectangle. Smear with melted butter. Sprinkle with brown sugar, cinnamon and raisins, if desired. Roll up, cut into slices and arrange in greased pie or cake pan. Let rise again. Repeat with other half of dough. Bake at 357° for 15 to 20 minutes. Turn out of pan and cool.

Sally Hedrick

Almond Puff Pastry

Serves 12

CRUST
1 cup flour
1 stick butter, cold
2 tablespoons water

TOPPING
1 cup water
1 cup butter
1 teaspoon almond
   extract
1 cup flour
3 eggs

FROSTING
3 cups unsifted
   confectioners sugar
1 teaspoon almond
   extract
¼ cup butter
¼ cup milk

CRUST

Cut butter into flour until it is pea-size. Add water and mix only until dough forms a ball. Divide in half and pat each half into an 8 × 12-inch oval.

TOPPING

Put butter and water in saucepan. Heat until butter melts and water just boils. Remove from heat and immediately add almond extract and flour all at once. Beat until mixture forms a ball. Add eggs, 1 at a time, beating well after each addition. Dough will become glossy. Spread each crust oval with half of topping. Bake at 350° for 1 hour. Cool.

FROSTING

Combine ingredients and beat until smooth. Frost pastries and sprinkle with sliced almonds or other chopped nuts.

Pamela Wojtowicz

Plum Bread

Makes 1 loaf

1 cup cut-up purple plums
1 cup sugar
½ cup butter
1 teaspoon vanilla
2 eggs
2 cups flour
½ teaspoon nutmeg
½ teaspoon baking soda
¼ cup yogurt
1 teaspoon baking
   powder
1 cup chopped nuts

Cream butter. Gradually add sugar and vanilla; beat until fluffy. Beat in eggs, 1 at a time.

Combine dry ingredients. Add to creamed mixture alternately with yogurt. Stir until well blended. Add plums and chopped nuts. Mix well.

Pour into greased 9 × 5-inch loaf pan. Bake at 350° for 50 to 55 minutes, until toothpick comes out clean.

Cool in pan.

Louise Cohen

German Apple Bread

Makes 1 loaf

2 cups flour
1 teaspoon salt
4 teaspoons baking
   powder
⅓ cup sugar
2–3 medium apples
2 tablespoons butter
2 tablespoons
   shortening
1 egg
1 cup milk

Sift flour, salt, sugar, and baking powder. Work in butter and shortening using fingers or pastry cutter.

Beat egg and add to milk. Add egg–milk mixture to flour mixture and pour into greased pan. Top with sliced apples, sharp ends down. Sprinkle with sugar and cinnamon.

Bake at 350° for 1 hour.

Glaze with confectioners sugar and water or cream frosting when cool.

Mrs. Ruth Matejka

Lemon Bread

Makes 2 loaves

1 cup butter
1¾ cups sugar
2 teaspoons baking powder
½ teaspoon salt
4 eggs, slightly beaten
2½ cups flour
1 cup milk

¾ cup coarsely chopped walnuts
Peel of 2 lemons, grated
Juice of 2 lemons
⅓–½ cup sugar

Cream sugar and butter together; combine baking powder, salt, and eggs. Stir in flour and milk, alternating ingredients. Add nuts and lemon rind.

Pour batter into 2 very well greased and floured loaf pans. Bake at 350° for 1 hour or until done.

While bread is baking, mix sugar with lemon juice. When bread is done, remove from oven and pierce tops with a toothpick, making small holes. Pour lemon-sugar mixture over hot loaves.

Cool loaves on a wire rack.

Patty Perkins Andringa

Tex-Mex Cornbread

Serves 4 to 6

1 cup yellow cornmeal
½ teaspoon baking soda
4 tablespoons oil
2 eggs
1 cup buttermilk, sour cream, or plain yogurt or any combination

2 canned green chiles, rinsed, seeded, and chopped
Pinch of salt
1 cup grated sharp Cheddar cheese

Combine all ingredients in a large bowl. Mix well, making sure that cheese and chiles are well distributed. Grease a 5 to 6-inch iron skillet. Pour in batter.

Bake for 20 to 25 minutes at 450°.

Slide out of pan, cut into wedges, and serve with butter and cheese.

VARIATION

In order to make more spicy, add more green chilies.

Francine M. Swift

Zucchini Bread

Makes 2 loaves

3 eggs
2 cups sugar
1 cup oil
3 cups flour
1 tablespoon cinnamon
1 tablespoon vanilla
1 teaspoon salt

1 teaspoon baking powder
2 teaspoons baking soda
2 large zucchini, grated
1 cup coarsely chopped pecans

Beat eggs until frothy. Stir in sugar, oil, and vanilla; beat mixture until thick and lemon-colored. Sift together dry ingredients. Stir into egg mixture alternately with zucchini. Fold in pecans.

Pour into 2 buttered and floured loaf pans and bake at 350° for 1 hour, or until tester comes out clean. Cool in pans for 10 minutes, then invert onto rack.

Helene R. Berman

VARIATION

In addition to zucchini and pecans, the following may be added: 1 cup grated carrots
1 cup raisins
1 cup sweet pitted cherries
½ cup chopped dates

Bake at 350° for 45 to 60 minutes

Sharon Press

Howard's Country Crêpes

Makes about 20 crêpes

This is an adaptation of the Cornmeal Cakes served at the Farmington Country Club in Charlottesville, Virginia.

½ cup all-purpose flour
1 cup white water-ground cornmeal
1 teaspoon baking powder
½ teaspoon salt

1½ teaspoons sugar
1 large egg
1½ pints milk
2 ounces melted butter, bacon grease or shortening

Combine dry ingredients. Add egg, milk, and butter. Mix thoroughly. This makes a very thin batter. Crêpes should be cooked on a very hot griddle; griddle should be well greased.

Stir batter each time, as cornmeal drops to bottom of bowl. For best results, use about 1½ tablespoons batter for each crêpe. Batter will keep for 48 hours.

Try these wrapped around filet of trout or serve with strawberry jam, or even just with butter.

Howard de Franceaux

SEAFOOD

Fish
Cookery

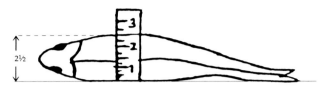

A simple way to determine how long to cook fish is to measure the fish at its thickest point and cook it for 10 minutes per inch. To measure, lay the fish on a flat surface on its side and measure at its tallest point as in the diagram above. Measure filets and steaks the same way; rolled filets by their diameter. For frozen fish, double the cooking time.

These instructions pertain to fish only, not to shellfish or crustaceans.

Filet of Fish with Cashews

Serves 4 to 6

1 whole fish (2–3 pounds) or fish filets
¾ cup crushed cashews
1 egg yolk
Butter or oil for basting
Salt and freshly ground pepper
Juice of 1 lemon
1 tablespoon melted butter
1 tablespoon sherry
2 tablespoons butter for frying

Season fish with salt and pepper. Grill, basting well with lemon juice, butter, or oil.

Mix crushed nuts with egg yolk and melted butter to form a paste. Fry paste in butter until golden brown. Deglaze pan with sherry to loosen nuts.

Spread nuts over fish and serve very hot with wedges of lemon and sprigs of fresh parsley.

Embassy of Kenya

Psari-Plaki
Baked fish

Serves 6 to 8

1 striped bass, 3–4 pounds (bream or haddock can be substituted)
4 small onions, chopped fine
1 clove garlic, chopped fine
Chopped fresh parsley
½ cup tomato juice, from fresh, ripe tomatoes, if possible
½ cup dry white wine
Salt and freshly ground pepper
Thick slices of fresh tomatoes (or drained, canned tomatoes)
½ cup olive oil (or salad oil)
Lemon juice

"One cannot travel to the Greek Islands without being aware of the marvelous scent of the sea. This recipe is synonymous with Greece. With a little Ouzo it will take your imagination to the Greek fishing villages."

Clean, wash, drain and salt fish. Slice into steaks and put aside. Mix onions, garlic, 4 tablespoons parsley, tomato juice, wine, salt, and pepper.

Grease a roasting pan with oil and lay a thick bed of chopped parsley over bottom.

Arrange slices of fish in pan and spread some of onion mixture over them. Top each with a slice of tomato and pour oil over all. Sprinkle generously with lemon juice and bake in a moderate oven (350°) for about 1 hour. Serve garnished with sprigs of fresh parsley.

Andreas Makris
NSO Member

Mrs. Weiss' Baked Fish

Serves 8 to 10

1 whole fish
   (approximately 4–6
   pounds)
   Lime juice
2 cups dry white
   wine
1 clove garlic,
   chopped fine
2 large onions,
   chopped fine
8–10 tomatoes, chopped
1 bay leaf
1 tablespoon tomato
   paste
1 cup tomato juice
1 cup water
1 tablespoon butter
½ cup olive oil
   Salt
   Pepper, freshly
   ground
   Fresh coriander,
   chopped
   Fresh parsley,
   chopped

On day before, clean fish and cover with a mixture of salt, pepper, lime juice, and wine. Add coriander and parsley. Marinate in refrigerator.

On following day, remove fish from marinade and place it in a baking dish. Strain marinade and reserve. Sauté garlic and onions in olive oil until golden brown. Add tomatoes and let simmer. Add strained marinade, tomato paste, tomato juice, water, and bay leaf. Add salt and pepper. Let simmer until sauce is thick. When ready, add butter and stir. Remove from heat and strain.

Brush fish with melted butter and olive oil. Pour some of sauce over fish. Bake fish in moderate oven. When fish is done, transfer to a serving dish and pour remaining sauce over it. Serve with mashed potatoes.

For a colorful dish, add ½ cup of chopped cooked spinach to the mashed potatoes.

Mrs. Antonio F. Azeredo da Silveira
Wife of the Ambassador of Brazil

Paupiette of Lemon Sole with Crabmeat & Coriander Sauce

Serves 2 to 3

3 3-ounce lemon sole filets
½ pound crabmeat
½ pound butter
¼ cup white wine
2 dashes Worcestershire
Lemon juice from 2 lemons
Salt and freshly ground pepper to taste
Water
½ bunch coriander

Roll crabmeat in each 3-ounce filet of sole. Season as desired with salt and pepper and lemon juice. Sprinkle on rolled filets a dash of paprika for color and a little melted butter. Broil 5 minutes; bake another 10 minutes in a 400° oven. Add water to bottom of pan as needed to keep fish from burning.

To make sauce, use pan that was used to cook filets. Add lemon juice, Worcestershire sauce, white wine, and butter. After butter is melted, add coriander to sauce and mix together. Pour sauce over paupiettes of lemon sole.

Chef Ki Choi
Wintergarden Restaurant at The Watergate

Dilled Monkfish

Serves 4

4 monkfish filets (approximately 2 pounds)
½ cup melted butter
2 tablespoons lemon juice
2 tablespoons white wine
Chopped fresh dill
Dash of Tabasco

Put two gashes in each filet.

Mix a sauce using butter, lemon juice, white wine, chopped dill, and Tabasco.

Pour sauce over filets, and broil for 10 to 20 minutes, turning once.

Monkfish is a relatively new but tasty fish in town. It can be tough if not cooked long enough.

Mrs. A. A. Sommer

Grenadin de Saumon Roti

Serves 6

2½ pounds boned and skinned salmon filet
10 tablespoons butter
5 garlic cloves
¼ pound fresh girolles (wood mushrooms) or dried Polish mushrooms, soaked in warm water for 15 minutes (available in gourmet sections of most food stores).
7 ounces pearl onions
Chicken stock
Sugar
1 tomato

1 tablespoon fresh thyme
1 tablespoon fresh chives
Clarified butter

Cut 2½ pounds of boned and skinned salmon filet into 4 lengthwise strips. Trim off sharp edges and cut each strip into 1½-inch lengths to form oval shapes.

Sauté in 3 tablespoons of butter in a preheated pan ¼ pound fresh girolles (wood mushrooms) and 2 unpeeled, smashed garlic cloves. Season to taste with salt and pepper. Cook approximately 1½ minutes. Discard garlic and set aside.

Cook pearl onions in chicken stock. Remove from stock while still crisp and sauté in 1 tablespoon of butter with a pinch of sugar until light brown in color. Set aside.

Finely dice one peeled and seeded tomato. Mince 1 tablespoon each fresh thyme and chives. Set aside.

Heat pan with clarified butter. Cook grenadins of salmon 3 minutes per side over medium flame. Remove and arrange on each plate. Spoon around salmon 1 tablespoon girolles interspersed with 4 or 5 of pearl onions.

Melt 6 tablespoons of butter over low heat. Add 3 cloves smashed garlic, diced tomatoes and herbs; bring to a boil. Discard garlic and drizzle over each salmon arrangement.

Chef Yannick Cam
Le Pavillon Restaurant

Baked Stuffed Red Snapper

Serves 4 to 6

3–3½ pounds whole red snapper, cleaned
¼ pound each of coarsely chopped filet of haddock, shelled, raw shrimp, cooked ham and artichoke hearts
1 hard-boiled egg, finely chopped
1 medium-size onion, chopped
1 medium-size green pepper, chopped
3 cloves garlic, minced
4 tablespoons highest quality olive oil
2 tablespoons lemon juice

2 whole lemons
½ cup dry white wine
2 tablespoons butter
2 tablespoons flour
4 tablespoons minced fresh parsley
Pimento slices
Salt
Ground white pepper

Preheat oven to 400°.

Rub white pepper and salt into cavity of fish. Place in lightly oiled baking pan.

Sauté onion, garlic and green pepper in 2 tablespoons olive oil until onion is transparent but not brown. Add haddock, shrimp, ham and artichokes. Cook over medium heat while stirring for 3 or 4 minutes. Add 3 tablespoons wine and cook 3 or 4 more minutes until shrimp is done. Add hard-boiled egg.

Stuff fish with mixture. Brush fish with 2 tablespoons each of lemon juice, white wine and olive oil. Reduce oven to 325°. Bake in middle of oven for about 40 minutes or until fish flakes when pierced with fork. Transfer fish carefully to platter and keep warm.

SAUCE

Strain juices and add remaining white wine. Boil until reduced to about ¾ cup. Add butter and flour and whisk until smooth. Simmer until sauce begins to thicken. Remove from heat and add 4 tablespoons minced fresh parsley. Cut strips of pimento (about ½ inch slices) and place vertically across fish. Form a row of thin lemon slices from tail to gills. Pour sauce over entire fish and serve on a bed of parsley.

Adel Sanchez
NSO Member

Yellowtail Snapper or Rockfish Meunière

Serves 2

2 yellowtail snapper filets (8 ounces) or	2 tablespoons dry sherry
2 rockfish filets (8 ounces)	3 tablespoons white port
Flour	1 tablespoon Maggie brand seasoning flour
3 tablespoons butter	2 teaspoons lemon butter (fresh lemon juice and butter mixed)
1 pound fresh mushrooms, sliced	Salt and freshly ground pepper
1 tablespoon parsley, chopped	

Flour fish filets on both sides. Sauté in butter over medium heat until browned.

Add sliced mushrooms, parsley, sherry and port. The addition of wines should ignite fish. Let filets flambé until flame dies out.

Add Maggie seasonings, salt, pepper, and lemon butter; put in a hot (450°) oven for 10 to 15 minutes. Serve at once.

Chef Kimsan Seng
Richard's Pier 20 Restaurant

Oven-Baked Smelts

Serves 8 as an appetizer
Serves 4 as a main course

2 pounds smelts, head and tail removed, fish cleaned of all bones	2 teaspoons salt
	½ teaspoon ground white pepper
4 ounces canned anchovies	2 tablespoons butter
2 cups heavy cream	Fresh dill for garnishing

Rinse fish and remove backbones. Sprinkle fish inside and out with salt and pepper. Lay fish in a shallow, buttered, oven-proof dish.

Mash anchovies into a paste and mix it with cream. Pour cream mixture over fish. Place in preheated 400° oven for 10 to 15 minutes. Do not cover.

Serve immediately from baking dish.

This dish is delicious served with steamed new potatoes seasoned with dill, boiled brussel sprouts, and small tomatoes.

Mrs. Jaakko O. Iloniemi
Wife of the Ambassador of Finland

Danish Fish Florentine

Serves 12

3½	pounds filet of sole
6	10-ounce packages chopped spinach, frozen
3	eggs
	16-ounces ricotta cheese
1½	pounds fresh mushrooms, caps only
2	cans cream of mushroom soup or 2 cups homemade cream sauce
½	stick butter
½	cup Parmesan cheese
1½	tablespoons sugar
1	teaspoon salt
	Butter for top

Cook spinach as directed on package. Drain thoroughly. Add sugar and salt to spinach; add ricotta and 3 eggs. Mix well.

Sauté mushrooms in ½ stick of butter. Add soup or, sauce. Cook on low heat. Grease 2, 2-quart casseroles or individual gratin dishes.

Place layer of spinach, then your fish; cover fish with mushroom sauce; top with cheese and butter pieces.

Cook in 350° oven for 50 minutes.

Can be done with frozen fish, but nothing is as good as fresh fish.

Susanne Misner

Ocean Quiche

Serves 6

1	pound fish filets, sole, flounder, pike or a combination of any
3	eggs, beaten
½	cup bread crumbs (preferably egg bread)
2	tablespoons wheat germ
2	tablespoons fresh parsley
1	large onion
2	ribs celery
5	tablespoons melted sweet butter
½	cup sour cream
½	cup white wine
	Salt and freshly ground pepper to taste
	Grated Parmesan cheese for top

Grind fish, onion, and celery. Add rest of ingredients and mix well. Sprinkle Parmesan on top generously.

Bake in buttered quiche pan or pyrex pie plate at 350° for ¾ of an hour to 1 hour, or until light brown. Can be eaten hot or cold.

Pearl Shalowitz

Soufflé de Poisson à la Florentine with Sauce Mousseline

Serves 6

½	pound skinless flounder, or sole filets
½	cup dry white wine
½	teaspoon salt
	Freshly ground pepper, to taste
2	tablespoons minced shallots or spring onions
3	cups cooked chopped spinach
3	tablespoons butter

3	tablespoons flour
1	cup boiling milk
½	teaspoon salt
	Freshly ground pepper, to taste
	Pinch nutmeg
1	egg yolk
5	egg whites
	Pinch salt
½	cup grated Swiss cheese

SAUCE MOUSSELINE

3	egg yolks
½	cup whipping cream
¼	cup fish liquor
6	ounces butter

Salt and freshly ground pepper, to taste
Lemon juice, to taste

Cut filets into 6 parts. Roll up fish filets and fasten with a toothpick. Poach fish 8 to 10 minutes in wine, ½ teaspoon salt, pepper, and shallots. Gently lift out fish and set aside. Boil down liquid to ¼ cup. Strain and reserve for sauce.

Cook spinach. Chop and "dry" by evaporating in a skillet over medium heat. Spread in bottom of buttered, oval, fireproof dish about 16 inches long.

Cook butter and flour about 3 minutes, but do not brown. Remove from heat, beat in boiling milk a little at a time and add remaining seasonings. Return to heat and boil, stirring 1 to 2 minutes. Off heat, beat in egg yolk. Cool to luke warm.

Beat egg whites and salt until stiff. Stir one quarter of them into soufflé base, then stir in ¼ cup cheese; fold, carefully, balance of egg whites into base.

Place rolled fish filets on spinach. Mound soufflé mixture over fish. Sprinkle remaining cheese over top. Bake 15 to 18 minutes in a preheated 425° oven or until soufflé has puffed and browned.

Serve with mousseline on the side.

SAUCE MOUSSELINE

Beat egg yolks, cream, and fish liquor over low heat until mixture gradually thickens into a light cream to coat a spoon.

Remove from heat; beat in butter, one tablespoon at a time until sauce thickens like a hollandaise. Add seasonings as necessary.

Albert J. Beveridge, III

Truite Grenobloise

Serves 1

8-ounce fresh water or sea trout
1 whole egg beaten
1 cup of croutons (diced French bread)
½ cup of diced lemon
2 tablespoons capers
2 tablespoons vegetable oil
1 pound butter
1 cup flour
Salt and freshly ground pepper

Salt and pepper trout, roll in egg, and dust with flour. Heat oil in large skillet and sauté trout on both sides until done.

Arrange trout on a serving dish, top with croutons, lemon, capers. Add butter to frying pan until chestnut color, pour over trout and serve with boiled potatoes.

Chef Roland Bouyat
The Bread Oven Restaurant

Tuna and Spinach "Sausage"

Serves 4

1½ pounds fresh spinach (or 3 boxes frozen spinach), cooked and drained
7-ounce can of white tuna in oil
6 flat anchovy filets
2 slices of good bread
½ cup half and half
1 lemon
Cheesecloth
2 jumbo eggs
3 tablespoons dry bread crumbs
¼ cup pignoli
Freshly ground black pepper
⅓ cup olive oil
1 tablespoon lemon juice

Put cooked, drained spinach and all other ingredients except olive oil, lemon juice, and lemon into food processor; chop coarsely. Shape resulting green mixture into a sausage-shaped form about 12 inches long. Wrap loaf in several layers of cheesecloth and tie both ends securely.

Place loaf in a close-fitting pan and simmer for 35 minutes. Allow to cool for 5 minutes and then remove cheesecloth. Let cool completely.

Cut loaf into ⅜-inch slices. Arrange them slightly overlapping on a platter. Sprinkle with olive oil and lemon juice and serve at room temperature; garnish with paper-thin lemon slices.

John L. Hurley, Jr.

Grilled Tuna

Serves 6

⅓ cup oil
2 teaspoons red wine vinegar
1 teaspoon garlic powder
1 teaspoon garlic salt
6 4-ounce tuna steaks, ½ inch thick
1 tablespoon butter
½ pound mushrooms, sliced
2 ounces currants

½ teaspoon garlic powder
⅛ teaspoon white pepper
1 teaspoon fresh parsley
½ teaspoon salt or to taste
1 thin slice lemon per serving
1 sprig parsley per serving

Combine first 4 ingredients. Place tuna in dish in one layer and cover with oil mixture. Marinate several hours or overnight.

Heat butter until sizzling. Sauté mushrooms, currants, and remaining seasonings for 30 seconds, stirring to combine. Remove immediately.

Grill tuna over charcoal 30 to 60 seconds per side until just opaque. Spoon 1½ ounces mushroom mixture across center. Garnish with lemon slice and parsley sprig.

This can also be served as an appetizer or first course.

The Pleasant Peasant Restaurant

Corn-Clam Bake

Serves 5 to 6

2 eggs
1 cup milk
1¼ cups coarsely crumbled soda crackers (12 large) or 18 Ritz crackers
7½ ounce can minced clams undrained or equal amount of fresh crab meat
1 cup frozen corn, thawed enough to separate

3 tablespoons minced green peppers
¼ teaspoon salt
½ teaspoon Worcestershire sauce
2–3 tablespoons butter, melted
2 tablespoons minced onion
½ cup grated Cheddar cheese

Preheat oven to 350°.

Beat eggs in mixing bowl. Add milk and crackers. Let stand long enough to soften. Stir in clams, corn and other ingredients, except cheese.

Pour into 1½-quart casserole. Bake 50 minutes or until firm. Sprinkle with grated cheese. Bake 5 minutes longer.

Kathryn C. Avery

Oysters Rockefeller

Serves 10 to 12
as an appetizer,
4 as a main course.
Makes 1 quart of sauce

1 bunch green onions
½ stalk celery
½ bunch parsley, leaves only
¼–½ cup broccoli heads, cooked and well drained
1 package (10 ounces) frozen leaf spinach, cooked and well drained
½ teaspoon anise seed
32 oysters

3 sticks butter, melted
¼–½ cup toasted bread crumbs
2 tablespoons Worcestershire sauce
½ teaspoon salt
½ teaspoon freshly ground pepper
½ teaspoon red pepper
1 tablespoon Pernod (or similar absinthe liquor)

SAUCE

Chop, then grind all greens and anise seed in blender or food processor using melted butter as liquid. Transfer to a bowl and add bread crumbs, Worcestershire sauce, salt, pepper, red pepper and Pernod. Store in covered container in refrigerator where it will keep several days. Freezes well, but if you freeze, do not add Pernod until you defrost and are ready to serve.

TO SERVE

Place oysters in shells. Have oysters at room temperature if possible. Place shells on shallow pan and set in 400° oven. When edges of oysters begin to curl, remove and pour liquid from each shell. Cover oysters with Rockefeller sauce and return to oven until slightly brown.

SHELLS

It is best to seek out medium-size deep oyster shells for this dish. Ask your local fish merchant to save you some when he shucks his oysters.

Janet Perry, NSO Member &
Richard Smith

Baked Mussels

Serves 4 to 6 as main course
more as an appetizer

5 dozen mussels, scrubbed and debearded
2 tablespoons melted butter
¼ cup olive oil
10 sprigs fresh parsley, chopped
3 cloves garlic, pressed
1 cup bread crumbs
½ teaspoon red pepper (cayenne)
Salt and freshly ground pepper to taste

Scrub mussels and throw away any that have opened. Pile mussels on a foil-covered cookie sheet with enough foil to enclose mussels for baking.

Melt butter and oil and pour over mussels. Sprinkle over that bread crumbs, parsley, garlic, salt and peppers.

Cover mussels tightly with foil and bake in a 375° oven for 30 to 40 minutes or until shells are opened. Serve hot with French bread to mop up sauce.

Pat VandeVort

Mussels with Saffron

Serves 6

4 pounds mussels, scrubbed and debearded
2 cups heavy cream
5 shallots, chopped
2 cups white wine
2 pinches of saffron
10 ounces mushrooms, sliced
3 carrots, julienned
2 zucchini, julienned
½ teaspoon freshly ground pepper

Steam open mussels with white wine, pepper and shallots. Remove and shell mussels. Strain and reserve broth.

Simmer carrots slowly in butter until tender. Separately sauté mushrooms and zucchini rapidly to retain crispness.

Add saffron to broth and reduce. Then add heavy cream and reduce again to an even creamier consistency.

Add mussels and vegetables. Bring to a slow boil and serve.

Chef Garard Vettraino
Jean-Pierre Restaurant

Coquilles St. Jacques Baumanière

Serves 4 to 6 as a
main course

1½ pounds of scallops
     (if sea scallops cut
     in quarters)
4 tablespoons softened
     butter
1 tablespoon chopped
     shallots
1 teaspoon salt
     Dash of white
     pepper
½ cup dry vermouth
1 cup heavy cream
1 tablespoon flour
     Minced fresh parsley
4–6 scallop shells for
     serving

Wash scallops and quarter, if necessary. Put scallops in a saucepan and add shallots, salt, white pepper, and vermouth. Bring this to a boil, then cover pan and simmer for 2 minutes.

Remove scallops, using a slotted spoon and place in scallop shells.

Remaining liquid should be cooked over a light flame until it is reduced by half.

To make sauce, add cream to liquid in saucepan and boil rapidly until syrupy. Then, to this add flour and butter, stirring butter over a low flame.

Pour sauce over scallops and sprinkle parsley over top. Heat scallops in a 450° oven for 5 minutes and they are ready to serve.

This is an easy and delightful dish to prepare. The scallops come out very tender. May serve as a first course.

*Erich Leinsdorf's version
of Hotel de la Poste's recipe
Burgundy, France*

Coquilles St. Jacques

Serves 4

½–1 pound sliced
    mushrooms
1 lemon
5 tablespoons butter
1 pound fresh
    scallops
1 cup dry white wine
¼ teaspoon ground
    thyme

1 bay leaf
½ teaspoon salt
    Dash of white pepper
3 tablespoons flour
1 cup cream
1 cup buttered bread
    crumbs

Preheat oven to 400°. Sprinkle mushrooms with juice of one lemon; sauté mushrooms in 2 tablespoons butter. In a saucepan, place scallops, wine or vermouth and seasonings. Simmer, covered, for about 10 minutes. Drain and reserve 1 cup of broth.

Make a white sauce from remaining 3 tablespoons butter, flour, broth and cream. When sauce is well blended add scallops and mushrooms.

Spoon mixture into a buttered casserole dish or into buttered shells and top with buttered bread crumbs. Bake for 10 minutes until browned.

Recipe doubles easily for larger dinner or could be served as an appetizer. Serve with brown rice.

Anne Keiser

Roof Terrace Crabcakes

Makes approximately
6 portions of
2 crabcakes each

1 medium onion,
    chopped
1 medium green pepper,
    chopped
2 pounds fresh lump
    crabmeat
1 whole egg
1 teaspoon chopped
    capers
1 tablespoon mayonnaise
    Butter for sautéeing
1 tablespoon lemon juice

1 tablespoon
    Worcestershire sauce
½ teaspoon Tabasco
    sauce
1 tablespoon finely
    chopped, fresh
    parsley
1 cup bread crumbs
    made from fresh
    white bread, crusts
    removed

Sauté onion and green pepper in butter and set aside.

Mix together rest of ingredients and add sautéed onion and green pepper.

Make into 3-ounce patties; roll each in bread crumbs.

Sauté in clarified butter approximately 3 minutes each side. Remove from heat and serve immediately.

The Roof Terrace at the Kennedy Center
Restaurant Associates

Imperial Crab

Serves 6

1½ cups homemade mayonnaise
3 teaspoons minced fresh parsley
3 egg yolks, well beaten
2 tablespoons Dijon mustard
¼ teaspoon white pepper
¼ teaspoon cumin
1 teaspoon Worcestershire
2 pounds jumbo lump crabmeat

HOMEMADE MAYONNAISE
4 egg yolks
½ teaspoon salt
⅛ teaspoon white pepper
Dash of cayenne
2 teaspoons white wine vinegar
1 teaspoon Dijon mustard
2 cups vegetable oil, at room temperature

Imperial Crab has brought us almost as much acclaim as our roast beef and potato skins.

To make homemade mayonnaise, place yolks in a stainless steel bowl and add salt, pepper, cayenne, vinegar, and mustard. Let sit for 30 minutes.

Blend with a whisk for 1 or 2 minutes. Gradually add oil in a steady stream while whisking constantly. Mayonnaise will become thick and stiff.

Whisk in 1 teaspoon of boiling water to seal. Refrigerate.

To prepare Imperial Crab, first preheat oven to 375°. Lightly butter 6 fluted baking shells.

In a large mixing bowl combine homemade mayonnaise, parsley, egg yolks, mustard, pepper, cumin, and Worcestershire. Mix well so that all flavors are blended.

Carefully remove all cartilage from crabmeat without breaking apart lumps. Place crabmeat in bowl containing mayonnaise mixture and gently combine.

Pile into buttered shells. Bake in preheated oven for about 10 to 15 minutes, or until hot, bubbly and lightly browned. Watch carefully to prevent burning.

Chef George Gianakos
The Prime Rib Restaruant

Shrimp Curry

Serves 8

4 pounds shrimp
1½ cups butter
3 onions, chopped
4 teaspoons garlic powder
4 teaspoons ginger powder
1 teaspoon turmeric powder
2 teaspoons chili powder or
6 green chilies

4 Cardamom pods
1 teaspoon cinnamon
4 cups coconut milk
   Salt to taste

Heat butter and sauté chopped onions until golden brown. Add all spices and salt with 2 tablespoons of water. Stir over low heat for a few minutes, add coconut milk. Add shrimp, cook 5 to 10 minutes until gravy thickens.

Serve with boiled rice.

Mrs. Tabarak Husain
Wife of the Ambassador of Bangladesh

Shrimp Madeleine

Serves 8

2 tablespoons dry English mustard
4 tablespoons butter
3 pounds raw shrimp, medium size
⅓ cup brandy
2 cups heavy cream
   Salt and freshly ground pepper

Mix dry mustard with a little water to make a light paste. Melt butter over high heat and sauté shrimp until all water has evaporated. Remove from heat. Then pour brandy over shrimp and ignite. When flames subside, add cream and cook, stirring all the time, until a smooth sauce is obtained. Add mustard paste and season to taste with salt and pepper. Serve in individual casserole dishes or on a platter; garnish with parsley.

Chef Roland Huet, Christian's Restaurant
New Orleans

Szechuan Shrimp

Serves 8 as an appetizer
Serves 4 as a main course

1 pound shrimp,
  shelled and deveined
  (Use 26 to 30 count
  shrimp for a main
  course; 41 to 60 count
  for an appetizer)
1 cup oil

MIXTURE 1
½ cup minced scallions
½ cup minced bamboo
  shoots, optional
¼ teaspoon minced fresh
  ginger
3 cloves garlic
¼ teaspoon hot pepper
  sauce or 1–2 seeded,
  dry red peppers,
  chopped

MIXTURE 2
2 tablespoons sugar
½ cup ketchup
3 tablespoons sherry
1 tablespoon soy sauce
1½ teaspoons sesame oil
  or 1 tablespoon
  sesame seed

MIXTURE 3
1 tablespoon
  cornstarch
3 tablespoons water

Heat oil to 400°. Have a large bowl with a strainer ready. Add shrimp to hot oil and stir fry until done, about 2 minutes. Pour oil and shrimp into strainer.

Heat 2 tablespoons of oil in skillet over high heat. Add mixture 1, and stir fry 1 minute. Add shrimp and stir fry 30 seconds. Add mixture 2, and stir fry 30 seconds. Add mixture 3 and cook until thickened, stirring all the while.

Serve hot as an appetizer or main course. The "hotness" can be varied by increasing or decreasing the amount of pepper sauce.

C. W. Gressle

Creole Seafood Gumbo

Serves 6 to 8

¼ cup butter
2 tablespoons flour
1 whole garlic, minced
2 onions sliced thin
½ green pepper, chopped
6 ribs of celery, chopped
2 shallots, chopped
4 cups beef consommé
1 large can peeled tomatoes
1 small can tomato paste
2 tablespoons Worcestershire sauce
¼ teaspoon allspice
½ teaspoon chili powder
3 bay leaves
1 teaspoon dried basil
Salt
Freshly ground pepper
Paprika
3 tablespoons chopped parsley

1 package frozen okra, cut (or fresh or canned)
1½ pounds cooked shrimp (par boil uncooked shrimp for 3 minutes)
1 cup crab meat or several whole crabs
3 cups rice (cook separately)
½ teaspoon gumbo filé

In a heavy kettle melt butter and make a dark brown roux with flour. When cooked to brown stage add garlic, onions, celery, green pepper and shallots; sauté slowly until tender.

Add tomatoes, tomato paste, consommé and okra. Add seasonings and cook uncovered 30 minutes. Add shrimp and crabmeat; continue cooking 20 minutes longer.

Adjust seasoning, reduce to simmer and add gumbo filé. Do not allow to boil after adding filé as it will gum up and form strings. Serve in a bowl over hot rice. This may be thinned with water, if necessary. When reheating, do not boil.

Parker C. Folse, Jr.

Eggplant with Seafood

Serves 6

3 medium eggplants
Oil for frying
2 large onions, sliced
1 tablespoon mild red paprika (Hungarian type)
  8-ounce can tomato sauce
4 fresh tomatoes, peeled, seeded, and chopped or 28-ounce can Italian tomatoes, drained
½ teaspoon oregano
  Pinch of cayenne pepper
1 pound cooked seafood (shrimp, crab, and white fish)
1 cup grated Parmesan cheese
½ cup melted butter

Halve eggplant lengthwise. Sprinkle with salt and let stand for 30 minutes.

Dry eggplant thoroughly; fry cut sides in oil until lightly browned. Bake in preheated 350° oven for approximately 10 minutes.

Add a little oil to frying pan and sauté sliced onion. Add paprika, tomato sauce, tomatoes, oregano, and cayenne pepper. Season and simmer slowly to a thick pulp.

Scoop pulp from eggplant. Add to tomato mixture; simmer for a few minutes. Mix with seafood and return to eggplant shells. Sprinkle with Parmesan and melted butter.

Brown in 425° oven for about 10 minutes. Serve this dish with homemade whole wheat bread.

Mrs. Donald Sole
Wife of the Ambassador of South Africa

Saucisson de Crustaces

Serves 4

3 ounces jumbo, all-lump crab meat
3 ounces lobster meat
3 ounces crayfish tails (meat)
5 ounces bay scallops
1½ ounces Cognac
4 ounces salmon filet
4 ounces sea scallops
4 ounces heavy cream
1 egg
Salt, freshly ground pepper, and nutmeg
Cognac
Pistachio nuts
2 feet of medium beef casing (available at Italian food specialty shops and custom butchers)

SAUCE
12 ounces ripe tomatoes
1 teaspoon tomato paste
3 teaspoons red wine vinegar
1 cup virgin olive oil
Salt
Freshly ground pepper
Freshly chopped tarragon
Freshly chopped parsley

Sauté lobster, crab, and crayfish meat in butter and deglaze with Cognac. Allow to cool. Sauté bay scallops in butter until three quarters done. Cool.

Grind salmon filet and sea scallops. Place this in a food processor. Blend briefly. Add egg and blend. Add salt, pepper, and nutmeg to taste. Add cream, a little at a time.

Mix sautéed and blended ingredients together and add pistachio nuts. Stuff this mixture in a medium beef casing. Poach at 180° for 45 minutes. Cool.

Carefully cut sausage and arrange slices on plate over the following sauce.

SAUCE

Blanch tomatoes for 10 seconds in boiling water; then plunge into cold water. When they are chilled, peel and cut tomatoes in half and squeeze to remove seeds and water. Push tomato pulp through a fine sieve, pressing down on it with back of a wooden spoon. Collect tomato purée in a bowl and refrigerate until ready to use.

Add tomato paste and vinegar to sieved tomatoes. Mixing continuously with a wire whisk, incorporate oil, a few drops at a time. Add salt, pepper, tarragon, and parsley.

Chef Pierre Chambrin
Maison Blanche Restaurant

Seafood Paella Bajamar

Serves 4

This dish comes from the Bajamar Restaurant in Madrid, Spain.

3½ ounces olive oil
2 teaspoons minced garlic
14 ounces Calasparra rice
7 ounces raw carabineros, peeled (variety of prawn)
14 ounces clams
1¾ pounds live crawfish or lobster, cut in half
9 ounces whole raw prawns
8 raw mussels
20 threads saffron
1 cup fried tomatoes
2½ cups fish broth
4 sweet red peppers, chopped
Peas
Salt, to taste

Using a paella pan (18 inches in diameter and 1½ inches deep), fry garlic in oil until brown. Add peeled seafood (shrimp and carabineros) and clams. After a while add rice and stir. Add fried tomatoes.

Add fish broth, saffron and salt. Add mussels, prawns, crawfish or lobster, placing them on top. Cover and cook 15 minutes. Place red peppers and peas on top and cook another 5 minutes.

Allow to settle a few minutes and serve with white wine.

Rafael Frühbeck de Burgos
NSO Principal Guest Conductor

Golden Caviar with Belon Oysters Wrapped in Spinach Leaves

Serves 1

6 Maine Belon oysters
6 impeccable spinach leaves
4 ounces golden caviar
Hazelnut oil
Excellent vinegar of your choice
Salt and freshly ground pepper

Shuck 6 oysters and keep their juice.
Poach oysters in their juice for 3 seconds.
Poach spinach leaves for 5 seconds in boiling salt water and dry on kitchen towel.
Toss oysters in hazelnut and vinegar dressing and wrap in spinach leaves.
On a large plate place 5 small portions of caviar around plate and one in center; position wrapped oysters on top.

Chef Jean Louis Palladin
Jean-Louis Restaurant at The Watergate

La Salade de Poisson Marine
Marinated Fish Salad

Serves 6

1 pound fresh salmon
1 pound fresh sea scallops
Juice of 10 lemons
Juice of 2 limes
2 teaspoons salt
½ teaspoon freshly ground pepper
1 teaspoon chopped fresh coriander (optional)
1 teaspoon chopped fresh dill
1 head Boston lettuce
1 head Belgian endive
2 tablespoons chopped shallots (optional)
2 tablespoons chopped parsley (optional)
2 tablespoons chopped green onions or chives (optional)
Black caviar
6 teaspoons vegetable oil

"My father and I developed this recipe, using the wonderful seafood available here in the Chesapeake Bay area."

Slice salmon into slivers. Place salmon and scallops in separate, deep earthenware bowls. Sprinkle evenly with lemon and lime juices; season with salt, pepper, coriander, and dill. Cover and marinate overnight in refrigerator.

Wash Boston lettuce and Belgian endive; dry completely. Place a bed of Boston lettuce on each of 6 chilled salad plates. Spread 4 spears of Belgian endive over lettuce leaves to form an "x." Layer salmon over endive, then scallops over salmon. If desired, garnish with a combination of shallots, parsley, green onion or chives, and top each with about 1 teaspoon of caviar. Pour about 1 teaspoon oil over each plate to moisten and glaze. Serve at once.

If scallops are large, slice before marinating.

Chef François Haeringer
L'Auberge Chez François Restaurant

Pâté de Coquilles St. Jacques

Serves 8

¼ pound fresh spinach, without stems
1 bunch watercress, without stems
¼ pound sorrel leaves, without stems
2 pounds scallops
2 eggs, separated
1 clove garlic
Salt and freshly ground pepper, to taste
2 branches tarragon
½ pound mushrooms
4 shallots
2 tablespoons olive oil

SAUCE
½ pound tomatoes, peeled, diced, and drained
1 cup ricotta cheese
½ cup yogurt
¼ cup heavy cream
1 teaspoon chopped parsley
½ teaspoon chopped tarragon
1 teaspoon ketchup
2 teaspoons Armagnac
Lemon juice and Tabasco sauce, to taste
Salt and freshly ground pepper, to taste

GARNITURE
4 strips of bass or filet of sole
2 pounds scallops
Chopped parsley
Wine for marinade

Prepare garniture ahead, marinating bass or sole and some scallops in wine, and then add chopped parsley.

To make pâté, blanch together spinach, watercress, and sorrel. Grind scallops. Add egg whites, garlic, salt, and pepper. Add blanched greens and leaves from tarragon branches. Blend well; add egg yolks and blend again.

Sauté mushrooms and shallots in olive oil.

Line bottom and sides of a mold with scallop-greens mixture. Add a layer of mushrooms and garniture. Then add another layer of forcemeat.

Place mold in a larger pan and add boiling water to reach about one-third height of mold. Bake in a 400° oven for about 50 minutes.

To make sauce, mix together tomatoes with ricotta cheese and yogurt in a blender. Add cream, parsley, tarragon, ketchup, Armagnac, lemon juice, Tabasco, salt, and pepper. Blend well.

Pour sauce over each individual slice of pâté.

Jean-Charles Berruet, The Chanticleer Inn
Nantucket Island, Massachusetts

Shrimp Remoulade

Serves 4 as a first course

1 pound cooked shrimp
½ cup olive oil
¼ cup vinegar
1 teaspoon salt
1 teaspoon paprika
¼ teaspoon pepper
4 tablespoons mayonnaise
8 tablespoons Creole mustard

3 tablespoons finely chopped parsley
½ cup chopped celery
½ medium onion, chopped

Rub bowl with garlic. Mix all ingredients together. Blend well. Add shrimp and chill. Allow mixture to marinate several hours before serving, preferably overnight. It is advisable to taste sauce before adding shrimp as sometimes it needs a little more of this or that.

Creole mustard is the distinctive ingredient in this recipe and other types of mustard should not be substituted.

Gerson Nordlinger, Jr.

Gravlaks

Serves 20

8 pounds fresh salmon, preferably from middle part
8 tablespoons salt
4 tablespoons sugar
4 teaspoons crushed, whole white pepper
Several big bunches of fresh dill

Filet salmon, leaving skin on. Rub mixed spices into meaty sides of fish.

Put a thick layer of chopped dill on a deep platter. Put one filet, skin down, on layer of dill. Then put a layer of chopped dill on filet and place other filet on top of first, skin up. Again, place a layer of chopped dill on top of whole dish. Weight dish down and refrigerate, turning the fish filets once a day for 3 to 5 days.

Turn dish once every day. Take it out, scrape off used dill and dry off filets. Slice filets thinly and serve with fresh dill and lemon, stuffed eggs, or spinach and a good mustard sauce, brown bread, and dry white wine.

Mrs. Knut Hedemann
Wife of the Ambassador of Norway

P O U L T R Y

&

G A M E

Arroz Con Pollo
Chicken With Rice

Serves 6

3-pound frying chicken or combination of favorite parts
½ cup olive oil
2 cups minced onions
3 cloves garlic
½ teaspoon red pepper
2½ teaspoons salt

1½ cups yellow or regular rice
28-ounce can tomatoes, undrained and chopped
10¾-ounce can chicken broth
5 ounces frozen peas
½ cup stuffed green olives
4-ounce jar sliced pimentos

Heat olive oil in large, heavy pan and brown chicken on both sides.

Remove chicken. Sauté onion, garlic, and red pepper about 3 minutes (onion will be golden).

Add rice, salt, and pepper and stir until rice is browned (about 8 minutes). Add tomatoes and chicken broth to rice mixture and stir.

Add chicken, cover pan, and simmer for 1 hour.

Add ½ cup water and stir. Add peas, olives, and pimentos, placing them on top. Simmer 20 minutes, or until peas are cooked. Serve from pan.

Luis Haza
NSO Member

Baja California Chicken

Serves 8

8 boned chicken breasts
Seasoned salt and freshly ground pepper to taste
2 cloves garlic, crushed
4 tablespoons olive oil
4 tablespoons tarragon vinegar
⅔ cup dry sherry

Sprinkle chicken with seasoned salt and pepper.

Crush garlic into oil and vinegar in a skillet. Sauté chicken pieces until golden brown, turning frequently. Remove; place in baking dish.

Pour sherry over pieces and place in 350° oven for 10 minutes.

Mrs. Ronald W. Reagan

Chicken Anna

Serves 10 to 12

12	chicken breasts or other chicken parts
4	tablespoons butter
3	cloves garlic, crushed
	Basil, salt, and freshly ground pepper to taste
3	heaping tablespoons gravy flour
1¼	cups dry white wine

1	pint sour cream
1	bunch chopped green onions, chopped
½–¾	pound fresh mushrooms, sliced
¼	cup chicken stock

This is a good "after-symphony" dish as it may be made ahead and popped into the oven to warm without loss of flavor.

Melt butter in large frying pan over medium heat. Add breasts and brown with crushed garlic. After browning, place chicken pieces in a flat roasting pan.

Season each piece with salt, pepper, and basil. Sprinkle chopped onion and mushrooms over all. Pour 1 cup wine over chicken. Cover with foil and bake in 350° oven for 45 minutes.

Deglaze frying pan with chicken stock. Add flour to make a sauce and reserve.

Remove baked chicken and mushrooms; deglaze reserved roasting pan with ¼ cup wine. Add sauce and blend in sour cream. Pour gravy over mushrooms and chicken. Place in oven to keep warm or serve immediately with rice pilaf or wild rice and spinach salad.

Anna Young

Chicken Jamaican

Serves 4

4	large, half chicken breasts, skinned
1	tablespoon butter
2	tablespoons light brown sugar
2	cups chopped onion
1	cup sliced mushrooms
	16-ounce can stewed tomatoes, chopped

1	tablespoon red wine vinegar
1–2	teaspoons salt
1	teaspoon pepper
½	teaspoon thyme
1	bay leaf
½	teaspoon rosemary or more to taste (optional)

Melt butter in large heavy skillet; electric fry pan is ideal. Add sugar and stir until bubbly. Add chicken and brown. Be careful not to let sugar scorch.

Remove chicken and keep warm. Sauté onion and mushrooms in butter mixture, adding butter as needed.

Return chicken to pan. Add rest of ingredients. Set electric skillet at 210° to 215°. Cover and simmer at least 45 minutes, basting now and then.

A good do-ahead recipe as taste improves with reheating

Sue Goetz Ross

Chicken with Lamb and Rice

Serves 6

3 whole chicken breasts
⅓ cup pine nuts, toasted lightly
1 cup ground lamb (½ pound)
2 tablespoons butter, melted
1 cup rice
½ cup toasted, slivered almonds

Salt, freshly ground pepper, and allspice
1 bay leaf
½ teaspoon coriander

Poach breasts in water with bay leaf and coriander for 10 minutes. Let cool in broth, debone, and cut into 2-inch squares. Reserve broth. In a frying pan, sauté lamb until no longer pink.

In a saucepan, combine lamb, pine nuts, rice, salt, pepper, allspice, and melted butter. Add 2 cups hot reserved broth. Cover and simmer 15 minutes.

Add chicken. Simmer 5 minutes longer.

To serve, mound rice on large platter; cover rice mixture with chicken and sprinkle with toasted almonds.

Leftovers may be turned into a very good cold salad by adding dressing to chilled mixture.

Embassy of Lebanon

Chicken à la Maria

Serves 10 to 12

¾ cup seasoned bread crumbs
¼ cup grated Parmesan cheese
6 whole, large chicken breasts, skinned, split, and boned
½ cup sliced green onion

2 tablespoons butter
2 tablespoons flour
1 cup milk
10-ounce package frozen, chopped spinach, thawed and well drained
4-ounce package boiled ham slices, diced

Combine bread crumbs and cheese. Dip chicken in crumb mixture to coat lightly. Arrange in a 13×9×2-inch baking dish. Reserve remaining crumb mixture.

In a saucepan cook onion in butter until tender. Blend in flour; stir in milk all at once. Cook and stir until thickened and bubbly. Cook and stir 1 minute more. Stir in spinach and ham.

Spoon spinach mixture over chicken; sprinkle with remaining crumbs. Bake uncovered, at 350° for 40 to 45 minutes.

James D. Kraft
NSO Member

Chicken Moghlai

Serves 8

8 whole chicken breasts, skinned, boned, and halved
Salt and freshly ground pepper to taste
Flour
½ cup butter
4 medium onions, chopped
4 garlic cloves, minced
1 tablespoon minced ginger
½ teaspoon cumin powder
½ teaspoon turmeric
¼ teaspoon cumin seeds
¼ teaspoon caraway seeds
¼ teaspoon cayenne

1 canned whole green chili, minced
1-pound can whole, peeled tomatoes, undrained
2 cups chicken stock or broth
2 pints sour cream
½ cup brown sugar
1 teaspoon saffron threads
½ teaspoon ground cardamom
¼ teaspoon ground cloves
¼ teaspoon nutmeg
2 tablespoons ketchup
2–3 teaspoons dried red pepper flakes
Chopped cilantro (as garnish)

Place chicken on cookie sheet. Season very generously with salt and lightly sprinkle with pepper. Dust thoroughly with flour.

Melt ¼ cup butter in 14-inch skillet. Brown half the breasts until golden on both sides. Remove and set aside. Add additional ¼ cup butter and brown remaining breasts. Set aside. Add onions to skillet and sauté over medium heat until soft. Stir in garlic and ginger and cook 2 minutes.

Add cumin powder, turmeric, cumin seeds, caraway seeds, cayenne, and chili. Stir in tomatoes, mashing with wooden spoon. Blend in chicken stock. Return chicken to pan and bring to boil. Reduce heat and simmer uncovered for 8 to 10 minutes.

Combine remaining ingredients except cilantro. Slowly stir into chicken mixture. Cook, covered, over low heat 30 minutes. Uncover and cook 45 minutes more, stirring frequently. Season to taste with salt and more red pepper flakes, if desired. Place in serving bowl and garnish with cilantro.

The sauce will have a curdled appearance, which is proper with this recipe. The texture will be smooth to the taste, however. Excellent cooked in advance and reheated.

Mrs. Zubin Mehta

Chicken Parmigiana

Serves 4

4 whole, boned and skinned chicken breasts
⅓ cup butter
1 egg
1 cup seasoned bread crumbs
15½-ounce jar spaghetti sauce or your own homemade
2 cloves garlic, crushed
½ teaspoon thyme
½ teaspoon oregano
8-ounce box thin, spinach noodles, cooked
6 slices mozzarella
5 ounces grated Parmesan cheese

Cut chicken breasts in half. Rinse in cold water and pat dry. Pound with a meat mallet until ¼ inch thick.

Heat butter in a large skillet. Beat egg in a medium bowl. Dip chicken in beaten egg and then into 1 cup seasoned bread crumbs.

Sauté chicken in butter, 2 minutes on each side. Pour spaghetti sauce into same pan. Add garlic, thyme, and oregano. Bring to a boil; cover and reduce to simmer for 20 minutes.

Place a slice of mozzarella cheese on top of each piece of chicken 5 minutes before end of cooking time. Sprinkle grated Parmesan cheese on top. Cover skillet.

Drain cooked noodles and place on a warmed serving platter with chicken on top.

Peggy Ahlfeld

Chicken Piquant

Serves 4

2 whole chicken breasts, skinned and boned
4 tablespoons butter
¼ cup flour
5 tablespoons capers
⅓ cup dry white wine
Salt and freshly ground pepper to taste

This recipe was selected by the Inaugural Committee as the entrée to serve President Reagan at the Inaugural Luncheon in the Capital Rotunda.

Cut chicken into strips. Melt butter in pan. Coat chicken in seasoned flour and sauté in melted butter until golden brown.

Deglaze chicken with white wine and capers. Reduce liquid to desired thickness. Season to taste. Serve with a garnish of chopped parsley.

Mrs. William French Smith

Chicken Rosemary

Serves 4 to 6

4 chicken breasts, split, boned, and skinned
2 cups homemade bread crumbs (French bread)
¾ cup flour
2 eggs
2 tablespoons dried rosemary
½ teaspoon dried thyme
½ teaspoon dried sweet basil
¼ teaspoon dried tarragon
2½ ounces Calvados
    Salt
    Finely ground black pepper
3 tablespoons sweet butter
4 tablespoons virgin olive oil (Greek is more aromatic)

Place breasts between sheets of waxed paper and pound until ¼ inch thick. Trim edges to pretty them up.

Dredge breasts in flour, seasoned with salt and pepper. Dip in beaten eggs. Mix bread crumbs with rosemary, thyme, basil, and tarragon. Roll chicken in mixture, forcing bread crumbs firmly on chicken. Chill on sheets of wax paper for at least 2 hours.

Add butter and olive oil to a large skillet and heat over medium heat. When foaming, add chicken and sauté over medium-high heat until golden. Turn and cook other side. Do not overcook. Light golden is best. Turn off flame.

Warm Calvados slightly and pour over chicken. Quickly flame Calvados, and shake pan. Serve immediately.

Vegetable combinations such as brussel sprouts and sautéed, glazed carrots or carrot purée and green beans go nicely with this dish. Chicken Rosemary is complimented by a good red wine.

John Weisman

Chicken Teriyaki

Serves 4

1 chicken, cut up

MARINADE
3 tablespoons soy sauce
1 teaspoon grated fresh
   ginger
2 teaspoons honey
2 tablespoons saké or
   pale dry sherry

Mix ingredients for marinade. Pour over chicken and turn to coat all sides. Marinate in refrigerator 5 or 6 hours.

Broil or barbecue 10 to 15 minutes on each side or until done.

Saké adds a slightly more unusual flavor.

Toshiko Kohno
NSO Member

Chicken Tikka

Serves 8

3 pounds chicken
1 cup yogurt
1 teaspoon crushed garlic
1 teaspoon crushed
   ginger
2 tablespoons lemon
   juice
2 tablespoons ground
   red pepper
2 tablespoons olive oil
   Salt and freshly
   ground pepper to
   taste

Skin and bone chicken and cut into 4 parts. Prick it well with a fork. In a large bowl, combine yogurt, ginger, garlic, lemon juice, red pepper, pepper, and salt. Marinate chicken in this mixture for 2 hours.

Thread chicken on skewers. Brush with olive oil and broil for 6 minutes on each side. Serve with sliced tomatoes, onion rings, and lemon quarters on a bed of lettuce.

Equally delicious Lamb Tikka is prepared by substituting lamb chops for chicken. Cook the chops a little longer.

Mrs. Shahida Azim
Wife of the Ambassador of Pakistan

Chicken Valenzuela

Serves 6

Terrific to take to ballgames, picnics, etc.

12 chicken drumsticks
2 tablespoons heavy soy sauce
2 tablespoons Worcestershire sauce
2 cups brandy
   Salt and freshly ground pepper
1 teaspoon thyme
12 strips bacon

Marinate chicken drumsticks in all ingredients except bacon for a minimum of 16 hours. Drain (reserving marinade for next time).

Wrap each drumstick in a strip of bacon. Place all in a roasting pan without rack and bake at 350° for 2 hours. Drain and serve hot, warm, or cold.

Velia Valenzuela

Curried-Ginger Chicken

Serves 8

1 chopped onion
½ stick butter
⅓ cup honey
1 teaspoon salt
1 teaspoon curry powder
¼ cup Dijon mustard
2–3 tablespoons chopped fresh ginger
4 whole chicken breasts, skinned and boned
½ cup toasted, slivered almonds

Cut chicken breasts in half to make 8 breasts. Cut each in half lengthwise and again in half, widthwise. Place in buttered, shallow casserole.

Brown onion in butter. Add honey, salt, curry, mustard, and ginger. Brush mixture on chicken.

Preheat oven to 350°. Bake covered 30 minutes plus uncovered 30 minutes. Sprinkle with almonds and serve over rice.

Dorothy Bourgin

Germaine's Lemon Chicken

Serves 4 to 6

2–3 chicken breasts split, boned, and skinned
White pepper and salt to taste
1 tablespoon pale dry sherry
¾ cup fresh lemon juice
1 egg white
½ cup all-purpose flour
½ cup cornstarch
½ cup water
1 teaspoon roasted sesame seeds
1 cup shredded iceberg lettuce
2 tablespoons vegetable oil
4 tablespoons ketchup
2 tablespoons soy sauce
1 tablespoon sesame oil
3 tablespoons sugar
¼ teaspoon ginger, chopped
½ teaspoon garlic, chopped
1 teaspoon scallion, chopped

½ teaspoon chili and garlic paste (optional)
1 tomato, sliced for garnish
½ lemon, sliced for garnish

Pour mixture of pepper, salt, sherry, and all but 3 tablespoons of lemon juice over chicken. Let marinate for 30 to 40 minutes.

Mix egg white, flour, cornstarch, and water. Coat pieces of chicken with this mixture and deep fry until light golden brown over medium heat. Drain and cut into bite-size pieces.

Arrange chicken, lettuce, tomato, and lemon on plate.

Heat vegetable oil. Add ketchup, soy sauce, sesame oil, remaining lemon juice, sugar, ginger, and garlic (and chili or garlic paste). Stir until just hot. Pour over chicken before serving. Sprinkle with scallion and sesame seeds.

Germaine Swanson
Germaine's Restaurant

Louise's Chicken Alouette

Serves 4

1 container Alouette or
  Boursin cheese
2 whole boneless
  chicken breasts
2 eggs, beaten
1 cup bread crumbs
½ cup melted butter
  Fresh parsley

Split chicken breasts and flatten between pieces of wax paper.

Cut cheese into four parts. Roll cheese into cylinder shape, place cheese in middle of chicken breast, and roll breast around cheese.

Dip rolled-up chicken breast in egg; then roll in bread crumbs. Place in baking dish seam side down. Cover with melted butter.

Bake at 350° for 20 to 30 minutes, basting occasionally. Garnish with fresh parsley.

Louise Millikan

Monterey Chicken Rice Bake

Serves 6 generously

½ cup cottage cheese
  3-ounce package
  cream cheese (room
  temperature)
½ cup sour cream
  10¾-ounce can cream
  of chicken soup
1 teaspoon salt
⅛ teaspoon garlic
  powder
  4-ounce can diced,
  green chiles

3 cups cooked chicken
  (in large pieces)
3 cups cooked rice
  (cooked in chicken
  broth)
1 cup grated Monterey
  Jack cheese
2 tomatoes, coarsely
  chopped
¾ cup corn chips,
  coarsely crushed

Blend cottage cheese, cream cheese, and sour cream until smooth. Add mixture to remaining ingredients except corn chips.

Pour into a shallow 2-quart baking dish. Sprinkle with corn chips. Bake at 350° for 25 to 30 minutes.

Turkey may be substituted for chicken.

Mrs. Frank E. Scott

Murgh Massallam
Chicken Curry

Serves 4 to 6

1 broiler chicken
½ teaspoon red chili powder or paprika
¼ teaspoon turmeric
¼ teaspoon each cinnamon, cloves, and cardamom powder or 1 teaspoon curry powder

Pinch of cumin
½-inch piece of ginger
3 garlic cloves
1 onion
1 large can tomato purée
2 tablespoons butter
1 tablespoon oil
Salt to taste

Clean and cut up chicken. Mince garlic, ginger, and onion. Mix with powdered spices and salt; smear over chicken. Set aside for half an hour.

Sauté chicken in butter and oil, adding any spices left over in pan. Cover with a tight lid and cook until all liquid evaporates.

Add tomato purée; cook until chicken is tender and gravy thick.

Serve with boiled rice or "nan" (unleavened bread) and green salad.

Mrs. Usha Narayanan
Wife of the Ambassador of India

Philippines Chicken and Pork Adobo

Serves 6 to 8

1 chicken, cut up
1½–2 pounds pork roast, in 2-inch cubes
1½–3 cloves garlic, crushed
¾ cup soy sauce
½ cup vinegar

1 bay leaf
1 teaspoon freshly ground black pepper
Peppercorns (optional)

Combine last 6 ingredients in large saucepan.

Put in chicken and pork; marinate for several hours (the longer, the better).

Cover and cook over medium heat for about 45 minutes, or until meat is tender.

After meat is done, it may be browned in a 350° oven for a few minutes. Use sauce as gravy over rice.

Elvi Moore

VARIATION

Add 2 to 3 large onions to the above. Use equal amount of chicken breasts instead of mixed parts and substitute red wine for vinegar.

Kenneth Pasmanick
NSO Member

Poulet aux Champignons

Serves 4

4 chicken breasts, boned, halved, and pounded thin
¼ teaspoon salt
5 tablespoons clarified butter
1 tablespoon chopped green onions
½ pound sliced mushrooms
¼ teaspoon rosemary
1 clove minced garlic
¼ cup dry white wine
1 cup whipping cream

Sauté mushrooms, onions, and garlic in butter without browning.

Add chicken breasts and rosemary. Cook breasts 2 to 3 minutes on each side. Remove to heated platter.

Add wine and salt to mushrooms and onions scraping drippings from bottom of pan. Add whipping cream; simmer until boiled down, and cream thickens. Pour sauce over chicken and serve. If sauce needs thickening, add a little cornstarch mixed with water.

Norma McCaig

Poulet Poulenc

Serves 4

4 boned chicken breasts, halved and pounded thin
¼ teaspoon salt
½ pint sour cream
½ teaspoon tarragon
½ cup freshly grated Parmesan cheese
½ cup bread crumbs
2 tablespoons butter

Salt chicken breasts. Mix sour cream and tarragon. Coat breasts in mixture.

Mix cheese and bread crumbs. Coat breasts with crumb mix. Place on a buttered cookie sheet. Dot with butter.

Broil until lightly browned, about 3 minutes or less on each side.

Norma McCaig

Poulet au Vinaigre

Serves 4

2 chickens (broilers),
  2 pounds each
2 carrots
1 stick celery
2 tomatoes
2 tablespoons oil
½ pound sweet butter
4 tablespoons red wine
  vinegar

½ cup white wine
2 cloves garlic, mashed
  Chopped parsley or
  tarragon
  Salt and freshly
  ground pepper

Cut chicken in quarters. Season. Cut carrots and celery in small pieces. Peel, seed, and slice tomatoes.

Sauté chicken with 2 tablespoons oil and 3 tablespoons butter. Brown on both sides. Add carrots and celery; sauté for 5 more minutes. Add vinegar, white wine, garlic, and tomatoes. Cover and cook for 25 minutes slowly.

Remove chicken from pan and place on serving dish. Reduce cooking liquid. Season and add 4 tablespoons butter. Pour over chicken and sprinkle with fresh tarragon or chopped parsley.

Chef Jean-Pierre Goyenvalle
Le Lion d'Or Restaurant

Puffed Chicken Pockets

Serves 8

1 box Pepperidge Farm
  Puff Pastry, thawed
6 ounces cream cheese
6 tablespoons melted
  butter
4 cups chicken, cooked
  and cubed
4 tablespoons milk

½ teaspoon salt
¼ teaspoon freshly
  ground pepper
2 tablespoons chopped
  pimento
1½ cups bread crumbs
1–2 tablespoons fresh dill,
  chopped (optional)

Blend cream cheese and 4 tablespoons butter. Add chicken, salt, pepper, milk, pimentos, and dill.

Thaw frozen puff pastry; roll out each sheet to yield 9, 3-inch squares. (One box of 2 sheets will yield 18 dough squares.) Place 1 to 2 tablespoons of chicken mixture in center of each square and pinch opposing sides together at center.

Baste with remaining butter. Roll in bread crumbs. Bake at 350° for 35 minutes, or until squares are puffed and brown. Serve hot.

These chicken squares can be made ahead and stored unbaked frozen. You do not need to thaw before baking.

Cookbook Committee

Stuffed Chicken Breasts With Curry

Serves 4

2 whole chicken breasts, split, skinned and boned
3 tablespoons white raisins
3 tablespoons butter
½ cup chopped onion
½ cup chopped celery
¼ teaspoon minced garlic
1 bay leaf
¼ teaspoon tarragon
1 cup apples, peeled and chopped in small cubes
Salt and freshly ground pepper to taste
½–1 cup heavy cream
1 teaspoon curry powder

In a skillet, sauté onion in butter. Add celery, garlic, bay leaf, tarragon, and apples. Simmer for about 3 minutes. Add raisins and cook another minute until all ingredients are soft. Set aside. When cool, spread mixture on chicken breasts that have been slightly flattened and roll up. Secure with wooden toothpicks if necessary.

Place chicken breasts seam side down in 1 tablespoon butter and cook on top of stove over medium heat for just 1 minute. Remove from pan and place in greased pyrex dish. Bake in preheated 425° oven for 10 minutes.

In another bowl, combine cream, curry powder, salt, and pepper. Pour cream mixture over chicken breasts and bake for 10 to 15 minutes, until golden brown. Serve with white rice and chutney.

Marta Istomin

Summer and Spice Chicken

Serves 4

Juice of 1 lemon
1½–2 pounds boneless chicken breasts, cut into small cubes
Salt and freshly ground pepper, to taste
1 tablespoon oil
1 cup yogurt
1 teaspoon chili powder, or to taste
Raw vegetables (carrots, cucumbers, red or green peppers, cauliflower, broccoli, jicama, or your choice), cut in sticks or slices for serving

Set aside 1 tablespoon lemon juice for dip and toss rest with chicken cubes. Then toss chicken with salt, pepper, and oil. Set aside.

In a small serving bowl combine yogurt with reserved lemon juice, chili powder, salt, and pepper to taste. Set aside (can be refrigerated and kept a week or more).

Thread chicken on small bamboo skewers. Grill skewers of chicken, preferably on a charcoal grill, for about 10 to 15 minutes, turning as it cooks, just until meat is opaque. Arrange on a serving platter with raw vegetables and yogurt sauce. Dip chicken and vegetables in yogurt as you eat them.

Phyllis Richman

Tanqueray Turkey

Serves 6 to 8

4–6 pound turkey breast
    (or whole turkey)
1 tablespoon curry
    powder
1 tablespoon fines
    herbes
1 teaspoon salt or salt
    substitute
1 teaspoon paprika

1 cup water
1 cup gin
1 orange, cut in half
1 onion
2 carrots
2 pieces of celery

Excellent diet dish!
If you are not on a diet,
it is especially good for
sandwiches with chutney.

Wash and dry turkey. Mix curry powder, herbs, salt, and paprika. Rub turkey inside and out with this mixture.

Place in pan with vegetables and orange. Roast uncovered at 350° for 3 hours. Baste with gin and water. When done, spoon off all fat from juices. Serve thinly sliced with pan juices.

Mrs. Donald L. Rogers

Roast Pheasants and Other Birds

Serves 4

2 pheasants (available
    frozen at many
    specialty markets)
Onion, celery, carrot,
    and parsley
Butter for roasting
    birds
2 strips bacon
Lemon pepper

SAUCE
1 small jar currant jelly
1 cup dry sherry
1 stick butter

Rinse birds thoroughly and pat dry. Salt and lemon pepper the cavity and stuff with onion, celery, carrot and parsley. Dot liberally with butter and put bacon over breasts and high part of legs to prevent drying out.

Melt butter and jelly in saucepan. Remove from heat and add sherry. Make more than you will use for basting to use as gravy.

Roast at 350° for 1½ hours (1 hour for quail; 2 hours for goose). Baste every 10 minutes with pan juices and sauce.

Reheat reserved sauce for gravy. It is important not to add pan juices to gravy sauce as they tend to be very gamey.

Recipe also works well with quail, duck and goose.

Anne Watson

Taming the Wild Goose

Serves 4

Chesapeake Bay
 wild goose
Onions
Celery
Carrots
Potatoes
Garlic
Red table wine

Clean and chop vegetables, except garlic. Rub inside and outside of bird with garlic. Put vegetables in cavity. Place goose breast up on rack over shallow pan (at least 2½ to 3 inches above pan; bird should not touch drippings).

Cook at 170° for 12 to 14 hours until drumstick moves easily. Baste frequently with wine and juices. Slow cooking does not dry out goose. When finished, discard vegetables.

Gravy can be made with red wine, drippings, and sautéed mushrooms. Serve with wild rice. Sherry or currant jelly sauce also make an excellent accompaniment to wild game.

G. Stuart Scott

Fruit Stuffing for Turkey or Goose

Makes about
2 quarts of stuffing.

1 cup chopped, soft, pitted, dried prunes
¾ cup chopped, dried apricots
6 cups day-old bread cubes
2 cups cut-up, peeled apples
¾ cup diced orange sections
½ cup chopped nuts (optional)
1 teaspoon salt
½ teaspoon poultry seasoning
½ cup orange juice
¼ cup melted butter

Pour boiling water over first 2 ingredients; then drain. Toss lightly with remaining ingredients.

Fred Begun
NSO Member

MEATS

B E E F

Cordon Rouge

Serves 6 to 8

1 tenderloin of beef (size
   depending on number
   of people: ½ pound
   per person)
8 ounces pâté de
   foie gras
Smoked bacon strips
Salt and freshly
   ground pepper

In a heavy casserole, sear meat on all sides briefly over high heat. Remove meat and make an incision lengthwise, so meat opens like a book.

Put slices of goose liver in opening. Close up. Season well on outside and wrap meat with slices of smoked bacon. Secure this with string at 3-inch intervals.

Return wrapped tenderloin to pan and cook over high heat until bacon is browned and crisped. Remove bacon and string before slicing meat.

Serve Cordon Rouge with French fries, baby peas, and artichoke hearts.

Anne-Sophie Mutter

Svíčková
Tenderloin of Beef in Sour Cream Sauce

Serves 4 to 6

3 pounds tenderloin of beef
3–6 ounces of bacon
2 cups sliced vegetables (onion, carrot, parsnip, and celery root)
½ cup butter
Salt and freshly ground pepper to taste
1 cup or more beef bouillon
8 peppercorns
8 whole allspice
1 bay leaf
Pinch of thyme
Flour
1 cup or more sour cream
Lingonberries

Lard meat with ½-inch thick bacon strips.

Brown vegetables in butter, add meat and brown on all sides. Pour in hot bouillon, salt, and seasonings. Roast in a 325° oven until tender (1 to 1½ hours), basting frequently.

Remove meat from pan, dust drippings with flour. Add more bouillon if needed, and simmer for 5 minutes.

Blend in sour cream and put sauce through a food processor to make creamy.

Serve with dumplings and wild lingonberries in sugar.

Rudolf Firkušný

Green Peppercorn Steak

Serves 4

4 New York strip steaks
2 tablespoons vegetable oil
5 tablespoons butter
1 tablespoon minced shallots
½ cup beef bouillon
⅓ cup brandy
2–3 tablespoons green peppercorns

Dry steaks; pound with green peppercorns; allow several hours to set.

Heat 2 tablespoons of butter and 2 tablespoons vegetable oil, add steaks and cook rapidly on both sides (approximately 2 minutes on each side). Remove from pan; keep warm.

Sauté shallots, add bouillon and boil down rapidly. Add ⅓ cup brandy. Turn off heat adding 3 tablespoons butter, one at a time. Pour sauce over steaks and serve immediately.

Mrs. Stephen Montgomery

Steaks with Two Mustards

Serves 2

2 small steaks, rib eye or Delmonico, well trimmed
1 tablespoon butter
1 tablespoon olive oil
2 ounces dry vermouth
2 tablespoons Worcestershire sauce
2 teaspoons tarragon mustard
2 teaspoons Dijon mustard
2 medium cloves garlic, pressed or finely chopped

Put butter and oil in a sauté pan or heavy skillet; heat over high flame to sizzling. Add steaks; sauté 1 to 2 minutes per side or until cooked to taste. Remove and set aside, keeping warm.

Deglaze pan with vermouth. Add Worcestershire sauce and reduce to 1 to 2 tablespoons. Press garlic into pan, cook a few seconds, and then add mustards. Stir; cook for a couple of minutes over lowered heat.

Add steaks and accumulated juices and turn in the sauce. Serve immediately.

Wayne B. Swift

Dad's Cowboy Steak

Serves 6 to 8

"Butter, steam, and shared anticipation are the secrets here."

3-pound sirloin steak
1 stick butter
Salt and freshly ground pepper, to taste
Small amount of flour

Put a big, heavy skillet on stove and let it get hot with a stick of butter in it. Heat slowly until butter bubbles up. In the meantime, salt steak well on both sides; then dredge it in flour, 2 or 3 times on each side.

Slide steak into hot butter in one big piece. Cover and let it get hot. Turn once, and cover; then repeat again and again until each side has been on heat twice and is nicely browned.

"When I was out in Cherry County, Nebraska, near Valentine," said my dad, "a cowboy told me that he could cook the best steak in the world." This is the way he did it; and for many years, I often cooked the steak, for a dinner when we had house guests. I would go to the butcher's, pick out the steak, and carry it home, with a pound of butter. Then the whole family would stand around the stove while I cooked the steak. Then when it was done, we would all rush to the table and eat it while it was steaming hot.

Mrs. L. W. Pogue

Flank Steak Cleland Style

Serves 4 to 6

Large flank steak or 2 small steaks (about 2½ pounds total)
3 tablespoons soy sauce
4 tablespoons olive oil
1 tablespoon thyme (crush dry herb between fingers to get more flavor)
6 tablespoons shallots, finely chopped
Tabasco (two shakes or approximately ⅛ teaspoon)
Juice of one lemon (2 to 3 tablespoons)

Trim excess fat and score lightly (⅛ inch deep) on both sides, cutting diagonally against grain.

Mix other 6 ingredients to make marinade. Marinate at room temperature, turning meat frequently, for 1 to 3 hours. Cook in broiler or on charcoal grill, 3 to 5 minutes each side or until done to taste.

Serve with Bearnaise Sauce.

Charles & Catherine Cleland

Buffet Brisket

Serves 8 for dinner and 18 to 20 for buffet

4–5 pound boneless brisket or tenderloin of beef
¼ cup crushed black peppercorns
1 tablespoon ground cardamom

MARINADE
⅔ cup soy sauce
½ cup cider vinegar
1 tablespoon tomato paste
1 teaspoon paprika
1 clove garlic

Trim meat of excess fat. Combine crushed peppercorns and cardamom; press *firmly* into all surfaces of meat.

Combine all ingredients for marinade. Place meat in a glass or other non-reactive container. Pour marinade over meat, cover with foil, and refrigerate for 24 hours, turning at least 4 times.

Drain meat completely, wrap well in heavy foil, and bake for 2 to 3 hours at 300°.

Open carefully, allow to rest ½ hour before serving. Slice diagonally, as thin as possible.

Margaret A. Morris

Beef Brisket in Beer

Serves 6

4 pounds brisket of beef (preferably first cut)
¼ cup chili sauce
1 clove garlic, minced
2 tablespoons brown sugar
1 can (12 ounces) beer
1 large onion, sliced
¼–½ pound mushrooms, sliced
Freshly ground pepper to taste

Mix together chili sauce, garlic, sugar, beer, and pepper. Pour over brisket. Add onions and mushrooms.

Cover with tight-fitting lid and roast at 350° for 3 hours or until meat is almost done.

Remove meat from pan. Cut off fat and slice thinly against grain. Return to pan. Roast uncovered for another ½ hour until brown.

Rebecca F. Shaw

Beef Brisket with Gruyère

Serves 4

2 pounds beef brisket, trimmed of fat and cut into cubes
3 tablespoons Dijon mustard
2 crushed garlic cloves
2 tablespoons vegetable oil
2 bunches green onions or 1 bunch leeks, cut to 1-inch lengths
1 teaspoon sugar
2 tablespoons Worcestershire sauce
8 ounces beef stock (may include dash of sherry)
8 ounces finely grated Gruyère cheese (milder cheese may be used if preferred)

Preheat oven to 350° if cooking immediately.

Place meat, mustard, and garlic in large bowl; stir together until meat is coated.

In large flameproof casserole, heat oil and fry meat, stirring constantly until lightly browned. (About 6 to 8 minutes).

Add leeks, sugar, and Worcestershire sauce. Pour stock over all. (At this point mixture may be refrigerated until next day).

Cook uncovered for 2 hours, stirring occasionally.

Sprinkle cheese over top and return to oven for 10 to 15 minutes until cheese is bubbly and brown. Serve immediately.

Tastes rich and delicious, but is simple to prepare.

Francine Krasowska

Green Pepper Steak Kunming

Serves 4 to 6

1 pound beefsteak, top round or chuck
4 tablespoons soy sauce
⅓ cup peanut oil
2 cups minced onion
1 large clove garlic (optional)
4 medium green peppers
1–2 cups sliced mushrooms
2 tablespoons crystalized ginger marinated in 3 tablespoons sherry
2 tablespoons peanut oil
4 teaspoons cornstarch
¾ cup hot water
1½ cups long grain rice
3 cups chicken broth

Cook rice according to package directions, substituting chicken broth for water.

Cut beefsteak (partly frozen for easy slicing) into thin slivers. Marinate in soy sauce.

Heat ⅓ cup peanut oil until hot in skillet or wok; add onion and garlic and sauté until transparent. Add green peppers, cut into narrow strips, mushrooms and crystalized ginger. Cook, stirring until tender-raw. Remove vegetables from pan.

Place 2 tablespoons peanut oil in skillet over high heat. Add cornstarch to meat in sauce; blend.

Turn meat into skillet; brown quickly. Add vegetables, hot water, and cook 2 minutes. Serve immediately over or with hot rice.

This entrée can be cooked and served in 30 minutes or less from start to serving. Serve with shrimp rolls, and wonton, egg drop, or sweet and hot soup before or after the meal.

Henry Schalizki and Bob Davis

Fruited Pot Roast

Serves 6 to 8

3–4 pound pot roast,
    browned in oil or
    butter

MARINADE

12 ounces mixed dried fruit (apricots, pitted prunes, pears, etc.)	1 bay leaf
	2–3 sliced onions
	1 teaspoon parsley
16 ounces beer	¼ teaspoon cinnamon
½ cup water	1½ teaspoons salt
1 clove garlic	¼ teaspoon freshly ground pepper
¼ cup brown sugar	

Brown pot roast in cooking oil.
    Pour marinade over roast. Cover and cook at 275° for 4 hours.

Noelle G. Vitt

Braised Star Anise Beef

Serves 4 to 6 as a main course or 8 to 10 as part of a Chinese meal

2 pounds boneless beef (chuck)
3–4 cups cold water
5 tablespoons soy sauce
2 tablespoons sugar
2 tablespoons sake or dry sherry
4 slices peeled fresh ginger root
1 whole star anise (available in oriental food stores)
1 tablespoon sesame oil

Place beef in heavy 3 to 4-quart pan and add water to cover. Bring to a boil over high heat and skim.
    Stir in soy sauce, sake or sherry, sugar, ginger, and anise and partially cover pan. Reduce heat and simmer for 2½ to 3 hours. (Careful it doesn't burn.) There should be about 1 cup liquid left in pan. Add oil and simmer about 10 minutes.
    Remove beef and slice into *very* thin slices. Discard ginger and anise, and pour sauce over beef in serving dish.
    To serve cold, let beef cool in sauce, then refrigerate.

Janet Perry
NSO Member

Carne Aporreada
Shredded Beef

Serves 4

2 pounds flank steak
   or very lean brisket
1 large onion, whole
2 whole cloves garlic
10 pepper corns
½ teaspoon salt

SOFRITO
¼ cup olive oil
1 medium onion, finely
   chopped
1 medium green
   pepper, seeded,
   deribbed, and finely
   chopped
½ teaspoon oregano
1 bay leaf
1 pound fresh peeled or
   large can of tomatoes
   drained and chopped
1 cup beef broth

Cut flank steak or brisket in half and place in a heavy 4-quart saucepan. Add enough water to cover 2 pieces of meat. Add onion, garlic, peppercorns and salt. Bring to a boil over high heat. Reduce heat, cover partially and cook for 1 hour or until beef is tender. Remove beef and allow to cool for a few minutes.

Separate meat fibers completely. With smooth side of meat mallet or other flat surface pound strings of beef, a few at a time and continue to separate fibers further until strings of beef are as thin as possible. Set aside.

In a large skillet heat olive oil and add onions, green pepper, garlic, oregano, and bay leaf. Sauté over medium-low heat until onions are transparent *but not brown* (about 10 to 15 minutes). Add tomatoes and broth; boil while stirring until most of liquid is evaporated. Sprinkle in beef, season to taste and simmer over low heat for 20 minutes.

For best flavor cook one day in advance and store in refrigerator.

Adel Sanchez
NSO Member

Beef Curry

Serves 2

1 pound stewing beef
   (mutton or pork)
2 ounces cooking oil
½ tablespoon salt
⅛ teaspoon turmeric
¼ teaspoon paprika
2 medium onions
½ teaspoon ginger
   powder
½ tablespoon Chinese
   soy sauce
1 small clove garlic
   Hot peppers (optional)

Cut meat into strips about 2 inches long. Mince onions and garlic. Season meat with salt, turmeric, paprika, and soy sauce.

In medium saucepan, heat cooking oil. When hot, put in onions and garlic. Add seasoned meat and cook until brown. Add water to cover meat and simmer for about 30 minutes or until tender. Serve with steamed rice.

Mrs. Kyaw Khaing
Embassy of Burma

Ragout of Beef

Serves 6

2 pounds round steak
3 tablespoons butter
½ pound mushrooms
12 small white onions
6 carrots
1 mashed clove garlic
1 tablespoon tomato
   paste
2 tablespoons chopped
   parsley
1 tablespoon flour
2 cups red wine

Cut meat in bite-size pieces and brown in hot butter. Remove meat from pan and brown onions, mushrooms and carrots. Add garlic, tomato paste, flour and parsley. Stir until smooth. Place meat, vegetables and seasonings in casserole and pour wine to within 1 inch of top of meat. Cover and simmer until meat is tender, (1½ to 2 hours).

Hilda Tiger

Hussar Style Cubed Beef

Serves 4 to 6

2 pounds round steak, cut in ½ to ¾-inch cubes
3 tablespoons cooking oil
1 large onion, chopped
1 clove garlic, chopped
2 tablespoons flour
½ pound fresh mushrooms, sliced
½ cup chopped celery
1 cup sour cream
8-ounce can tomato sauce
1 teaspoon salt
⅛ teaspoon freshly ground pepper
1 tablespoon Worcestershire sauce

Brown cubes in oil. Add onion and garlic; cook until golden.

Stir in flour and cook about 3 to 5 minutes. Add remaining ingredients. Mix thoroughly.

Turn into greased 3-quart casserole. Bake uncovered in 325° oven until meat is tender (about 1½ hours).

Serve on egg noodles.

Eileen Sterling

Padoc's Chili

Serves 8 to 10

3 pounds lean beef, coarsely ground
3 12-ounce cans whole tomatoes
2 cups chopped onions
½ cup brown sugar
1 can Taco sauce
2–3 tablespoons salt
1 tablespoon freshly ground black pepper
4 teaspoons paprika
6 teaspoons chili powder
1 green pepper, chopped
3 12-ounce cans red kidney beans

Cook in 2 batches. Put beef, onion, paprika, chili powder, and salt in frying pan; cook until meat is well done.

In gallon container put in tomatoes, pepper, sugar, and taco sauce and bring to boil. Place beef mixture into tomatoes; boil slowly for 4 hours.

Next day, simmer 2 hours. Add beans and simmer 2 more hours.

Dr. W. Dabney Jarman

Hunt County Chili

Serves 4

2–4 dried ancho peppers
or 2–4 tablespoons
chili powder
1 pound lean beef,
cubed or coarsely
ground
1 teaspoon oregano
1 teaspoon crushed
cumin seed
1 teaspoon salt
1 teaspoon ground
cayenne pepper
1 teaspoon Tabasco
1–2 cloves garlic, peeled
and crushed
1 tablespoon Masa
Harina or corn meal
Water

To prepare dried anchos, carefully open peppers, removing seed and stems. In a saucepan, cover peppers with water, bring to a boil, and simmer for 20 to 30 minutes. Drain peppers; reserve liquid. Carefully scrape flesh from skins. Pulp, chop, or purée flesh; discard skins. *Do not* touch face, especially eyes, until you have washed your hands thoroughly with soap and warm water. Carefully scrub all wooden utensils used in pepper preparation, for "elevated" flavor of ancho remains.

Brown meat in a heavy skillet (preferably iron or enameled iron). You may need a little cooking oil if meat is especially lean. Add pepper pulp (or chili powder), reserved pepper liquid, plus enough water to cover meat by 2 inches. Bring it to a boil, reduce heat, and simmer covered for 30 minutes. Remove from heat, add oregano, cumin, salt, cayenne, Tabasco, and garlic. Return to heat, bring back to a boil, and simmer covered for 45 minutes. Stir only to prevent sticking. Remove from heat, add Masa, and return to simmer gently for 30 minutes, tasting frequently. Chill overnight, remove grease, and serve hot with side dishes of frijoles (red or pinto beans), chopped onion, and for Californians, grated cheese.

The old rule of thumb is 2 peppers per pound of meat, unless you know better. This is not one of the super-hot versions. It is slightly milder than the old standard "Two Alarm" chili. Three alarm chili is 3 peppers/pound, etc. Try the 2 pepper version first, escalate at your own risk!

Francine Morris Swift

Texas Chile Con Carne

Serves 6 to 8

1 green pepper, chopped fine
2 large onions, chopped fine
1 clove garlic, chopped fine
1 tablespoon butter or olive oil
3–4 tablespoons chili powder
2 tablespoons flour
1 teaspoon oregano
1 teaspoon ground cumin

2 pounds ground beef
1 can (21 ounces) tomatoes
1 cup water
2 tablespoons sugar
2 teaspoons salt
1 square unsweetened chocolate
2 cans (15 ounces each) kidney beans

Fry onion, green pepper, and garlic in fat until golden brown and transparent. Mix chili powder, flour, and all herbs together and stir into onion mix. Cook 3 minutes; then add tomatoes and water. Simmer and season with sugar, salt, and chocolate; stir until dissolved and cook 1 hour longer. The sauce should be about like gravy. It may be thinned with water and tomato sauce.

Brown beef and add to sauce. Cook about 1 hour. Add beans and cook until blended.

Cathy Tennyson

Pastel de Choclo de Chile

Serves 4 to 5

1½ pounds lean ground beef
1 handful of raisins
1 large or 2 small onions
1 teaspoon cumin seed
Paprika to taste

17-ounce can creamed corn
Sugar, to taste

Brown beef in skillet with butter and onions. Add salt to taste and enough paprika to make juice in skillet red in color; add cumin seed. Cook about 10 minutes or more; add raisins.

Remove from heat and place contents in a flat baking or serving dish. Spread creamed corn over top of mixture and sprinkle a bit of sugar on top of corn. Brown in oven until corn is golden brown.

The amounts of the ingredients vary according to personal taste.

Elizabeth S. Sanders

Relleno Con Carne

Serves 6

1 large eggplant, prebaked
5 medium zucchini, sliced thin
2½ pounds ground chuck
1 large onion, chopped
3 shallots, chopped
3 cloves minced garlic
1 tablespoon sweet marjoram, or to taste

1 tablespoon rosemary or to taste
Salt and freshly ground pepper
5 ounces Romano cheese, sliced

Prebake eggplant in a 350° oven for about 30 minutes. When done, cool and slice.

Sauté meat with garlic, onion, shallots, herbs and seasonings. Cook slowly until onion is transparent.

In a large pyrex dish, layer all ingredients as follows: slices of zucchini, ground beef, and slices of eggplant; repeat until all ingredients are used up. Cover top with slices of cheese. Bake covered with tin foil for 1 hour at 350°. Uncover for last 15 minutes to brown cheese.

Paula Morgan

Taco con Fuoco Casserole

Serves 8 to 10

10–12 tostados, crumbled
1 pound ground beef
1 tablespoon cumin
3 tablespoons chili powder
1 pound shredded Cheddar cheese
2 chopped Jalapeño peppers
2 16-ounce cans refried beans
1 cup chopped green onions

2 5-ounce cans hot Enchilada sauce
1–2 cups cottage cheese

Brown ground beef with cumin and chili powder.

Make sauce, puréeing enchilada sauce with cottage cheese.

Layer all ingredients as follows: tostados, beef mixture, cheese, and beans, pouring sauce between each layer. Casserole should end with tostados and cheese on top.

Bake at 350° for 30 to 35 minutes.

Alfhild Winder

Noodle Doodle

Serves 6 to 8

2 pounds lean ground beef
1 pound box medium noodles
1 large onion
1 cup grated Cheddar cheese
1 cup grated Parmesan cheese
  Fresh garlic
  Salt and freshly ground pepper to taste
1 jar stuffed olives
1 can button mushrooms
1 jar spaghetti sauce, or your own
  Butter
  Sunflower seed cooking oil

In a large pot bring to boil enough water to more than cover a pound of noodles. Add about 6 tablespoons of oil. Add noodles, stirring occasionally. Do not overcook. When done, drain noodles in a colander.

Mince onions and garlic. Cover bottom of large frying pan with oil. Brown onions, garlic, and beef.

Take a large casserole dish and grease bottom and sides with butter. Alternate layers of meat and noodles, adding to each layer grated cheese, olives, garlic, salt, pepper, mushrooms, and spaghetti sauce. Top layer should be cheese and spaghetti sauce. Dot entire top with thick pats of butter.

Put in a 350° oven (covered) until all of cheese is melted and casserole is hot and bubbly.

This dish begs for a green salad with vinaigrette dressing!

Milton Schwartz
NSO Member

Oxtails with Dried Fruit

Serves 4

1 oxtail, sectioned, (about 3 pounds)
2–2½ cups beef stock
1 medium potato, diced
1 medium turnip, diced
1 bunch (6–8) carrots, diced
1 large onion, grated
4 strips bacon, chopped
¼ cup chopped parsley
1 tablespoon butter
¼ cup seedless raisins
12 dried peaches, quartered and plumped in the wine
1 cup red wine
Juice of 1 lemon
Salt and freshly ground pepper to taste (omit if using canned beef broth)

Season oxtails. Add beef stock and bring to boil. Simmer for 1½ hours.

Add potatoes, carrots, and turnips; simmer gently until meat is tender.

Sauté onion, bacon and parsley in butter. Add raisins, peaches, wine and lemon juice. Add to meat and simmer until dried fruit is soft.

Make a day ahead so fat on top can be removed.

This should be served like a stew.

Mrs. Elizabeth Sole
Wife of the Ambassador of South Africa

Rognons de Veau au Calvados et Moutarde

Serves 4

4 kidneys
¼ cup chopped shallots
4 ounces Calvados
Salt and freshly ground pepper to taste
3 tablespoons butter
2 tablespoons oil
1 cup heavy cream
2 tablespoons Dijon mustard
Fresh chervil, chopped for garnish

Cut kidneys in half, then in slices about ½ centimeter thick. Salt and pepper them.

Sauté in oil and butter very fast, for about 4 minutes, remove kidneys from pan and set in strainer.

Add shallots to pan with Calvados (do not flame). Add heavy cream and reduce sauce. Add Dijon mustard. Put kidneys back into sauce and bring to a fast boil.

Garnish with chopped chervil.

Jean-Charles Berruet, The Chanticleer Inn
Nantucket Island, Massachusetts

Brains Vinaigrette

Brains

Court Bouillon

VINAIGRETTE
½ pint oil or more if necessary
⅓ as much vinegar
Freshly ground pepper
A few capers
Onion, chopped
Parsley, chopped
Chervil
Tarragon
Chives

"United Nations Recipes for War Rationed Cooking" published during WW II

First carefully remove thin membrane which entirely covers brains. Try not to tear them as they are very delicate. Then soak brains in cold water with a little vinegar and salt to remove all blood. When they are white put them in boiling "court-bouillon" (see below) to cover; skim and simmer gently for ½ hour. The brains are then lifted out and ready to prepare in various ways.

Our favorite way is with sauce vinaigrette. Keep brains in large pieces, sauté gently in butter or margarine, and serve with following sauce.

SAUCE VINAIGRETTE

To oil and vinegar add salt, freshly ground pepper, a few small capers, finely chopped onion, parsley, chervil, tarragon and chives. Stir well. This is very good with only onion, parsley and chives, if other herbs are not available.

COURT BOUILLION

Court bouillion is used for many things, especially fish, when a little vinegar is added to keep fish firm. It is simply salted water to which has been added minced carrots, onions, parsley and any herbs or seasonings you care for, such as bay leaf, thyme, celery, and whole peppers. In some cases milk is added; sometimes wine; sometimes a slice of lemon.

Brains are delicious mixed with sweetbreads and mushrooms in a rich white sauce. Leftover chicken, hard-boiled eggs, gnocchi, asparagus tips, elbow macaroni or other things may be added to make this an ample and substantial dish.

Hans Kindler
First NSO Music Director
1931–1949

Lamb with Green Beans and Cashews

Serves 5 to 6

1½ pounds lean ground lamb
1 pound fresh green beans or ¾ pound frozen green beans
5–6 large cloves garlic, chopped
1 tablespoon lemon juice
½ teaspoon salt
2 tablespoons dry sherry
½ cup dry-roasted, unsalted cashews

Brown lamb in a heavy skillet and drain off fat. Add chopped garlic and sizzle briefly. Remove lamb and garlic from skillet.

Cook beans (covered) in same skillet using smallest possible amount of water and *no salt*.

When beans are barely tender, add lamb and garlic, lemon juice, sherry, and salt. Simmer until most of liquid is gone. Sprinkle with cashews and serve immediately.

This is almost a stir fry type recipe and can be done in a wok.

David R. Whaley
NSO Member

Charcoal-Grilled Lamb with Sauce

Serves 8 to 10

6-pound leg of lamb, boned, fat removed, and butterflied
1 cup olive or vegetable oil
⅔ cup lemon juice
3 cloves crushed garlic
2 bay leaves
6 sprigs parsley
2 teaspoons salt
½ teaspoon freshly ground pepper
1 tablespoon dried sage
1 tablespoon rosemary
1 tablespoon dried thyme

SAUCE
½ cup beef stock
¼ cup red wine
2 tablespoons chopped shallots
3 tablespoons butter
3 tablespoons chopped parsley

Be sure all fat is removed from lamb.

Combine oil, lemon, garlic, bay leaves, parsley sprigs, salt, pepper, and ½ teaspoon each sage, rosemary and thyme. Marinate meat in this mixture 24 hours, turning occasionally.

Drain meat; reserve marinade. Sear each side of lamb on a hot grill; then cook 45 minutes to 1 hour, brushing with reserve marinade. Outside will be crusty and inside pink.

SAUCE

Combine stock, wine, shallots, and remaining spices. Boil rapidly and reduce to ½ cup. Remove from heat; add softened butter and chopped parsley. Pour over sliced meat. Great with taboulleh.

Norma Dugger

Hunan Lamb

Serves 6 to 8 as part
of a multi-course
Chinese dinner

3-pound leg of
 lamb (weight
 includes bone)
½ cup peanut oil
12–16 dried hot red
 peppers
12 cloves of garlic,
 peeled
1-inch cube ginger,
 sliced thin
2 scallions
 (including green
 portion) sliced in
 1½-inch lengths
½ pound rock sugar*
2 teaspoons salt
2 tablespoons chili
 paste with garlic*
¼ cup *dark* soy
 sauce*
1¾ cups beer

*available in oriental
groceries

Cube lamb into bite-size pieces. Boil enough water to cover meat; add lamb to boiling water and cook for 3 minutes, stirring occasionally. Drain; chill with cold water.

Heat peanut oil in wok. Add garlic and cool for 10 seconds. Add dried peppers and ginger; cook until peppers and garlic are dark brown. Add scallions and cook 20 to 30 seconds. Add lamb; cook (stirring) for 1 minute. Add rock sugar, chili paste, soy sauce, and salt. Stir to blend and cook 1 minute.

Transfer to casserole and add beer. Cook for 45 minutes to 1 hour until meat is tender but not overcooked. Temperature for cooking should be medium heat to keep mixture below boiling point.

Henry Fogel

Shish Kebab Marinated in Orange Juice

Serves 4

1 pound lean lamb, cut into 1½-inch cubes
Onions, green peppers, tomatoes for skewering

MARINADE
¼ cup brown sugar
⅛ teaspoon ground cloves
¼ teaspoon dry mustard
⅓ cup chopped onion
Grated rind of ½ orange (about ½ tablespoon)
⅓ cup orange juice
¾ cup ketchup
1½ cups water

Combine all marinade ingredients in a saucepan. Bring to a boil, and reduce heat. Simmer uncovered for about 30 minutes. Remove from heat and cool. Pour over lamb and marinate for at least 8 hours or overnight.

Skewer lamb cubes alternately with tomatoes, onions, and green peppers. Baste periodically while broiling. Remaining marinade can be strained and used as a sauce for accompanying rice.

The lamb absorbs the orange flavor beautifully. Not good with beef.

Arthur Lieb

Kleftiko

Serves 2

½ pound lamb, cubed
1 teaspoon salt
1 teaspoon freshly ground pepper
1 teaspoon oregano
1 teaspoon thyme
2 tablespoons corn oil

¼ cup lemon juice
4 small potatoes
1 cup corn oil
2 bay leaves
3 tomatoes, cut in thick slices

Cube meat and sprinkle with lemon juice. Add salt, pepper, oregano, thyme and 2 tablespoons oil to meat. Seal tightly in foil. Cook in oven at 300° for 3 hours.

Peel and halve potatoes. Put in pyrex dish; add oil, salt, pepper, and bay leaves. Place tomatoes on top of potatoes. One hour before meat is done, put in oven.

Add potatoes to meat in foil for last 15 minutes of cooking time. Serve with mixed salad.

Kleftiko is made of lamb or goat meat in Cyprus, cooked in sealed pots or pyrex dishes. Here I wrap the lamb in foil.

Mrs. Andrew Jacovides
Wife of the Ambassador of Cyprus

Stuffed Lamb Breast

Serves 4

1 cup cooked rice
1 tablespoon raisins or currants
1 tablespoon pine nuts
Parsley to taste
Salt and freshly ground pepper to taste
1 lamb breast
1 tablespoon grated onion
2 tablespoons butter
1 tablespoon tomato sauce
⅛ cup water

Sew breast on two sides leaving one side open for stuffing. Season it with salt and pepper.

Sauté onions in butter. Add raisins, pine nuts, parsley, salt, pepper, and rice. Cook this mixture in a skillet a few more minutes.

Fill breast cavity with stuffing and sew edges together. Stuffing will expand so do not fill cavity completely.

Place meat in a baking dish, and bake uncovered in a low 300° to 325° oven until evenly browned, approximately 2 hours.

Add tomato sauce, and cook for 5 more minutes. Add ¼ cup water, cover pan, and cook until tender.

Mrs. Sükrü Elekdag
Wife of the Ambassador of Turkey

Ballinaclough Stew

Serves 6

3 pounds end of neck or shoulder lamb chops
2 pounds potatoes, quartered
1 pound onions, sliced
1 pound carrots, sliced
4 sticks celery, sliced
Salt and freshly ground pepper to taste
4 ounces frozen peas
1 package dried vegetable soup
6 cups water

Trim fat from meat. In large skillet add meat and cover with a layer of cut vegetables. Sprinkle salt and pepper over this layer. Repeat this process until all meat and vegetables have been used. Add water and bring to a boil over high heat. Simmer for 1½ hours over reduced heat.

Mix vegetable soup with 1 cup boiling water. Add this to stew. Simmer for 10 minutes. Add frozen peas for last 5 minutes. Add a little more water if it seems to get too dry.

Mrs. Carol O'Colmain

Lamb Chops Satay Style

Serves 6

6 lamb chops

MARINADE

1 tablespoon whole
    pickling spice
    Lemon pepper
1 very small piece
    galangal (Malaysian
    ginger)
1 very small piece
    turmeric
1–2 dried chillies
3 small onions
1 clove garlic
1 clove fresh ginger
1 teaspoon sugar
    Salt to taste
    Cooking oil
    Juice of 1 grapefruit

GRAVY

2 teaspoons cooking oil
1 clove garlic
1 tablespoon peanut
    butter or 1
    tablespoon roasted,
    ground nuts
3 small onions,
    shredded
2 chillies, ground, or
    Tabasco sauce to
    taste
    Lemon pepper
1 tablespoon sugar
½ cup water (or
    tamarind juice)
1 small piece shrimp
    paste *or*
1 teaspoon anchovy
    paste
    Salt

Wash and dry lamb chops. Combine all marinade ingredients and grind to a paste. Add juice of grapefruit. Mix and pour over chops. This can be done in the morning and left until dinner time.

Grill or barbecue chops, basting with oil, and serve with gravy.

GRAVY

Heat cooking oil in a saucepan. Fry shredded onions and garlic until golden brown. Add ground chillies and lemon pepper. Fry 1 more minute. Add peanut butter and stir; add water and remaining ingredients all the while stirring and bring to a boil.

Mrs. D. Azraai Zain
Wife of the Ambassador of Malaysia

Sha-Khul Mahshie
Stuffed Eggplant Casserole

Serves 8

2–3 large eggplants

STUFFING
 1 pound ground lamb
 ½ cup pine nuts
 2 onions, chopped
    Salt and freshly
      ground pepper to
      taste

TOMATO SAUCE
    3-ounce can tomato
      paste
 1 onion, finely chopped
 ½ teaspoon sugar
    Salt and freshly
      ground pepper to
      taste
 1 tablespoon butter or
      cooking oil.
 1 cup water

Peel eggplant and slice in ½-inch thick rounds. Put butter or oil in shallow pan and broil eggplant until brown. Turn and brown on other side. After all eggplant is cooked, line bottom of a slightly oiled baking dish (9 × 13 inches) with one layer of eggplant slices.

Place about 2 tablespoons stuffing on each slice and cover with another layer of eggplant slices. Pour tomato sauce over eggplant and bake at 350° for ½ hour.

STUFFING

Sauté chopped onion until soft; add pine nuts and lamb. Salt and pepper to taste and cook until lamb is slightly browned.

SAUCE

Sauté onion in butter or oil. Add tomato paste, sugar, salt, pepper and ⅓ cup water. Cook for 10 minutes. Add rest of water and simmer for 30 minutes.

This is a traditional Lebanese dish which is usually served over a bed of rice.

Tom Hier

Kibbeh Bil Sineych
Baked Kibbi

Serves 6

2 cups fine Bulgur
2 pounds lean lamb, ground very fine
1 large onion, ground very fine
  Salt and freshly ground pepper to taste
½ cup of water

FILLING
1 pound ground lamb
  Salt, freshly ground pepper and allspice to taste
¼–½ cup pine nuts
1¼ cups clarified butter

Rinse bulgur in large amount of water. Drain and squeeze out moisture handful by handful. Mix with ground meat and onion; grind together twice more. Add water as needed to mixture to make a stiff paste.

Butter a flat 10 × 14-inch baking sheet. Spread half of kibbi on it. Brown rest of lamb in ¼ cup butter; add seasonings and pine nuts. Spread over kibbi. Score in squares or diamonds with a knife; loosen edges with a knife.

Pour rest of butter over top to cover it and bake in a 400° oven for 30 minutes or until golden brown. Serve hot or cold.

Embassy of Lebanon

Pork Tenderloin with Sesame Seeds and Mushroom Sauce

Serves 6

1½ pounds pork tenderloin, cut into ½-inch slices	½ cup sliced green onion
1 tablespoon cooking oil	½ teaspoon dried thyme
Salt and freshly ground pepper to taste	½ tablespoon sesame seeds, toasted
10½-ounce can consommé	½ pound mushrooms, sliced
½ cup chopped celery	2 tablespoons butter
	2 tablespoons mustard
	3 tablespoons flour
	2 tablespoons parsley, chopped

Slowly brown tenderloin pieces in oil. Sprinkle with salt and pepper; then drain off fat.

Add consommé, celery, green onions, and thyme. Cover and simmer for about 40 minutes or until meat is tender. Remove meat from skillet.

In a separate pan, sauté sliced mushrooms in 2 tablespoons butter. Add flour and stir for 2 minutes.

Slowly add flour and mushroom mixture into consommé mixture in skillet. Cook, stirring occasionally, until thick and bubbly.

Add parsley and sesame seeds. Heat thoroughly and pour over tenderloin pieces.

Linda Font

Stuffed Pork Loin Braised with Bourbon

Serves 6 to 8

3-pound pork loin, boned
8–10 prunes
1 or more cups beef broth
¼ pound prosciutto or smoked ham, cut into thin slices
½ cup shelled pistachio nuts
½ cup Dijon mustard
⅔ cup dark brown sugar
2 tablespoons cooking oil
⅔ cup bourbon
Salt and freshly ground pepper to taste
Thyme, sage, and parsley to make bouquet garni
½ teaspoon arrowroot or cornstarch (optional)

Preheat oven to 375°.

Dry meat. Cut a deep pocket in pork from within 1 inch of either end of meat. Cut prosciutto or ham into strips.

Steep prunes in about 1 cup of beef broth. Remove prunes, but save liquid.

Insert prosciutto or ham strips, pistachios, and prunes into pork pocket. Press meat back in place and tie securely. Paint meat with mustard; then roll in brown sugar.

Heat oil in a heavy, ovenproof, cooking pot and brown meat in it, turning to brown evenly, for about 10 to 15 minutes. The sugar will caramelize, so be careful it does not burn.

Remove pot from burner. Pour half bourbon over meat and set aflame. When flame goes out, pour in remaining beef broth. Cover pot and set into a preheated 375° oven to cook for 1¾ hours.

Halfway through cooking, turn meat. Season with salt and pepper; add bouquet garni. Lower heat to 350°.

About 10 minutes before end of cooking time add liquid saved from prunes.

This pork may be served hot or cold; best served cold only in summer. When pork is served hot, remove meat to a warm platter, strain cooking liquid and remove fat. Return liquid to pot and set over heat. Bring sauce to boil, adding remaining bourbon and stirring to dislodge sediments. Sauce may be thickened by bringing to a boil with arrowroot or cornstarch mixed with a little cold water. Taste and correct seasoning.

Whether pork is served cold or hot, slice it and lay it over a bed of watercress. If served hot, coat meat lightly with sauce and serve remaining sauce on the side.

Lonie Landfield

Indonesian Pork Kabobs

Serves 6

2 pounds lean pork
¼ cup peanut butter
3 tablespoons soy sauce
2 tablespoons ground coriander
1 tablespoon ground cumin
½ teaspoon chili powder
1 clove crushed garlic
1 tablespoon lemon juice

SAUCE
1 cup soy sauce
2 tablespoons pineapple juice
1 clove crushed garlic
¼ cup sherry
¼ teaspoon salt
½ teaspoon minced fresh ginger root

Cut meat into 1-inch cubes.

Make a paste of peanut butter, soy sauce, spices, garlic, and lemon juice. Add meat to paste and mix well. Let marinate ½ hour.

Thread cubes of meat onto skewers and broil slowly for about 20 to 30 minutes, 6 inches from heat. Turn to brown all sides.

For sauce, mix soy sauce, pineapple juice, garlic, sherry, salt, and ginger root; bring to boil. Let cool and strain. This sauce also may be used as a dip.

Serve meat over rice with sauce on the side. Accompany with a light, colorful Beirut Salad made of two parts chopped tomato, one part chopped green peppers, and one part chopped Spanish onion; no dressing or seasonings needed.

Jackson Bain

Pork Saté

Serves about 8 people as an entrée and about 30 for a cocktail appetizer

3 pounds pork tenderloin or <u>fresh</u> ham, cut into 1½-inch cubes (for cocktails cut into ¾-inch cubes)
¾ teaspoon salt
Freshly ground pepper to taste
1 tablespoon ground coriander
1 tablespoon ground cumin
½ cup salad oil
1 clove crushed garlic
1 tablespoon brown sugar
1 tablespoon vinegar
4 tablespoons soy sauce
Dash of ginger

SATÉ SAUCE
4 tablespoons chunky peanut butter
¼ cup chopped peanuts
2 tablespoons brown sugar
1 tablespoon vinegar
2 tablespoons water
3 tablespoons soy sauce

Bamboo skewers can be purchased at oriental food stores.

Soak skewers in water at least ½ hour before threading meat so meat does not stick to skewers. For an entrée, thread 3 or 4 cubes on a skewer; for an appetizer 2 or 3 cubes.

Combine salt, pepper, coriander, cumin, salad oil, garlic, brown sugar, vinegar, soy sauce, and ginger to make marinade. Marinate meat overnight.

Remove meat and put on skewers. Broil meat 4 inches from heat for about 15 minutes, basting occasionally, or cook in a 450° oven for about 30 minutes.

Meanwhile, make saté sauce by mixing together peanut butter, brown sugar, vinegar, water, and soy sauce over low heat, stirring constantly (thin with hot water if necessary).

Pour sauce over satés and sprinkle with peanuts. Serve with rice if used as an entrée.

Kathryn C. Avery

Choucroute Garnie
Garnished Sauerkraut

Serves 4 to 6

6 slices bacon, cut up
½ cup chopped onion
27-ounce can sauerkraut, drained and rinsed to reduce sourness
2 medium carrots, sliced on the diagonal
1 tablespoon sugar
8–10 juniper berries (optional)
6 whole black peppercorns
2 whole cloves
1 bay leaf
1 large sprig parsley
¾ cup chicken broth
½ cup dry white wine
4 potatoes, peeled and quartered
4 smoked pork chops
4 knockwurst (diagonally scored)

In large skillet, cook bacon and onions. Drain off fat. Add sauerkraut, carrots, and sugar to skillet, and stir.

Loosely tie juniper berries, peppercorns, bay leaf, and parsley in cheesecloth bag; bury in center of sauerkraut.

Add broth and wine. Bring to boil. Reduce heat and simmer covered for 10 minutes. Add potatoes, pushing them into sauerkraut. Simmer covered for 15 minutes more.

Put meat on top. Simmer covered for 20 minutes. To serve, discard herb pouch, arrange sauerkraut and potatoes on platter, and top with meat.

This dish is good reheated.

Ilene Cox

Country Winter Dish

Serves 3 to 4

1½ pounds pork tenderloin *or*
1½ pounds Canadian bacon
3 large yellow onions
4 tablespoons butter
4 tart, cooking apples, red or green, sliced
Salt and freshly ground pepper, if using tenderloin

Slice tenderloin into ¼ to ½-inch slices. Peel and slice onions to same thickness.

Add 4 tablespoons butter to an iron skillet. Cook onions until yellow; remove from skillet.

Brown meat slices on both sides in same skillet. Return onions; add apples. Steam gently on top of stove until hot and tender. Do not overcook apples.

Serve with mashed potatoes, a light, green tossed salad and beer (not wine).

Malan Strong

Civet de Porc à la Marcassin

Serves 4 to 6

2 pounds diced, lean
   pork
2 cups red wine
2 cups cold water
1 cup red wine vinegar
1 cup minced carrots
2 tablespoons flour
1 cup minced onions
1 clove garlic
2 bay leaves
1 tablespoon lard or oil
5 juniper berries
6 black peppercorns
1 tablespoon red currant
   jelly

In a deep crock or stainless steel or enameled pan, combine wine vinegar, cold water, bay leaves, peppercorns, carrot, juniper berries, and diced pork; marinate for a couple of days.

Remove meat from marinade and pat dry with a paper towel. It will remain very moist.

In a saucepan, brown meat on all sides in hot fat. After meat is browned, add marinade and all its ingredients; bring to boil. Reduce heat and simmer for about 1½ to 2 hours, or until meat is very tender. Remove meat and strain sauce.

In separate saucepan, over low heat, beat ¼ cup of sauce with flour. When smooth, add rest of sauce and currant jelly.

Pour gravy over meat; serve immediately. May be served with any vegetable.

Chef Roland Bouyat
The Bread Oven Restaurant

Szegediener Gulyas

Serves 6 to 8

2 pounds pork
1 pound sauerkraut
2 onions
1 pint sour cream
2 tablespoons butter,
    oil, or bacon
    drippings
1 teaspoon paprika
2 tablespoons tomato
    paste
    Salt, to taste
1 tablespoon caraway
    seeds
½ cup water
1 tablespoon flour

Cut meat into 2-inch cubes. Mince onion and brown in butter or oil; add meat and brown a little longer.

Add paprika, tomato paste, salt, caraway seeds, and water; simmer until meat is tender, adding more water if necessary. Add sauerkraut and simmer a little longer.

Before serving, add flour and sour cream. Mix well and serve piping hot.

Serve with boiled potatoes on a cold winter's night.

Franziska Mayer

Ham Loaf with Dressing

Serves 4 to 6

1 pound ground cured
    or smoked ham
½ pound ground fresh
    ham (pork)
1½ cups dry bread
    crumbs
2 medium eggs, beaten
¾ cup milk
    Freshly ground
    pepper to taste

DRESSING
¼ cup vinegar
½ cup water
¼ cup sugar
1 tablespoon mustard

Mix meat, bread crumbs, eggs, milk, and pepper well. Form into a loaf shape, and place in loaf pan.

DRESSING

Melt sugar in water and vinegar; stir in mustard. Pour over loaf. Bake at 350° for 1½ hours, basting frequently.

John and Annie Glenn

Sausage-Spinach Bread

Serves 8 to 10

1½ pounds Italian sweet sausage, cooked and drained
2 packages, frozen chopped spinach, steamed
½ pound whole milk mozzarella cheese, grated

Garlic powder
Salt and freshly ground pepper
1 loaf frozen white bread dough

Defrost bread dough and roll out to size of large pizza. Fry sausage; drain. Steam spinach; drain and squeeze out excess moisture when cool. Grate mozzarella.

Mix sausage, spinach, and cheese together. Spread over dough. Sprinkle liberally with garlic powder; salt and pepper to taste.

Roll up dough with filling as you would a jelly roll. Bake on oiled cookie sheet at 350° for 25 to 30 minutes or until golden brown. Slice like bread.

Can be served as an appetizer or as a meal with a green salad.

Lili Chookasian

Karelian Stew

Serves 8

1 pound stewing pork
1 pound stewing beef
1 pound stewing lamb
¾ pound veal kidneys (optional)

Salt, to taste
Whole white peppercorns or allspice
2–3 large onions

Preheat oven to 350°. Cut meats into 1-inch cubes and layer them in deep ovenproof casserole dish. Add onions and seasonings. Pour in enough water to just cover meats. Cover casserole with a tight-fitting lid.

Let simmer in oven for about 1 hour. Lower heat to 300° and let simmer for an additional 2 hours. The slower the dish cooks, the tastier it will be. Serve with baked potatoes, pickles, and pickled red beets.

Originally, salt was the only seasoning used. The meat yields a delicious flavor and aroma during the slow cooking. Today, however, peppercorns and onions are added. In some parts of Finland even carrots and bay leaves are considered essential. Karelian Stew used to be served with dark sourdough rye bread dipped in the liquid.

Kaarina Kaurinkoski
Embassy of Finland

Hungarian Stuffed Cabbage

Makes 32 rolls

3 heads cabbage
5½ pounds meat loaf mixture or lean ground pork
4 eggs
Chopped parsley
Spareribs, about 2 pounds
2–3 onions, grated
Salt and freshly ground pepper, to taste
Pinch of marjoram
Paprika

1½ cups long grain rice
4 large cans sauerkraut, drained
1 large can tomato purée
Sour cream, optional

To prepare cabbage:
Core cabbages, plunge whole into boiling water until they're soft enough to pull leaves apart. Cool a little and separate 32 large leaves. Use a paring knife to shave off the large rib of leaves, so they can be rolled up easily around filling. Reserve remaining cabbage.

FILLING

Soak 1½ cups rice in hot water for 30 minutes, changing water frequently to keep it hot or parboil for 8 minutes.
Combine meat loaf mixture, eggs, grated onions, salt and pepper to taste, and marjoram. Drain rice, and add to meat loaf mixture. Place meat mixture in cup of each cabbage leaf, loosely fold over sides of leaf, and roll up; tuck ends of leaf into each roll.

ASSEMBLY

Chop reserved cabbage. In a large pan with a tight-fitting lid, place a layer of chopped cabbage, followed by a layer of sauerkraut. Add a layer of cabbage rolls, then another layer of sauerkraut and some spareribs. The number of alternating layers of cabbage, rolls, and sauerkraut will depend on size of pan. Top with remaining spareribs.
Cover tightly and cook slowly over very low heat for 1½ hours. Pour large can of tomato purée over contents and continue cooking until well done, 2 to 3 hours. When serving, sour cream may be added to the entrée. Serve with mashed potatoes and good rye or pumpernickel bread.

This dish is ideal for reheating as the flavor keeps improving.

Donald Havas
NSO Member

Klaps
à la
Konigsberg

Serves 4 to 6

1½–2 pounds meat
(3 parts pork to
1 part beef, finely
ground)
1 grated onion
2 whole eggs, beaten
2 hard rolls, soaked
in milk and
squeezed almost
dry
Salt, freshly
ground pepper,
and nutmeg to
taste
¼ cup finely chopped
parsley
1 quart beef stock or
bouillon

SAUCE
4 tablespoons butter
4 tablespoons flour
1 chopped onion
1–2 finely ground
anchovies or
anchovy paste
3 egg yolks, beaten
with 1–2 teaspoons
vinegar
Capers (optional)

Add grated onion, eggs, minced rolls, seasonings, and parsley to meat; mix well, tossing lightly as not to toughen meat.

Form into small, 2-inch balls. Bring beef stock to a boil and drop meat balls carefully into boiling liquid. Cook gently about ½ hour or until done. Balls may retain a pink color. Remove with slotted spoon and set aside. Save broth for sauce.

To make sauce, brown flour in butter. Add onion and anchovy paste; sauté onion. Add broth, a little at a time; then add egg-vinegar mixture. Let cook, stirring constantly until sauce thickens.

Pour sauce over meatballs and serve with boiled potatoes.

Anne R. Keller

V E A L

Veal Cutlets in Port

Serves 4 to 6

1½ pounds veal cutlets
1 onion, chopped
3 tablespoons butter
¾ cup port wine
Juice of ½ lemon
1 cup heavy cream
Dash of cayenne
pepper
⅛ teaspoon thyme

Brown veal and onions in butter. Cover and simmer for 25 minutes or until tender. Remove meat and keep warm.

Add remaining ingredients to pan drippings. Heat, stirring, but do not boil. Serve over meat.

Using port wine is the key.

Chester Ludgin

Sautéed Veal Scallops in Sour Cream Sauce

Serves 2 to 4

4 large veal scallops, sliced ⅜ inch thick and pounded to ¼ inch thick.
3 tablespoons unsalted butter
¼ cup finely chopped onion
3 tablespoons vegetable oil

SAUCE
Pan drippings and onions from skillet
2 tables vermouth
1 cup sour cream
1 cup shredded goat cheese (Montrachet)
Salt and freshly ground pepper to taste

Heat 1 tablespoon butter and 1 tablespoon oil in a heavy skillet over moderate heat. When foam subsides, add onions and cook 3 to 5 minutes or until transparent. Scrape with spatula into a small bowl and set aside.

Add remaining butter and oil. When foam subsides, add veal and fry over moderate heat until golden brown (4 to 5 minutes each side). Remove to heated platter and warm in 220° oven while making sauce.

Return veal to skillet. Baste with sauce and let simmer for a few minutes. Serve at once.

SAUCE

Deglaze pan with 2 tablespoons vermouth. Add cooked onions. Cook over high heat, stirring constantly, 2 to 5 minutes. Reduce heat and stir in sour cream and cheese, a little at a time. Stir until melted and smooth, but do not boil. Add seasonings.

Leonard Slatkin

Escalope de Veau à la Moutarde

Serves 3 to 4

8 veal scallops
⅓ cup flour
  Salt and freshly
  ground pepper
4 tablespoons butter
2 tablespoons minced
  shallots

¼ cup dry white wine
½ cup heavy cream
1 tablespoon Dijon
  mustard
  Fresh chopped parsley

Place veal scallops on flat surface and pound thin. Blend flour with salt and pepper; coat scallops.

Heat butter in a large skillet until hot (not brown). Add scallops. Cook quickly until golden (about 2 minutes) and turn. Remove to warming dish; keep warm.

Add shallots to skillet and cook briefly, stirring. Add wine and cook, stirring, until nearly evaporated. Add cream, and continue stirring as it comes to a boil. Cook about 30 seconds and then remove from heat. Stir in mustard. Do not cook further. Pour over scallops and serve. Sprinkle with parsley.

This sauce can also be made ahead, heated up and poured over baked chicken.

Paul R. Ignatius

Veal Birds in Tomato Sauce

Serves 2 to 4

4 veal scallops
4 prosciutto ham
  slices, thinly sliced
4–6 sage leaves
½ cup flour
¼ cup butter
  Salt and freshly
  ground pepper

SAUCE
2 1-pound cans Italian
  plum tomatoes
2 teaspoons Italian
  seasoning
½ teaspoon basil
¼ cup butter

Salt and pepper veal scallops. On each piece of seasoned veal, place a similarly-sized slice of proscuitto and one sage leaf.

Roll up from end and tie with thread. Roll in flour and sauté in butter. Finish cooking veal birds in a well-seasoned tomato sauce for about 15 minutes.

SAUCE

Crush tomatoes in pan; add herbs and butter. Cook until some but not all liquid is reduced. Pour over veal birds and cook over low heat for 15 minutes.

Henryk Szeryng

Super Scallopine

Serves 4

8 veal scallops
1 avocado, sliced thin
2 fresh tomatoes, sliced
8 slices Jarlsberg or
    Swiss cheese
    Lemon pepper and
    flour
3 tablespoons butter

Pound veal between sheets of wax paper. Sprinkle with lemon pepper and dredge with flour.

Melt butter in skillet and brown veal briefly. Cover veal with tomato slices and avocado slices. Top with cheese. Cover and cook over moderate heat for 5 minutes or until cheese is melted. Serve immediately.

Anne Watson

Veal and Peppers

Serves 2

10 ounces veal scallops
 2 green peppers, sliced
     thin
     Medium-size red
     onion, sliced thin
 1 cup canned tomatoes
     Freshly ground
     pepper and herbs, to
     taste
     A few fresh
     mushrooms, sliced,
     if desired

Cut veal in strips. Clean, stem and seed peppers; cut in strips.

Place onion and peppers in Silver-Stone fry pan. Add sliced mushrooms, if desired. Stir to prevent burning. If it sticks, add a little water. Remove onion and pepper and save to add to veal.

Brown veal (takes seconds), and add onion and peppers. Add 2 or 3 medium-size mushrooms, if desired. Add tomatoes with juice. Cover and simmer about 15 minutes.

This is a low calorie recipe with only 250 calories per serving. Use only non-stick cookware or "Pam" or its equivalent. Veal may be substituted with chicken, turkey slices, crabmeat, or shrimp.

Ralph E. Becker

Caraway Veal Paprika

Serves 6

½ pound fresh
    mushrooms, sliced
3 medium-size onions,
    sliced
3 tablespoons butter
2 pounds boneless veal,
    cubed
1 can (6 ounces) tomato
    paste
½ cup water, more if
    necessary
1 tablespoon Hungarian
    sweet paprika

1 bay leaf
1 teaspoon salt
½ teaspoon caraway
    seeds
¼ teaspoon freshly
    ground pepper
½ cup sour cream

Sauté mushrooms and onions in butter for 5 minutes. Brown veal cubes separately; add to mushrooms' and onions.

Add tomato paste, water, paprika, bay leaf, salt, caraway seeds, and pepper. Cover and simmer for 2 hours or until veal is tender, adding more water if necessary.

Just before serving, stir in sour cream. Serve with noodles.

Cookbook Committee

G'Schnetzletz

Serves 4 to 6

¼ cup butter
3 tablespoons chopped
    onion
1 pound veal cutlets, cut
    into 1-inch strips
½ pound sandwich-
    steak, cut into 1-inch
    strips
    Flour
    Salt and freshly
    ground pepper

¼ teaspoon tarragon
½ cup dry white wine
1 tablespoon lemon
    juice
1 cup sour cream

Sauté onion in butter. Dredge meat in flour. Add to onion and fry until brown. Season with salt and pepper.

Add tarragon and wine. Cover and cook for 10 minutes, or until done. Add lemon juice. Slowly stir in sour cream.

Heat thoroughly, but do not boil.

Miran Kojian
Former NSO member

Veal Basket Royal

Makes 8 baskets

3 pounds veal, extra lean
1 bunch watercress, chopped
1 large shallot, chopped
1 cup chablis wine
1 cup whipping cream
1 teaspoon butter
3 teaspoons flour
   Salt and freshly ground pepper
3 cups oil
1 loaf solid white bread

For each basket, cut a 2 × 4-inch rectangular-shaped piece of solid white bread and fry in oil at 350° or until light brown all around; set aside when done. When cool, remove center section to form a basket design.

Put soft butter into a bowl; add flour with a fork and mix together. It will become a sticky paste.

With a sharp knife, remove all remaining fat from veal and cut meat into strips. In a cooking pan, melt butter until brown and sauté veal a pound at a time. Set aside.

Sauté shallot and watercress together for 30 seconds. Pour in wine and let boil for 1 minute; then pour in whipping cream. When it starts to boil, add roux one teaspoon at a time and stir sauce until thick.

Put veal back into sauce and mix well for a couple of minutes. Place veal mixture into bread basket and serve.

Ridgewell's Caterer, Inc.

Slavic Veal Stew

Serves 4 to 6

1½ pounds boneless veal shoulder
¼ cup flour
1 teaspoon salt
¼ teaspoon freshly ground pepper
⅓ cup beef broth
8 slices bacon, diced
½ cup chopped onion
2 teaspoons paprika
   Fresh parsley

Place bacon, onion and paprika in a heavy 10- or 12-inch skillet. Cover and cook slowly, stirring frequently, until bacon and onions are lightly browned.

Cut into 1-inch cubes. Coat meat by shaking it in a plastic bag containing flour, salt, and pepper.

With a slotted spoon, remove bacon mixture to a small dish, leaving bacon fat in skillet. Add meat to skillet, and brown slowly on all sides. Return bacon mixture to skillet and add with ⅓ cup hot water.

Cover and simmer, stirring occasionally. Add small amounts of water as needed. Cook for 45 to 60 minutes, or until meat is tender when pierced with a fork. Transfer meat and sauce to a warm platter and garnish with parsley.

William Arsers
NSO member

Osso Bucco

Serves 4 to 6

1 onion, finely chopped	¾ cup white wine
1 carrot, finely chopped	3 tablespoons V8 juice
1 large stalk of celery, finely chopped	2 tablespoons beef consommé
½ cup olive oil	1 tablespoon chopped rosemary
6 veal shanks	2 tablespoons chopped parsley
3 tablespoons flour	1 clove garlic
Salt and freshly ground pepper	

Brown onion, carrot and celery in oil in large casserole. Dredge shanks in flour and add them to vegetables. Brown evenly and then set upright to retain marrow. Season with salt and pepper and pour wine over them.

When wine has partially evaporated, dilute V8 juice with a little clear stock and pour it over meat. When liquid begins to boil, cover casserole, reduce heat and simmer slowly for about 1½ to 2 hours.

Before removing pan from heat, add chopped rosemary and parsley, as well as two drops of garlic juice.

Place meat in a warm dish and cover with vegetables. Skim off fat and pour some sauce over meat and vegetables. Serve remaining sauce separately.

Mary-Jo Campbell

Kalv Sylta
Jellied Veal

4½ pounds veal on bone	1 tablespoon vinegar
Water to cover	1 envelope unflavored gelatin, softened in ¼ cup stock
10 white peppercorns	1 tablespoon salt
5 allspice	
1 bay leaf	
2 cloves	
1 onion	
White pepper	

This recipe dates back to my grandmother's day. I have never had a Christmas without it. It is an old Swedish recipe, always prepared for the Christmas holidays, but is served any time of the year.

Trim veal of excess fat and place in large kettle. Add water to cover and bring to boil. Add seasonings and onion, using plenty of seasoning (extra white pepper). Cover and simmer until meat is tender, about 2½ hours.

Lift out meat and let it cool. Do not waste any of liquid. Cube or mince meat or run through a food processor. Return bones to liquid and boil further.

Strain off bones, herbs, and spices; pour stock back into kettle. Return meat to liquid and bring to boil. Season and stir in gelatin. Boil a few minutes longer.

Pour mixture into molds and set in refrigerator to jell, 3 or 4 hours. It is best prepared the day before. Bread pans make good molds.

Makes about 2 pounds jellied veal. Do not freeze.

Mrs. Warren E. Burger

Marinated Sweetbreads

Serves 6

1½ pounds veal sweetbreads, cut into ½-inch cubes
2 tablespoons butter, clarified
Salt and freshly ground pepper
4 leaves fresh basil, chopped
1 teaspoon shallots, chopped
1 green onion, top only
1 tomato, peeled, seeded, and diced
2 cloves garlic
2 tablespoons olive oil
1 teaspoon sherry vinegar

12 fava bean pods, shucked (Italian lima beans)
1 cup chicken stock

Cut sweetbreads into ½-inch cubes. Sauté in butter over high heat until cooked, approximately 3 minutes. Transfer sweetbreads to a plate and season to taste with salt and pepper.

Finely chop and add to sweetbreads basil, shallots, green onion, and tomato, reserving 2 tablespoons of tomato for garnish.

Cut garlic cloves in half. Soak them in olive oil and sherry vinegar. Toss with above mixture and let marinate for 5 minutes.

Shuck fava beans and peel skin from each bean. Cook 4 minutes in chicken stock. Remove from stock and add to marinated sweetbread. Toss, drain off marinade and set aside.

Arrange individual portions on 6 plates and drizzle each with 1 teaspoon of the marinade. Sprinkle with diced tomato.

Chef Yannick Cam
Le Pavillon Restaurant

P A S T A
&
R I C E

Agnolotti alla Crema

Serves 4

PASTA
¾ pound flour
3 eggs
   Pinch salt
1 egg to brush dough

FILLING
4 ounces ricotta cheese
4 ounces mortadella
2 ounces spinach

SAUCE
6 ounces heavy cream
1½ ounces butter
1½ ounces Parmesan cheese

PASTA

Form mound of flour on a working surface. Break eggs into center and add a pinch of salt. Stir in flour. Gradually knead with your fingers and heel of your hand for at least 10 minutes, until dough is very elastic. Let rest for about 15 minutes wrapped in parchment.

Feed dough through a pasta machine several times until it becomes smooth and firm. Divide dough in half and roll out each piece in fairly thin sheets.

Place small mounds of filling on one sheet at regular intervals. Cover with second sheet of dough which has been brushed with beaten egg. Cut mounds with a round cutter. Gently lift each round with a spatula and place on a cookie sheet.

FILLING

Wash spinach well. Cook in boiling water until just tender; drain and let cool. Grind spinach, mortadella, and ricotta cheese through a food mill and mix until smooth.

SAUCE

Place cream, butter, and Parmesan cheese in a sauté pan and let simmer to a creamy consistency. In plenty of boiling, salted water, cook agnolotti until tender, yet firm. Drain and add to cream sauce. Serve immediately.

Chef Pierre Dupont
1789 Restaurant

Asparagus and Prosciutto Lasagne

Serves 6

¼ pound fresh green
   pasta, whole flat
   sheets
¼ pound fresh regular
   pasta, whole flat
   sheets
½ cup Parmesan cheese,
   freshly grated
2 tablespoons butter
   Salt and freshly
   ground pepper

SAUCE
1 onion, minced
1 garlic clove, minced
1 bay leaf
2 tablespoons olive oil
2 tablespoons butter
¼ pound thinly-sliced
   prosciutto or
   Westphalian ham,
   chopped
2 pounds asparagus,
   trimmed and sliced
1 cup dry white wine
1⅓ cups heavy cream
2 tablespoons flour

Cut tips off asparagus and reserve. Slice remaining stalks thinly on diagonal.

In a large, heavy skillet, sauté onion, garlic and bay leaf in oil and butter over moderate heat until onion is golden. Add prosciutto and cook for 1 minute, stirring. Add sliced asparagus stalks and cook, stirring again for 1 minute. Add wine and bring to boil. Cover and simmer for 5 minutes. Uncover and cook over moderately high heat until wine is evaporated.

Mix cream with flour and stir into asparagus mixture. Again bring to boil, stirring. Simmer for 1 minute, season with salt and pepper and remove from heat. Discard bay leaf. Cut pasta into 10-inch lengths.

Cook pasta in boiling, salted water in batches for 3 minutes; it will not be very soft. Drain and cool in ice water; dry on paper towels.

Blanch asparagus tips, drain and cool under water. Pat dry.

Butter a 9 × 12-inch baking dish. Begin with a layer of yellow pasta, add one third of sauce and sprinkle with ⅓ cup Parmesan cheese. Add another layer, this time using green pasta, then half of remaining sauce. Again sprinkle ⅓ cup Parmesan. Add layer of yellow pasta, remaining sauce and ⅓ cup Parmesan.

Cover mixture with green pasta, scatter asparagus tips over top and sprinkle with remaining ½ cup Parmesan. Dot with butter and bake in a preheated 400° oven for 25 minutes, until golden and bubbly. Let rest for 5 minutes before serving.

Fresh sheets of pasta are sold at Vace, Pasta, Inc., or other specialty stores that sell fresh pasta.

Carol Becker

Irena's Lasagne with Bolognese Sauce

Serves 8 to 10

2 pounds fresh flat sheets of pasta (green or yellow)
2 pounds fresh ricotta
2 pounds mozzarella, grated
2 cups freshly grated Parmesan cheese
1 stick unsalted butter

BOLOGNESE SAUCE
3 carrots, finely diced
3 onions, finely diced
3 celery stalks, finely diced
1 slice bacon, finely diced
3 tablespoons olive oil
¼ pound chicken liver, chopped
1 pound lean ground beef
1 pound lean ground veal or pork
1 cup dry red wine
2 teaspoons salt
Freshly ground pepper to taste
2 2-pound cans peeled plum tomatoes
4-ounce can tomato paste
½ cup water

SAUCE

Sauté carrots, onions, celery, and bacon in large 4 to 6-quart enameled pot until onions are golden. Add chicken livers, beef and veal; brown. Break up any lumps in ground meat and then add wine. Cook until wine evaporates.

Add salt, pepper, tomatoes, tomato paste, and water; bring to a boil. Cover and lower heat. Simmer 3 hours.

Preheat oven to 350°.

Cut pasta into 10-inch lengths and cook in boiling salted water *al dente*, about 4 to 5 minutes. Drain and pat dry. Cook in batches.

Ladle a thin layer of Bolognese sauce into 2, 9 × 12-inch ovenproof dishes. Layer with pasta, another layer of sauce, a layer of ricotta, ⅛ of mozzarella, and ⅛ of Parmesan. Continue these layers until ingredients are used up. (Don't worry if there are leftovers.) Finish with a layer of cheeses.

Dot with butter. Bake for ½ hour. Cool for 10 minutes before cutting.

Carol Becker

Etta's Lasagne Impottite

Serves 6 to 8

1 package lasagne noodles
1 pound ricotta or cottage cheese
1 pound mozzarella cheese, sliced
1 cup grated Parmesan cheese
3 hard-boiled eggs, sliced

SAUCE
   No. 2½ can Italian tomatoes
2 cans water
   6-ounce can tomato paste
1 tablespoon salt
½ teaspoon crushed basil
1 tablespoon grated Parmesan cheese
1 teaspoon fresh parsley
½ cup chianti wine

POLPETTINI
1 pound ground meat (half pork, half beef)
¼ cup fresh bread crumbs
½ teaspoon salt
   Freshly ground pepper to taste
¼ cup water
2 tablespoons grated Parmesan cheese
1 egg
1 tablespoon fresh parsley
1 garlic clove, minced
3 tablespoons cooking oil

MEATBALLS

Mix ground meat and next 8 ingredients thoroughly; shape into tiny, marble-sized meatballs. Brown in cooking oil. When done, remove and set aside.

SAUCE

Mix Italian tomatoes and following 6 ingredients in same saucepan used to brown meatballs. Cook for 2 hours. Add meatballs and wine; cook an additional 1½ hours.

LASAGNE

Bring 6 quarts of water to a rapid boil. Add salt and cooking oil; then add lasagne a few pieces at a time so they will not stick. Cook about 20 to 25 minutes. Drain well. Pass cold water through lasagne to keep them from sticking.

To assemble lasagne, cover bottom of a 14 × 10 × 2-inch baking dish. Layer lasagne, sauce, polpettini, eggs, mozzarella, ricotta, and Parmesan cheese. Repeat until

Continued

all ingredients are used, ending with lasagne, topped with mozzarella and grated cheese. Bake 20 minutes in 375° oven. Let set 15 minutes before cutting into squares.

Team this with a tossed salad, red wine, and Zabaglione for dessert.

Armand Sarro
Former NSO Member

Fettuccine with Broccoli and Chicken

Serves 4 as main course
Serves 8 as first course

1 pound white fettuccine, fresh
½ cup sesame oil
1 cup diced chicken breast
2 teaspoons minced garlic
2 teaspoons slivered ginger
3 cups (packed) broccoli flowerets
½ cup sherry
⅓ cup soy sauce
3 tablespoons butter
½ cup grated Parmesan cheese
½ cup toasted almond slices

"Nice combination of Italian and Chinese"

Cook fettuccine al dente. Drain and pour one cup cold water over it. Drain again.

Heat oil in a wok until it is smoking hot. Stir fry chicken for 30 seconds. Add garlic, ginger, and broccoli. Stir fry 1 minute. Add sherry and soy sauce; simmer 1 more minute.

Add fettuccine and butter to wok. Toss. Add cheese and toss again. Garnish with toasted almonds. Serve with more cheese if desired.

Mark David, Woods Restaurant
New York City

Linguini Rosa

Serves 8 as a first course

2 pounds fresh tomato linguini
6 medium to large shallots, finely chopped
16–20 medium-size white mushrooms washed, peeled, finely sliced and rubbed with lemon juice, if not used immediately
2 cups heavy cream
6–8 tablespoons butter
1 cup Parmesan cheese
Freshly ground pepper
Salt

Use enamelled cast iron pot large enough to accommodate all cooked linguini. Sauté shallots to translucency and soften in a small portion of butter. Add mushrooms and sauté to desired doneness. Remove to a bowl with slotted spoon.

Put remaining butter and ⅔ of cream in saucepan, simmering over medium heat for at least a minute until thickened. Never boil cream.

Bring 6 quarts of water to a boil and add 2 tablespoons salt. Drop in linguini; cover when it returns to a boil. Pasta is cooked when returned to the boil. Drain immediately.

Return cooked, drained pasta to enamelled pan containing butter and cream. Place over low heat under linguini and toss with sauce. Add mushroom-shallot mixture, remaining cream, and all cheese. Toss until well coated. Taste and correct seasoning. Serve immediately.

Fresh pasta of any type is available at a number of specialty stores.

Mary S. Odyniec

Seafood Pasta LeCompte

Serves 4 to 6

1 pound vermicelli, capellini, or thin spaghetti
1 pound crabmeat, more, if you wish
1 package of langoustinos or large cooked shrimp
1 pint sour cream or plain yogurt
  Cottage cheese (optional)
3 tablespoons mayonnaise
  Pinch sugar

Juice of 3 lemons (plus grated rind of 2 lemons)
¼ pound butter
  Salt and freshly ground pepper
  Dash of bitters (optional)

SAUCE

Combine melted butter, sour cream or yogurt, lemon juice and grated rind, salt and pepper. A dash of bitters added to sauce will perk up taste.

Cook pasta about 1 minute less than "al dente."

Oil an oven-proof casserole dish. Place one third of pasta at bottom of dish. Place one third of crab meat on top of it, spreading carefully in a thin layer. Dribble one third of sauce over crabmeat.

Beat mayonnaise into rest of lemon-butter sauce. Put another layer of pasta (one third of total) into dish. Add cottage cheese, if desired, and crab meat and langoustinos or shrimp, reserving a few to decorate top layer. Dribble another third of sauce over that layer. Now top your dish with remaining pasta, a layer of crab meat, remainder of langoustinos or shrimp, and rest of sauce.

Place in a 400° oven for about 20 minutes. By this time, casserole should be bubbling. Allow to rest for awhile to blend flavors; then serve.

This dish can be made with tuna or any other flaked fish. The addition of dill to the sauce is also an interesting variation. Best of all, the leftovers are delicious cold.

Calvin B. LeCompte, Jr.

Spaghetti Puttanesca alla Moffo

Serves 6

PASTA

3 cups flour
4 eggs
  Pinch of salt

SAUCE

¼ pound butter
3 tablespoons olive oil
4 medium garlic cloves, finely chopped
20 pitted and halved olives
1 tablespoon capers
6 fresh cherry tomatoes or ½ can peeled tomatoes
2 teaspoons chopped parsley
8 anchovy filets

To make pasta, mound flour on kneading board. Make a hole in middle of flour; add eggs and salt. With a fork, gradually stir eggs beginning at center of mound and working out until all flour is mixed. Knead dough until it is smooth and firm and begins to blister on outside.

Cover dough with a mixing bowl and let rest for 1 hour. Cut 2-inch squares and press with roller until very fine. Allow to dry about 10 minutes.

After all dough has been rolled out, flour kneading board. Fold rolled dough to 2 inches in diameter and then cut with a sharp, floured knife into ⅛-inch slices. After each piece is cut, open each piece of pasta and hang to dry fully.

SAUCE

Combine butter, oil, garlic and anchovies in saucepan over low heat. As soon as garlic begins to turn golden (about 30 seconds) add olives, capers, and tomatoes. Stir another 30 seconds over high heat.

After sauce is made, boil pasta. The secret to making very good pasta is to be sure you have a large pot and a lot of water, much more than you think you need. As soon as pasta comes to top of water, it should be drained and put on a serving platter ready for the sauce.

Pour sauce over pasta and sprinkle with chopped parsley. Serve immediately.

A pinch of salt should be added to the water before pasta is put in, but in the case of Puttanesca, I do not put in salt because the anchovies are so salty.

Anna Moffo

Tomato Angel Hair Pasta with Basil & Crab

Serves 4

¾ pound butter
4 teaspoons chopped, fresh shallots
4 teaspoons chopped, fresh basil
4 teaspoons chopped, fresh parsley
6 cups fresh, peeled tomatoes
1 pound fresh, backfin crabmeat
1¼ pounds angel hair pasta

Melt butter in saucepan. Add shallots, basil, parsley, and tomatoes. Bring to boil. Add crabmeat.

Douse pasta in boiling water for 90 seconds. Drain and add to hot sauce. Serve at once.

Chef Monroe Duncan, Suddenly Last Summer Restaurant Norfolk, Virginia

Cold Linguini and Ham

Serves 4

8 ounces linguini
1 tablespoon olive oil
1 cup parsley leaves, coarsely chopped
1 cup thinly-sliced ham
1 cup Racquet Club dressing

RACQUET CLUB DRESSING
12 tablespoons salad oil (not olive)
4 tablespoons white wine vinegar
1 teaspoon salt
1 teaspoon white pepper
1 teaspoon freshly ground black pepper
1 teaspoon sugar
Dash paprika
4 tablespoons Durkee's dressing

Cook linguini until al dente. Drain, run under cold water, and toss with olive oil.

Mix parsley with Racquet Club Dressing. Toss with linguini, add ham and toss again. Serve at room temperature or slightly chilled.

DRESSING

Put all ingredients in jar and shake well. Good on almost any salad.

Pat and Bob Schieffer

July 4th Pasta Salad

Serves 8 to 10

1 pound rotelle, twists, or fettuccine
1 bunch parsley, chopped
   6-ounce can small pitted black olives, drained
2 4½-ounce cans chopped black olives
   8-ounce can artichoke hearts, or more, drained and cut in quarters
1 bunch scallions, chopped
1 green pepper, chopped fine
1½ cups dressing
3–5 pieces cooked chicken, diced
¼ pound sliced salami, chopped

DRESSING
½ cup fresh lemon juice
¾ cup olive oil
¼ cup mayonnaise
½ teaspoon seasoned salt
   Freshly ground pepper

Cook pasta until al dente. Drain and put in large bowl. While pasta is still warm, add remaining ingredients and dressing. Toss well.

Refrigerate at least 4 hours, tossing occasionally. Serve with sliced tomatoes sprinkled with fresh basil, olive oil, vinegar, and salt.

If to be used at a picnic or when refrigeration is unavailable, mayonnaise can be omitted.

Joan C-C Oppenheimer

Don's Casserole à la Symphony

Serves 4 to 6

1 pound orzo pasta
10-ounce package frozen peas
1½ sticks butter
2 large garlic cloves, finely chopped
4 whole chicken legs, split or 8 thighs
½ pound bay scallops

½ pound large shrimp, peeled, deveined
12 small fresh clams, scrubbed clean
8 baby lobster tails (optional)
Salt and freshly ground pepper
3 cups water

Cook orzo according to directions, adding frozen peas the last 5 minutes. Melt butter and add garlic.

In a large saucepan, cook chicken legs in 1½ cups water with salt and pepper. Steam until chicken is tender. Remove chicken, set aside, and add ¾ cup of chicken broth to butter and garlic mixture.

In same saucepan, add all seafood to about ½ inch water and steam until clams open. Remove seafood, set aside, and add ¾ cup of seafood liquid to butter and garlic mixture.

Grease a 3-quart pyrex casserole. Mix liquid with orzo-pea mixture. Place half of mixture in bottom of casserole. Add a layer of chicken and seafoods, then rest of pasta and peas. Place last of chicken and seafood decoratively on top; cover. Place in 350° oven for 45 minutes.

Donald Havas
NSO Member

Pierogis

Serves 4 to 6

DOUGH
2 cups flour
1 large egg
½ teaspoon salt
⅓–½ cup water

FILLING
1 cup hot mashed potatoes
½ cup grated cheese, extra sharp
1 beaten egg
½ teaspoon salt
¼ teaspoon pepper, freshly ground

Mix flour, egg and salt. Stir in water to form stiff dough. Divide in half, and roll paper thin. Cut circles with a large biscuit cutter. Set aside while making filling.

Mix potatoes, grated cheese, egg, salt, and pepper.

Fill each circle with heaping teaspoon of filling. Fold in half, moisten edge with water and press to seal.

Drop in boiling, salted water and cook 3 to 5 minutes (they will start to rise to top of water). Remove with slotted spoon. Place in single layer on serving dish.

Serve by pouring melted butter over top or with sour cream on the side. Can be kept in a 300° oven, covered with foil, for up to an hour. Uncooked pierogis may be frozen or refrigerated several hours ahead.

Sandy Wheeler

Slava's Siberian Pelmeni

Serves 4 as a main course
Serves 6 as a first course

Pelmeni have been made in Siberia for centuries and frozen in the snow outside the house. Travellers would carry them frozen, then cook them in melted snow over a campfire.

DOUGH
1 whole egg
1 egg yolk
  Salad oil to make 1 cup liquid with eggs
1 cup water
4–4½ cups flour

FILLING
¾ pound lean ground beef
½ pound lean ground pork
½ large onion
2 cloves garlic
½ teaspoon freshly ground pepper
¼ cup water
  Salt to taste

DOUGH

Make a well in center of flour. Measure eggs and oil to make 1 cup and add to well. Add water, then mix thoroughly until dough can be gathered into a compact ball. Knead, folding over until dough is smooth and elastic. Refrigerate for at least 1 hour, wrapped in slightly floured wax paper.

FILLING

Chop onion and garlic very finely and mix with meat, pepper, salt, and water. Meat should be light and fluffy in consistency. If it feels heavy and dense, add more water. Mix thoroughly.

Roll out dough, one quarter at a time, until almost paper thin. To keep dough from sticking and shrinking during rolling, make a quarter turn every 5 or 6 rolls.

Cut out 1¾-inch circles of dough with a biscuit cutter. Put a teaspoon of filling in center, fold over edges, and crimp together firmly with fingers. Then bring together corners of finished semi-circle, making a triangular pouch. Store finished raw pelmeni on well-floured cookie sheets. Pelmeni can be frozen or cooked at this point.

To cook, place pelmeni (about 25 to 30 at a time) into 6 quarts of well-salted, boiling water. Stir carefully to prevent sticking at bottom. Cook 3 minutes, timing when pelmeni start rising to surface.

Remove from boiling water with slotted spoon. Sprinkle lightly with melted butter, and serve with all or any of the following: sour cream, freshly ground black pepper, vinegar, or soy sauce.

Mstislav Rostropovich
NSO Music Director

Anne's French Pizza

Serves 4 as main course
Serves 6 to 8 as first course

CRUST

1½ cups flour
1 teaspoon baking
    soda
¼ teaspoon salt
½ cup butter
¼ cup ice water

TOPPING

1 medium sweet
    onion, sliced
½ pound fresh spinach
    destemmed,
    washed, and dried
2–3 tomatoes, seeded
    and skinned or
    canned tomatoes,
    seeded and drained
    Fresh mushrooms
    Oregano, basil,
    thyme (fresh, if
    available)
½ pound Gruyère
    cheese, grated
1–2 cloves garlic
    (optional)

Mix flour, baking soda, salt, butter, and ice water to make a rich dough. Chill.

Roll out chilled dough in oblong shape. Pat into a 9 × 13-inch pan, extending up sides. Bake for 20 to 25 minutes at 350° until browned. Remove and cool.

TOPPING

Starting with onions, layer vegetables on cooled dough. Sprinkle with herbs. Top with cheese and chopped garlic.

Bake about 20 minutes in 325° to 350° oven until cheese melts.

When used as appetizer, serve at room temperature.

Amy E. Foster

Bohemian Peach Dumplings

Serves 3 to 4

½ pound dry cottage cheese
1–2 cups flour
2 eggs
Pinch of salt
6 small peaches
Melted butter
Sugar

Buttered graham cracker crumbs
Additional sieved cottage cheese

Put cottage cheese through sieve. Add eggs and salt. Mix together and add flour gradually until dough is soft and sticks together. Divide dough into 6 portions and flatten out.

Put peach which has been blanched in center of dough and press dough firmly around it to make small ball. Place gently in boiling, salted water for 11 to 15 minutes. Drain and serve with melted butter, sugar, buttered graham cracker crumbs and additional sieved cottage cheese.

Fresh ripe plums may be substituted. Dumplings may be served as a main course or for dessert.

Betty Soukup

Zwetschken- "knödel"
Plum Dumplings

Serves 4 to 6

This recipe can only be done during the Italian prune season in the fall.

2 pounds potatoes, cooked and mashed while warm
1–2 eggs
Scant ⅓ cup farina
2 heaping cups flour
Italian prunes, in season

½ cup bread crumbs
3 tablespoons butter, melted
Sugar

Peel and mash potatoes while warm. When potatoes have cooled, mix in flour, eggs and farina. Take bits of dough (with floured hands) and spread thinly around each prune. Repeat this process until dough is all used up.

Bring water to boil in a large kettle. Add a little salt and then, gently, with a slotted spoon, add covered prunes to simmer about 15 mintues or until dough is cooked. Lift out carefully so dough doesn't split and prunes burst. Brown bread crumbs and mix with melted butter. Toss "knödel" in this. Serve immediately with lots of sugar on top. Zwetschkenknödel may be served as a main course or for dessert.

Rudolf Serkin

Noodle Kugel

Serves 6

½ pound broad noodles
1 pound ricotta or
   cottage cheese
½ cup raisins
¾ cup chopped apples
⅓ cup sugar
3 eggs
1 teaspoon cinnamon
   Pinch of salt
2 tablespoons butter

Cook and drain noodles.

Blend cheese and noodles. Combine raisins, apples, sugar, eggs, cinnamon, and salt; add to cheese and noodles.

Melt butter to grease casserole dish. Bake at 375° for 45 minutes.

Elise Rosenthal

Trioletta

Pineapple, Cheese, Noodle Squares

Makes approximately
30 squares

8 ounces fine egg
   noodles
¼ pound butter
5 eggs, beaten
2 pounds cottage cheese
   (large curd)
   12-ounce can crushed
   pineapple, drained

1 pint sour cream
¾ cup sugar
½ teaspoon salt
1 teaspoon vanilla

Cook noodles according to directions and drain. Melt butter. Pour half into baking dish. Put noodles into mixing bowl. Add remaining butter, drained pineapple, salt, and vanilla; mix well. Fold sour cream into beaten eggs and add to mixture. Finally, add cottage cheese and sugar, stirring gently until blended.

Pour into a 10×13×2-inch baking dish over melted butter. Bake at 425° for 45 minutes or until top and sides are light brown. Let cool and cut into 2½ inch-squares. Can be served hot or cold.

Samuel Levy
NSO Member

Beautiful
Baked Rice

Serves 8

5 tablespoons butter
2 cups rice
¼ cup onion, minced
½ teaspoon garlic, minced
3 cups chicken broth
3 sprigs parsley
2 sprigs thyme or ½ teaspoon, dried
1 bay leaf
  Pinch cayenne or Tabasco

Melt 2 tablespoons butter in heavy saucepan or oven-proof dish. Sauté onion and garlic, stirring with a wooden spoon, until onion is clear.

Add rice and stir briefly over low heat until well coated with butter. Stir in stock, making sure there are no lumps in rice. Add remaining seasonings.

Cover with tight-fitting lid, and place in 400° oven. Bake 20 to 25 minutes. Remove cover and discard parsley and thyme. Using a 2-prong fork, stir in remaining butter. Rice can be made up to 2 days ahead and reheated very slowly in a 200° oven for 1 hour.

Mrs. Kenneth Gaarder

Black Rice

Serves 12

4 cups uncooked rice
2 teaspoons salt
4 tablespoons oil
6 cups Coca Cola
2 cups water
1 cup raisins

Heat oil and fry rice lightly.
Mix Coca Cola with water and salt; add to rice.

Let boil uncovered until it begins to dry; add raisins; stir with a fork and cover. Over low heat cook until rice is completely dry and fluffy.

Maribel G. de Amado
Wife of the Ambassador of Panama

Sausage-Wild Rice

Serves 10 to 12

2 packages wild and long grain rice mix
2 cups thinly sliced celery
1 cup chopped onion

4 tablespoons butter
1 pound hot Italian sausage
1 cup toasted, slivered almonds

Prepare rice according to package instructions.

Sauté celery and onion in butter. Add to this mixture sausage (casing off, sliced in bite-size pieces).

Brown meat with celery and onion; drain well before adding to rice. Add toasted almonds and place in casserole dish. Bake at 300° for 30 minutes (cover for first 20 minutes only).

Dorothy S. Wheeler

Wild Rice with Almonds and Water Chestnuts

Serves 6 to 8

1 cup wild rice
¼ cup butter
½ cup slivered almonds
2 tablespoons snipped chives
1 can water chestnuts, drained
3 cups chicken broth

OPTIONAL:
½ cup celery
¼ teaspoon sage

Wash and drain wild rice in a sieve for 2 minutes under running water (removes sand).

Melt butter in large skillet. Add rice, almonds, chives, or onions. Cook and stir over low heat for about 20 minutes until almonds are golden.

Heat oven to 325°.

Pour rice mixture into ungreased 1½-quart casserole. Add water chestnuts. Heat chicken broth to boiling; stir into rice mixture. Cover tightly and bake 1½ hours (or longer if necessary) until liquid is entirely absorbed.

May be made early in day, set aside, and reheated by covering casserole with foil and setting over boiling water for 30 minutes (longer if rice has been refrigerated).

VARIATION

For water chestnuts substitute ¼ pound fresh, sliced mushrooms, sauteéd.

A favorite Minnesota recipe. Delicious starch course with or without gravy.

Virginia MacLaury
Helen Gaul

Shahjanhani Biryani
Spiced Saffron Rice

Serves 8

½ cup plus 2 tablespoons butter
1 whole chicken breast, skinned, boned, and cut into bite-size pieces
4 medium onions, minced
1 tablespoon ginger, minced
2 garlic cloves, minced
16 whole cloves
4 4-inch cinnamon sticks
2 teaspoons turmeric
2 teaspoons cumin seeds
1½ teaspoons ground nutmeg
1½ teaspoons ground mace
¾ teaspoon cardamom seeds
¾ teaspoon cayenne

2 cups uncooked, converted rice
4 cups chicken stock or broth
2 teaspoons salt
1 teaspoon sugar
1½ teaspoons saffron threads
2 medium onions, cut lengthwise into thin strips
¾ cup dark raisins, plumped in water
¼ cup light raisins, plumped in water
½ cup unsalted cashews, sautéed in butter
½ cup shelled pistachios
½ cup slivered almonds, sautéed in butter
Silver leaf, optional (available at Indian grocery)

Melt 2 tablespoons butter in 6-quart pan. Sauté chicken over medium heat until golden. Remove and set aside.

In same pan melt ½ cup butter. Add minced onion and cook until soft. Stir in ginger and garlic; sauté briefly.

Stir in cloves, cinnamon sticks, turmeric, cumin seeds, nutmeg, mace, cardamom seeds, and cayenne. Add ½ cup butter. When melted, mix in rice, and cook over medium heat until golden, stirring frequently. Stir in stock, salt, sugar, and saffron threads. Return chicken to pan. Bring to boil, cover, and cook over low heat for 45 to 50 minutes, until liquid has been absorbed.

Melt ¼ cup butter in medium skillet. Cook onion strips until well browned. Drain on paper towels.

Arrange rice on platter. Layer in following order: dark raisins, light raisins, cashews, pistachios, almonds, onions, and if desired, silver leaf.

Mrs. Zubin Mehta

VEGETABLES

Artichoke Bottoms

Serves 4 for luncheon
Serves 6 to 8 as an appetizer

8 artichoke bottoms,
   frozen or canned
8 tablespoons pâté
8 tablespoons chopped
   mushrooms, sautéed
   in 1 tablespoon butter

MORNAY SAUCE
2 tablespoons butter
2 tablespoons minced
   onion
2 tablespoons flour
1 cup hot milk
   Pinch ground nutmeg
1 teaspoon salt
   Few grains white
   pepper
2 sprigs parsley,
   chopped
¾ cup dry white wine
2 tablespoons grated
   Gruyère or Swiss
   cheese
1 egg yolk
1 tablespoon sweet
   butter
2 tablespoons whipped
   cream (optional)

Place 2 tablespoons butter in shallow dish in 450° oven. Remove when melted. Place artichoke hearts in dish. Fill each bottom with 1 tablespoon pâté and 1 tablespoon mushrooms. Cover with foil and bake 3 to 5 minutes. Remove.

Spoon 2 to 3 tablespoons mornay sauce over each and glaze under broiler.

MORNAY SAUCE

Melt butter, add onion, and cook to light brown. Add flour and stir in milk, nutmeg, salt, pepper, and parsley. Cook until thick and smooth. Add wine and cook until thick.

Stir in cheese; cook until melted and smooth. Stir in egg yolk, and sweet butter; cook until thick. Add whipped cream if desired.

Cookbook Committee

Smothered Cabbage

Serves 4 to 6

Having always resented overcooked vegetables, I prize this quick method of preparing cabbage for its flavor and convenience.

1 small, tight head cabbage
2 shredded lettuce leaves
1 small Bermuda onion, sliced
   Pinch of sugar
   Vegetable oil for frying
   Caraway seeds, optional

Salt and freshly ground pepper, to taste

Shred cabbage, as you would cole slaw; rinse it in lukewarm water first, then in cold water to crisp it.

Heat vegetable oil briefly over moderate heat in a heavy fry pan. Add shredded cabbage, salt and pepper to taste. Cover tightly for about 2 minutes; toss cabbage briefly. Add lettuce leaves to provide moisture for steaming and a few thinly-sliced rounds of onion. Cover tightly again and let cook for another 3 minutes.

Remove cover and sprinkle a pinch of sugar on cabbage; add caraway seeds, if desired, and toss cabbage briefly. Serve immediately.

Calvin B. LeCompte, Jr.

Broccoli Soufflé

Serves 4 to 6

3 cups broccoli
   8-ounces sour cream
½ cup grated Parmesan cheese
6 tablespoons butter
4 egg yolks
5 egg whites
2 tablespoons chopped onion

½ teaspoon freshly ground pepper
1 teaspoon lemon juice
   Dash salt

Peel and trim broccoli. Drop in boiling water for 2 minutes. Drain and pat dry.

Place broccoli and all ingredients *except* egg whites in a food processor fitted with steel blade. Process, scraping sides once or twice for 2 minutes or until puréed. This can be done ahead and stored in refrigerator.

Whip egg whites until stiff and fold into purée. Pour into buttered baking dish that has been dusted with Parmesan cheese.

Bake in preheated 375° oven turned down to 350° and bake for 30 to 40 minutes.

Pam Kloman

Carrot Soufflé

Serves 4

1 pound carrots
3 eggs
½ cup sugar; less if carrots are sweet
3 tablespoons flour
1 teaspoon baking powder
1 teaspoon vanilla
1 stick butter (¼ pound)
  Dash of cinnamon
  Dash of nutmeg

TOPPING
¼ cup crushed corn flakes or bread crumbs
2 tablespoons brown sugar
2 tablespoons butter
  Dash cinnamon and nutmeg
¼ cup chopped walnuts, optional

Cut up carrots. Cook well. Strain and purée them in a food processor. Cool carrots. Add 3 eggs to purée. Blend in sugar, flour, baking powder, vanilla, butter, and seasonings.

Grease in oven-proof casserole dish. Preheat oven to 350°. Mix topping and put on top of carrot mixture.

Bake uncovered for 1 hour and serve hot.

Cookbook Committee

Zippy Carrots

Serves 3 to 4

6 carrots, ½-inch slices
2 tablespoons grated onion
2 tablespoons horseradish
½ cup mayonnaise
  Salt and freshly ground pepper
  Paprika
  Bread crumbs

Cook carrots until tender. Drain but reserve ¼ cup carrot water. Mix carrot water with onion, horseradish, mayonnaise, salt, and pepper.

Place cooked carrots in flat casserole. Pour carrot water mixture over carrots. Top with sprinkle of bread crumbs and paprika. Bake at 375° for 15 minutes.

Margaret Dean

Curried Cauliflower

Serves 4 to 6

1 quart yogurt
1 cup chopped onion
1 tablespoon ginger powder
1 clove garlic, pressed
½ teaspoon turmeric
1 teaspoon salt
½ teaspoon cinnamon
2 cardamom pods, seeds only
4 cloves
6 tablespoons butter
½ teaspoon black mustard seeds
½ teaspoon cumin seeds
1 large head cauliflower, about 3 pounds, flowers only
2 tomatoes, peeled, seeded and chopped
2 bay leaves
1 teaspoon methi powder (available in Indian stores), or 1 tablespoon of chopped coriander leaves

Put the first 9 ingredients in blender and blend for 3 minutes.

In a heavy pot, heat butter to foaming, add bay leaves, mustard seeds and cumin seeds, and cook while stirring for 2 minutes. Add cauliflower and cook until golden.

Sprinkle methi, or coriander leaves over cauliflower and add sauce from step one.

Cover pot and simmer for 15 minutes.

Stir in tomatoes, cover vessel and simmer 5 minutes. (Two beaten eggs, optional, can be added with tomatoes, which improve the taste.)

Cookbook Committee

Concombres au Beurre
Baked Cucumbers

Serves 6

6 cucumbers (each about 8 inches long)
2 tablespoons wine vinegar
1½ teaspoons salt
⅛ teaspoon sugar
3 tablespoons melted butter
1 teaspoon fresh dill, minced
3–4 tablespoons minced green onion
⅛ teaspoon freshly ground pepper
Minced parsley

Peel cucumbers. Cut in half lengthwise; scoop out seeds. Cut into lengthwise strips about ⅜ inch wide. Cut strips into 2-inch pieces.

Toss cucumbers in a bowl with vinegar, salt, and sugar. Let stand for at least 30 minutes. Drain. Pat dry in towel.

Toss cucumbers in baking dish with butter, herbs, onions, and pepper. Set uncovered in middle level of a preheated oven (375°), for about 1 hour (or less) tossing 2 or 3 times, until cucumbers are tender, but still have a suggestion of crispness and texture. Sprinkle with minced parsley and serve.

VARIATION

To make creamed cucumbers, boil gently 1 cup heavy cream until it is reduced by one half. Add salt and freshly ground pepper to taste and fold into hot cucumbers.

Shirley Koteen

Stuffed Aubergines

Serves 8

4	medium eggplants
2	onions, finely chopped
2	cloves crushed garlic
4–6	ounces thinly-sliced, fresh mushrooms
4	large ripe, red tomatoes, skinned, seeded and chopped
1	tablespoon tomato purée
	Pitted black olives
3	ounces browned bread crumbs
3	ounces grated Gruyère cheese
½	pint stock (beef or chicken)

5–6	chopped anchovy filets
2	tablespoons chopped parsley
	Marjoram, thyme, and oregano

Cut eggplants in half, lengthwise; scoop out pulp, leaving shells intact. Salt and drain shells for about 30 minutes; then rinse and dry carefully.

Fry onions, eggplant pulp, and mushrooms gently in some butter until very soft. Add fresh tomatoes, tomato purée, herbs, garlic and stock, stirring well. Add anchovies and olives. Cook briefly.

Mix bread crumbs, cheese and parsley, and add cooked tomato mixture.

Rub skin of each halved eggplant shell with olive oil and pile mixture into each half.

Bake in a covered dish in a moderate 350° oven until shells have softened and are cooked through.

Yehudi Menuhin

Baked Eggplant

Serves 4 to 6

1 large eggplant
2 eggs
Flour for dipping
Salt
Tomato sauce (recipe
  listed under Sauces
  and Relishes)
Grated Parmesan
  cheese

In Spain, this is served as a first course before a meat course. Here, I think it would make a nice luncheon main course, or it could be served as a vegetable side dish.

Make tomato sauce.

Slice eggplant fairly thin; dip in salted flour, and then in beaten egg.

Fry in ½ inch of olive oil and set aside. Pre-heat oven to 450° or 475°.

In a baking dish, put a layer of eggplant, a layer of sauce, and cover with Parmesan cheese. Repeat until all the eggplant is used, ending with a layer of cheese on top.

Bake in a hot oven until cheese is lightly browned.

Carlos Montoya

Stuffed Eggplant Casserole

Serves 4

1 large eggplant
1 cup chopped onion
1 cup chopped fresh
  mushrooms
1¼ teaspoons sweet basil
  or oregano
1 teaspoon salt
¼ teaspoon freshly
  ground black
  pepper

2 tablespoons butter
1 cup cooked beef
  (ground)
½ cup dry bread crumbs

Preheat oven to 350°.

Wash eggplant, wrap it in aluminum foil and bake for 50 minutes, or until partly done. Cut in half, remove pulp to within ½ inch of outer skin. Chop pulp.

Sauté onions, mushrooms, and seasonings in butter and add to eggplant pulp. Add meat and bread crumbs; mix well. Spoon mixture into eggplant shells and fit them into a casserole.

Bake long enough to heat them, 15 to 20 minutes. Garnish with parsley or grated Parmesan cheese.

Leontyne Price

Yancey Green Beans

Serves 6

2 packages (10 ounces
  each) frozen cut
  green beans or
  equivalent fresh
  green beans
3-ounce package
  cream cheese
¼ cup sour cream
2 tablespoons heavy
  cream
¼ cup chopped walnuts
¼ teaspoon
  Worcestershire sauce
¼ teaspoon salt

Cook beans according to package directions (or fresh green beans until just done). Drain well.

Blend cream cheese, cream and sour cream in small saucepan. Set pan in larger pan containing a small amount of boiling water. Stir cream mixture until heated. Add Worcestershire sauce, salt, and walnuts. Pour heated sauce over beans and serve immediately.

Joan Yancey

Creamed Leeks

Serves 6

2 bunches leeks
1 cup heavy cream
1 ounce water
2 tablespoons butter
  Salt and freshly
    ground black pepper
    to taste

Clean leeks (soak in water and separate to get all sand out). Dice into ¼-inch pieces. Use all of white and only light green part of stalks.

Place water and butter in a pan large enough to hold leeks. Add leeks and cook over medium heat for 20 to 25 minutes. Be careful it does not burn or stick. Stir occasionally. Season with salt and pepper.

When leeks are tender, add heavy cream and reduce cream until consistency is thick. Correct seasonings.

Cookbook Committee

Leeks and Ham with Cheese Sauce

Serves 4 to 6

1 bunch leeks or about 4 stalks
6 slices ham, cut in half
2 tablespoons butter

CHEESE SAUCE
2 tablespoons butter
2 tablespoons flour
¼ teaspoon salt
1 pinch freshly ground pepper
1 cup milk
½ cup grated Swiss cheese

Preheat oven to 375°.

Wash leeks and cut each into 3 pieces. Simmer over low heat in a little salted water until done (about 15 to 20 minutes). Drain and let cool.

Grease a baking dish with 2 tablespoons butter. Wrap half a ham slice around each leek and fasten with a toothpick. Arrange side by side in baking dish.

CHEESE SAUCE

Melt butter. Add flour, salt and pepper. Stir until smooth and bubbly. Gradually add milk, stirring constantly until thickened. Add cheese. Stir until cheese is melted.

Pour sauce over leeks and bake until top is slightly brown. (About 30 minutes).

Miran Kojian
Former NSO Member

Spring Mushrooms

Serves 4

2 pounds mushrooms
1 bunch spring onions
6 slices bacon
4 tablespoons butter
1 bunch fresh parsley, chopped

1 pint sour cream
2 tablespoons or more fresh dill
   Salt and freshly ground pepper

Wash mushrooms, remove stems and dry mushroom caps.

Put about 4 tablespoons butter in a frying pan and melt. Add mushrooms and chopped spring onions, including light green part of onion stems. Add dill, salt, and pepper to suit your taste. Cook about 5 minutes over hot burner, turning mushrooms.

At this point remove mixture from stove and transfer to a casserole. Add sour cream and half chopped parsley.

Fry bacon until crisp. Drain thoroughly, crumble, and reserve.

About 20 minutes before serving, place casserole in a preheated 400° oven. Sprinkle a blanket of chopped parsley on top. Sprinkle crisp, crumbled bacon over all.

Mary Armstrong Amory

Stuffed Mushrooms

Serves 6

12 very large fresh mushrooms
½ pound Italian ricotta
2 eggs
½ cup cracker crumbs
½ cup raw wheat germ
   Chopped fresh parsley to taste
1 teaspoon chopped basil to taste

1 heaping tablespoon Romano grated cheese
   Salt and freshly ground pepper to taste
   Chopped garlic or onion (optional)

Wash mushrooms, remove stems and chop reserving them for later. Oil large pan and put mushrooms in being sure cap side is down; sauté lightly.

Mix together ricotta, eggs, cracker crumbs, raw wheat germ, parsley, basil, grated cheese, salt, and pepper. (Remember that cheese is very salty.) Add to filling reserved chopped mushrooms.

Fill caps, mounding slightly. Grate more cheese on top, sprinkle with a dash of paprika and drizzle over tops a little olive oil.

Bake in oven 15 to 20 minutes at 400°. Chopped garlic or onion is also good in filling. If filling is too dry, add more ricotta.

Mrs. Ramon Scavelli

Pissaladière Provençal

Onion and Tomato Tart

Serves 6 to 8

1	partially baked 9- or 10-inch tart shell
4	tablespoons butter
3	pounds onions (to make 6 cups) finely chopped
2–3	peeled garlic cloves finely chopped
2	tablespoons olive oil
2	pounds fresh tomatoes peeled, seeded, juiced and chopped
1	tablespoon tomato paste

2	teaspoons dry basil
1	teaspoon oregano
1	teaspoon salt
	Freshly ground pepper
1	tablespoon dry bread crumbs
24	flat anchovies drained
24	black olives
1	tablespoon olive oil
1	tablespoon Italian parsley, finely chopped

Melt butter in 10 to 12-inch skillet over moderate heat. Stir in onions and when well coated with butter, simmer for 10 minutes covered. Stir occasionally.

Uncover after 10 minutes. Add garlic and cook for 30 minutes over low heat, stirring occasionally until all liquid is evaporated and onions are translucent.

Put olive oil in another pan and set over high heat. Add chopped tomatoes and bring to a boil. Stir frequently and let boil until almost all liquid is gone. Remove from heat; stir in oregano, basil and tomato paste. Combine onions and tomatoes; add salt and pepper. Taste for seasonings.

Preheat oven to 375°. Place partially cooked pastry shell (still in its tart pan) on a cookie sheet. Spread bread crumbs in bottom to absorb any excess liquid and prevent a soggy shell. Spoon in onion and tomato mixture and smooth to edges of crust. Make a lattice work of anchovies across tart. Place an olive in each resulting square. Dribble one tablespoon olive oil on top.

Bake in center of oven for 30 minutes or until onion and tomato mixture is lightly browned. Serve either hot or at room temperature. Sprinkle with chopped parsley just before serving.

The onion mixture can be prepared earlier in the day, as can the pastry shell, and combined just before baking. Filling is also delicious over broiled fish or chicken.

Mrs. Harry E. Gould

Potatoes Supreme

Serves 6

2 pounds potatoes
1 pound onions
¼ pound bacon
Salt and freshly ground pepper to taste
2 cups dry white wine
2 cups sour cream
½ pound grated Swiss cheese
1½ tablespoons butter

Peel potatoes.

Cut potatoes, onions and bacon into cubes. Place in buttered casserole. Salt and pepper to taste. Mix well. Pour wine over potatoes.

Cook uncovered at 325° for 1 hour and 15 minutes. Do not allow to get mushy.

Add butter, Swiss cheese and sour cream. Blend carefully until cheese is melted. Adjust seasoning.

Return to oven at 300°. Bake until bubbly, about 25 minutes.

Great on a buffet table!

Marty Platt

Twice Baked Potatoes Cottage Style

Serves 4

2 medium baking potatoes
½ cup low-fat cottage cheese
¼ cup buttermilk or low-fat yogurt
½ tablespoon minced onion

Dash freshly ground pepper
Paprika
Fresh, minced parsley

Scrub potatoes in cold water with vegetable brush. Pierce each potato in several places with fork. Bake at 400° for 45 minutes or until tender

Cut hot potatoes in half lengthwise. Scoop out inside of potato, leaving skins intact for re-stuffing. With wire whisk, beat potato with remaining ingredients, except paprika and parsley, until fluffy. Do not add too much liquid as mixture can become runny.

Put mixture back into skins; sprinkle with paprika and parsley. Bake 10 minutes or until golden brown.

Each portion contains 75 calories.

Ralph E. Becker

Vegetable Mousse

Serves 4 to 6

1 pound carrots, cut in chunks
1 package frozen artichoke hearts
2 tablespoons butter
1 package frozen, chopped spinach, defrosted and squeezed dry
1 medium onion, chopped fine
3 tablespoons chopped, fresh dill or 1½ tablespoons dried dill
5 large eggs
1 cup heavy cream
½ cup Parmesan cheese
½ cup milk
   Salt and freshly ground pepper
   Nutmeg, to taste

Thoroughly grease sides and bottom of a loaf pan. Line with wax paper and grease again. Set aside

Cook or steam carrots in small amount of water and drain. Cook artichoke hearts and drain.

Melt butter in medium-size pan and add spinach, onion, and dill. Sauté over medium heat until onion is tender and spinach is dry.

Combine eggs, cream, milk, cheese, salt, pepper, and nutmeg and blend until smooth.

In a food processor, combine a third of egg mixture with each of above vegetables. Process each briefly until blended. Arrange in layers, spreading each out evenly. Put artichokes on bottom, followed by carrots and then spinach.

Cook in a bain marie (sit loaf pan in a larger pan filled with water a third up sides of loaf pan), for 1¼ hours in a 375° oven. Let stand 10 minutes. Invert onto serving dish. Remove wax paper. Let stand 20 minutes before serving or refrigerate and serve very cold.

Howard de Franceaux

Spinach Casserole

Serves 4

2 10-ounce packages
   frozen spinach
6 ounces cream cheese,
   softened
¼ pound butter, melted
   and seasoned with
   salt and freshly
   ground pepper
¼ cup bread crumbs
   (half plain and half
   seasoned)
¾ teaspoon sage

Cook and drain spinach well.

Mix softened cream cheese with half of butter and add to spinach.

Grease a 9-inch pyrex pie plate or small shallow casserole. Pour in spinach mixture.

Add remaining butter to bread crumbs and sage. Spread over top of spinach.

Bake at 350° for 30 minutes.

Cookbook Committee

Don's Hungarian Spinach

Serves 6

2 10-ounce packages
   frozen, chopped
   spinach
4 tablespoons butter
4 tablespoons flour
½ teaspoon salt
¼ teaspoon garlic salt
¼ teaspoon freshly
   ground pepper
1½ cups light cream
2 eggs

Prepare spinach according to package directions and drain thoroughly.

Melt butter over low heat and blend in flour and seasonings. Add cream, stirring constantly. Cook 1 to 2 minutes.

Remove from heat and stir about 6 tablespoons of sauce into slightly beaten eggs. Return mixture to sauce and blend well. Combine with spinach.

NSO Member

Spicy Spinach

Serves 4 to 6

2 10-ounce packages chopped spinach, cooked; no salt (save ½ cup spinach liquid)
2 tablespoons butter
2–3 ounces onions
½ cup evaporated milk
¾ teaspoon celery salt
¾ teaspoon garlic
1 teaspoon Worcestershire sauce
Dash of red pepper
6-ounce roll Jalapeña cheese
Croutons, sautéed in butter

Melt butter and sauté onions until tender. Add evaporated milk and spinach liquid. Add black pepper, celery salt, garlic, Worcestershire sauce, and red pepper. Add Jalapeña cheese, cut up; melt into sauce.

Add drained spinach. Put in casserole and top with bread croutons that have been sautéed in butter.

Cook until bubbly at 350° for 30 minutes.

Very hot; serve with Tex-Mex menu.

Lynda Johnson Robb

Butternut Squash and Snow Peas

Serves 4 to 6

½–1 pound snow peas
4 cups butternut squash, sliced
1 medium onion, sliced
3 tablespoons butter
1 cup sour cream
½ teaspoon salt
Freshly ground pepper to taste
Fresh dill, chopped or
1 teaspoon dried dill

Cook or steam squash until done but firm. Drain well.

Sauté onion in butter. Add sour cream to sautéed onions.

Blanch snow peas and drain. Pour squash and snow peas onto platter. Cover with sour cream sauce. Sprinkle with pepper and dill. Serve immediately.

Linda Tyson Font

Stuffed Summer Squash

Serves 4

5 yellow (summer)
    squash, use large but
    not old squash
4 hard-boiled eggs,
    chopped
1 large onion, chopped
    Olive oil
    Salt and freshly
     ground pepper
     to taste
    Parsley
    Bread crumbs
    Stewed tomatoes, fresh
     or canned

Cut summer squash lengthwise. Scoop out seeds carefully and discard. Parboil squash in salted, boiling water until just tender. Cut off necks from 8 halves. Scoop some pulp from each squash. Set aside. You should now have 8 squash "boats."

Coarsely chop necks and extra squash. Set aside. Chop onion. Sauté onions and squash in olive oil until onion is transparent. Remove from heat and pour entire contents into large bowl. Add chopped eggs, chopped parsley and enough bread crumbs to hold mixture together. Add a bit more oil if necessary. Season to taste. Stuff squash boats with mixture.

Place a layer of stewed tomatoes in shallow pan or dish. Place stuffed squash on top. The boats should fit snugly into pan. Do not use too large a pan or boats will spread and possibly split. Pour remaining stewed tomatoes over squash.

Bake uncovered for approximately 30 to 45 minutes or until thoroughly hot. Serve with additional stewed tomatoes if desired.

Virginia C. Mars

Sweet Potato Casserole

Serves 6 to 8

3 cups mashed, cooked
   sweet potatoes
½ cup granulated sugar
½ teaspoon salt
2 eggs
⅓ stick butter
½ cup milk
1 teaspoon vanilla

TOPPING
1 cup brown sugar
1 cup chopped nuts
⅓ cup flour
⅓ stick melted butter

Mix together sweet potatoes, sugar, salt, eggs, and butter. Add milk and vanilla last.

Pour into a greased baking dish. Sprinkle topping over sweet potato mixture and bake at 350° for 30 to 35 minutes.

Edna E. Powers

Apples and Yams

Serves 8 to 10

2 pounds canned yams
1 teaspoon salt
   Freshly ground
   pepper
4 tablespoons butter
   melted
½ cup brown sugar
4 tablespoons butter
½ teaspoon nutmeg
2 medium apples,
   peeled, thinly sliced

Combine yams, salt, pepper and melted butter and mash together.

Mix together brown sugar, 4 tablespoons butter and nutmeg. Line an 8-cup baking dish with brown sugar mixture. Cover with sliced apples and top with yam mixture. Dot with butter.

Bake at 350° for 1 hour.

Cookbook Committee

Christmas Tomatoes

Serves 6

6 medium large tomatoes	¾ cup grated Parmesan cheese
10-ounce package frozen spinach (chopped)	1½ teaspoons dried basil
1 stick butter (½ cup)	1 teaspoon dried oregano
1 bunch (6–8) spring onions	1 tablespoon fresh parsley, chopped
1–1½ cups bread crumbs	

Cook spinach in small amount of water to thaw. Drain. Squeeze out moisture so spinach is dry.

Cut off stem ends of tomatoes and scoop out pulp (leaving ½-inch shell). Sprinkle inside of tomatoes with salt and invert on rack. Reserve pulp.

In skillet, melt butter. Sauté chopped spring onions with basil, oregano and parsley. Add spinach and ½ cup tomato pulp (chopped) and heat through. Add bread crumbs so mixture holds together but is not dry. Add Parmesan cheese and mix well.

Stuff tomatoes with stuffing mix. Sprinkle top with Parmesan. Place in lightly-oiled pyrex dish just large enough to hold tomatoes.

Bake 20 to 25 minutes at 350°.

Joan H. Lewis

Turnips Bordelaise

Serves 6

2 pounds white turnips	1 shallot
4 tablespoons butter	½ cup coarse bread crumbs
Salt and freshly ground pepper	1 tablespoon minced parsley
Water, about ½ cup	
2 cloves garlic	

Peel turnips and cut into walnut-size pieces. Melt 3 tablespoons of butter. Add turnips, salt and pepper to taste, and a small amount of water. Cover pan and cook slowly over low heat, until turnips are cooked through and liquid has been absorbed.

Mince garlic and shallot; mix with bread crumbs and parsley. Add 1 tablespoon butter to pan. Add bread crumb mixture and toss turnips to coat. Brown briefly over moderately high heat, shaking pan often.

Pamela Powers

Frituritas De Yucca
Yucca Fritters

Serves 12

1 package frozen yucca
2 eggs
1 teaspoon anise seeds
1 tablespoon butter
3 tablespoons milk
½ teaspoon salt
½ teaspoon sugar
1 cup cooking oil

Thaw yucca. Grate it coarsely. Add all other ingredients except cooking oil and mix until well blended.

Heat oil in a medium-size frying pan. After oil has become very hot, reduce heat to medium. Take 1 teaspoon of yucca mixture and drop it carefully into cooking oil. Let it get a light golden color and turn only once to cook other side as well. Repeat until all yucca dough is fried.

Drain on a paper towel before serving. Fried yucca can be kept hot and crispy in a warm oven for up to 30 minutes. Serve with meat as you would potatoes.

Mrs. Carlos Despradel
Wife of the Ambassador of the Dominican Republic

E-Z Zucchini

Serves 4 to 5

4 medium-large zucchini (about 1¾ pounds), chopped
½ cup stale bread crumbs, cracker crumbs, unprocessed bran, wheat germ, or a mixture of any of these
1 medium onion, chopped
½ pound Cheddar cheese, grated
¼ teaspoon garlic salt
Freshly ground pepper, to taste
2 eggs and ⅓–½ cup milk beaten together with a fork

Lightly butter a baking dish.
Mix all ingredients together right in the baking dish.
Bake about 40 minutes at 325°.

Anne Price

Stuffed Zucchini Pike Place Market

Serves 6 to 8

6 large zucchini
3 tablespoons olive oil
3 medium onions, minced
3 cloves garlic, mashed
10 parsley sprigs, leaves only
½ teaspoon salt
1 teaspoon black pepper, freshly ground
½ teaspoon garlic salt
½ cup fresh basil leaves (cut into strips) or 2 tablespoons dried basil

2 pounds Italian sausage (mix them up, hot and mild)
3 slices sourdough bread
¾ cup milk
¾ cup Parmesan cheese, grated
Italian salad dressing

Zucchini should be about 2½ inches thick and approximately 6 to 7 inches long.

Cut off stems and parboil whole in boiling, salted water for about 12 minutes. Drain and cool.

Cut zucchini lengthwise into halves. Scoop out pulp and set aside.

Place olive oil in a skillet and heat. Add onions, garlic, parsley, and basil. Sauté for about 4 minutes.

Remove sausage from its casing and place meat, broken into small pieces, in mixture. Add salt, pepper, garlic salt, and other seasoning. Cook for about 15 minutes. Remove from heat.

Preheat oven to 350°. Soak sourdough bread in milk until milk is absorbed; squeeze out milk from bread and shred bread. Add shredded bread, cheese, and zucchini pulp to skillet with sausage mixture. Blend well for about 3 minutes.

Stuff zucchini with mixture. Oil baking pan with olive oil, arrange zucchini in pan, and sprinkle a few drops of olive oil over top. Bake for approximately 30 minutes.

Immediately before serving, spoon about 1 tablespoon salad dressing over each zucchini. Zucchini may be served hot or cold.

Llewelyn G. Pritchard

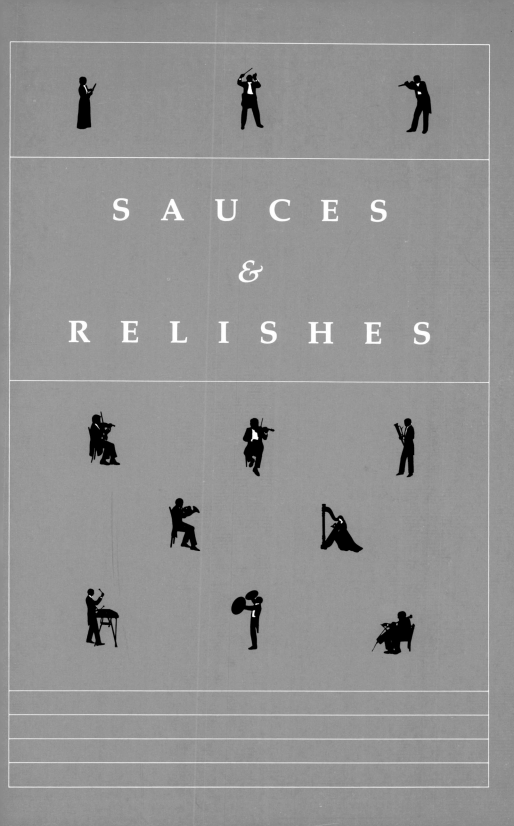

SAUCES

&

RELISHES

Fresh Tomato Sauce

Makes 4 cups

1 clove garlic, minced
½ cup finely chopped onions
3 tablespoons olive oil
¼ cup finely chopped celery
3 cups diced, ripe tomatoes or 1 large can Italian style tomatoes
½ teaspoon sugar
1 teaspoon salt
Freshly ground pepper, to taste
1 teaspoon dried basil or 1 tablespoon fresh basil
1 small bay leaf
2 tablespoons tomato paste

Sauté garlic and onion in olive oil in heavy pan. Add celery, diced tomatoes, sugar, salt, pepper and bay leaf. Cook mixture for 20 minutes. Press through coarse sieve. Stir in tomato paste and heat.

Cookbook Committee

Mushroom Sauce

Makes about 2 cups

½ pound fresh mushrooms, sliced
2 tablespoons butter
Salt and freshly ground pepper to taste
2 tablespoons dry sherry
1 tablespoon brandy
3 tablespoons heavy cream
1 tablespoon flour
1 tablespoon Dijon mustard

Sauté mushrooms in butter for 5 minutes until soft. Add salt, pepper and sherry.

Warm brandy. Light brandy and pour flaming over mushrooms. Shake pan until flame dies.

Blend cream, flour, and mustard. Add to mushrooms. Simmer, stirring until slightly reduced and thickened. Good served over steak or hamburgers.

Cookbook Committee

Pesto-Genoese
Fresh Basil Sauce

Makes 1 cup

2 cups fresh basil leaves
½ cup olive oil
2 tablespoons pine nuts (blanched almonds may be substituted)
2 cloves mashed garlic
1 teaspoon salt
⅔ cup freshly grated Parmesan or 4 parts Parmesan to 1 part sharp Romano cheese
4 tablespoons butter

Put basil, olive oil, pine nuts, garlic, and salt in a blender or food processor and mix at high speed. Stop from time to time and scrape ingredients down toward bottom of blender cup with a rubber spatula. Add grated cheese and butter; blend briefly.

Before spooning pesto over pasta, dilute pesto with a tablespoon or so of hot water in which pasta was boiled. If adding to other sauces, various liquids can be used to blend it.

To make pesto for freezer, mix all ingredients in blender but do not add cheese or butter. Spoon mixture into a jar and seal tightly; freeze. Before using, thaw overnight in refrigerator. Mix grated cheese and butter; add to completely thawed mixture.

Pesto may be added to soups, vegetable dressings, salad dressings and dips. A little goes a long way.
Pesto can stand in refrigerator a month or longer.

Cookbook Committee

Meat Spaghetti Sauce

Serves 6

1½–2 pounds ground meat (hamburger or a combination of beef, pork, and veal)
3 cloves garlic
6-ounce can tomato paste
4 cups canned tomatoes (28 ounce can)
½ pound fresh mushrooms, sliced and sautéed in butter or olive oil)
1 whole bay leaf
8 whole cloves
¼ cup sugar
1 teaspoon salt
½–1 teaspoon crushed red pepper or ½ teaspoon Cayenne

Brown meat and garlic. Pour off accummulated fats. Add remaining ingredients. Simmer for at least 2½ hours. Remove cloves and bay leaf before serving.

Serve over extra thin spaghetti and sprinkle with freshly grated Parmesan cheese.

Charlotte D. Neil

Wine Barbeque Sauce for Poultry

Makes 1 cup

¼ cup salad oil
½ cup white wine
1 clove garlic, crushed
1 grated onion
½ teaspoon salt
½ teaspoon celery salt
½ teaspoon freshly
    ground pepper
1 teaspoon fresh thyme
1 teaspoon fresh
    marjoram
1 teaspoon fresh
    rosemary
    (If using dried herbs,
    use ¼ teaspoon each)

Mix all ingredients and let stand for 2 hours. Use to baste cornish hens or other poultry.

John Marcellus
Former NSO Member

Gourmet Poultry Marinade

Makes about 3½ cups

1½ cups salad oil
¾ cup soy sauce
¼ cup Worcestershire
    sauce
2 tablespoons dry
    mustard
1½ teaspoons salt
    Freshly ground
    pepper to taste
½ cup wine vinegar
1½ teaspoons tarragon
    and/or parsley
2 or more garlic cloves,
    crushed
⅓ cup fresh lemon juice

Mix all ingredients. Pour over chicken pieces and marinate for 12 to 24 hours, turning occasionally.

You can baste with leftover marinade, or refrigerate it to use again within the week.

Joan Searby

Mixed Pickled Vegetables

Makes 6 quarts

2 heads cauliflower, separated into small pieces
1 cabbage head, sliced into 6 pieces
1 bunch celery, cut into 3-inch strips
2 pounds green tomatoes, cut into quarters
1 package (1 pound) carrots, quartered
1 bunch dill
Hot pepper, optional
18 cloves garlic

BRINE
3 quarts water
1½ quarts white vinegar
1 cup salt (not iodized)
½ package pickling spice
Few sprigs of dill
½ cup sugar

Wash and drain vegetables. Cut as directed. Pack into 6 clean quart jars, adding 3 cloves of garlic, two sprigs of dill and a 1-inch piece of hot pepper to each. Prepare brine.

BRINE

Bring water, sugar, salt, pickling spice and dill to boil. Simmer for 10 minutes. Turn off heat and add vinegar. Allow to cool slightly. Pour brine into jars of vegetables enough to cover vegetables completely. Cover jars tightly. Store in cool place. Pickles will be ready to serve in 3 weeks.

Irene D. Johnson

Pickled Mushrooms

Makes 1½ pounds

1½ pounds small button mushrooms, washed and trimmed
1 cup white wine
½ cup distilled white vinegar
½ cup vegetable oil
1 bay leaf
10–20 whole black peppercorns
½ teaspoon salt
1 teaspoon tarragon
Parsley, for garnish
Hard-boiled eggs, for garnish

Mushrooms will keep refrigerated for about one year if stored in glass jars in their marinade.

Prepare marinade and add mushrooms. Bring to a boil and remove foam from surface of marinade. Allow to simmer for a few minutes. Leave mushrooms in marinade for 3 to 4 days. The mushrooms will have absorbed taste of marinade and be ready to serve. Discard marinade before serving.

Serving suggestion: Add chopped, hard-boiled eggs to mushrooms and garnish with lots of chopped parsley.

Cookbook Committee

Texas Sweet Pickles

Makes about 1 quart

5 large sour pickles, cut into rounds
4 tablespoons pickling spice
4 cups sugar
4 tablespoons oil

Put pickles in bowl, sprinkle with spices. Cover with sugar and pour on oil.

Cover and let stand overnight. Turn and let stand until it exudes its own juice.

Patrick Hayes

Kosher Dill Cucumbers or Tomatoes

Makes a lot!

10 pounds small whole
   cucumbers or small
   round green
   tomatoes
   Cloves of garlic
   Hot red pepper pods
   Peppercorns
   Fresh dill
3 quarts water
1 cup salt
4 cups vinegar

Wash and dry vegetables and pack in sterilized quart jars. For each jar add 1 peeled clove garlic, 1 hot red pepper pod, 4 to 6 peppercorns, and 1 generous sprig of fresh dill. Combine water, salt, and vinegar in saucepan, bring to boil, and pour at once over pickles. Seal jars.

David Howard
NSO Member

Beach Island Artichoke Relish

Makes about 6 to 8 quarts

3 quarts Jerusalem
   artichokes sliced
   (about 2–3 pounds)
1 quart onions, sliced
6 green peppers, sliced
3 pounds cabbage,
   sliced (optional, as
   filler)
½ gallon vinegar
   9-ounce jar prepared
   mustard

¾ pound flour
3 pounds sugar
1 tablespoon turmeric
1 tablespoon black
   pepper, freshly
   ground
3 tablespoons white
   mustard seeds

Soak vegetables overnight in 1 gallon of water and 2 cups salt. Take off any woody parts. Drain and blot dry.

Mix spices and add to vegetables; boil in vinegar for 10 minutes. Mix mustard and flour with some cooled liquid and add slowly. Boil 5 more minutes. Put into sterilized jars and seal. Excellent with roast beef and lamb.

Jerusalem artichokes are easily raised in this area. Artichoke plants may be found in some area nurseries. The roots are harvested after the first killing frost. They can be cut into chunks, steamed for several minutes (don't let them get mushy) and served with lemon and butter. The flavor is remarkably akin to globe artichokes.

G. Stuart Scott

Poor Man's Caviar or Russian Eggplant Relish

Makes about 6 cups relish

1 large eggplant
4 large green bell peppers
2 large onions
4–6 ounces tomato paste
Salt
Freshly ground pepper to taste

Roast eggplant and peppers in 375° oven until limp, about 45 minutes. Cool until easy to handle. Skin eggplant and remove most of seed pods; chop coarsely. Remove stems and ribs from peppers; skin and chop coarsely.

At this point there are several possible variations:

For classic Russian caviar add finely chopped onion, sautéed in olive oil until light golden, and tomato paste to eggplant mixture. Salt and pepper to taste. Mix well. Sauté in large skillet, mixing constantly with wooden spoon until all excess moisture is evaporated. Cool and serve at room temperature with crackers, pumpernickel or pita bread as appetizer or plain with cold roast meats as relish or vegetable. *OR*

Add finely chopped fresh onion and garlic to eggplant mixture. Salt and pepper to taste. Add lemon juice and scant tablespoon of homemade mayonnaise. Do not use commercial mayonnaise, as it changes flavor. Quantity of onion and garlic will depend on desired sharpness of finished relish. One small onion and 2 to 3 cloves of garlic are standard. *OR*

Add fresh, finely chopped onion (about 1 medium) and 2 to 3 seeded and chopped fresh tomatoes to eggplant mixture. Salt and pepper to taste.

The two versions with fresh onion are not sautéed to remove excess moisture. Therefore it is necessary to drain eggplant mixture (before adding onion and other ingredients) in sieve lined with double thickness of cheesecloth. Serve well chilled with crackers, pita bread, or buttered pumpernickel.

Both basic eggplant mixture and Russian relish freeze well. The onion and tomatoes in other versions tend to get watery on defrosting, and should be added to basic mixture after defrosting.

Nadya Efremov

Spiced New England Cranberry Relish

Yields about 6 jars relish

2 packages cranberries, washed and picked over
2 cups water
3 cups brown sugar, packed
1½ cups granulated sugar
1 cup vinegar
4 teaspoons ground cloves
4 teaspoons cinnamon

Put all ingredients except cranberries in a large pan and boil for 5 minutes. Add berries and boil until they "pop their skins." Skim off any foam. Pour into sterilized small jelly glasses (5 ounces). Refrigerate.

Marilyn Butts

Sue Davie's Mother-in-Law's Neighbor's Famous Homemade Hot Mustard

Yields about 2 cups mustard

4 ounces dry mustard
⅝ cup tarragon vinegar
⅝ cup cider vinegar
4 eggs
½ cup sugar
¾ teaspoon salt

Mix together first 3 ingredients. Refrigerate overnight.
    Beat together eggs, sugar and salt; combine with mustard mixture in medium saucepan. Cook over low heat 10 to 12 minutes or until thickened, stirring constantly. Chill thoroughly.

Mark Conrad

DESSERTS

C A K E S
&
T O R T E S

Mildred's Apple Cake

Serves 12 to 15

4 cups plus 2–3 extra apples, cut in wedges
2 tablespoons sugar
1½ teaspoons cinnamon
1 cup raisins
3 cups flour
1 tablespoon baking powder
1 teaspoon salt
2 cups sugar
4 eggs
1 cup oil
¼ cup orange juice
2½ teaspoons vanilla

Mix 2 tablespoons sugar with cinnamon and sprinkle over apples. Add more sugar if necessary. Add raisins and set aside.

Sift flour with baking powder and salt. Cream sugar and eggs. Add oil, orange juice, and vanilla to creamed mixture. Stir in dry ingredients.

Put half batter in greased tube pan. Add half apple mixture. Cover apples with remaining batter. Top batter with remaining apples. Be careful not to let apple mixture touch sides of pan; it might stick.

Bake at 350° for 1½ hours or longer.

Goes anywhere, always looks nice, is very moist, and stays fresh a long time.

Carol Sue Lebbin

Janet's Harvest Cake

Serves 12 to 15

4 cups diced and peeled apples
2 cups sugar
3 cups flour
2 eggs
1 cup cooking oil
1 teaspoon salt
1 teaspoon cinnamon
1 teaspoon nutmeg
2 teaspoons baking soda
1 teaspoon vanilla
1 cup chopped walnuts

Mix apples and sugar; let stand for 1 hour. Sift flour, baking soda, and spices. Beat eggs, oil, and vanilla together; add to apples. Stir in flour mixture and walnuts.

Bake in greased and well-floured tube or bundt pan at 350° for 1 hour, or until done.

Anne Merick

VARIATION

Use 1½ cups whole wheat flour, 1½ cups regular flour and ½ cup white sugar combined with ½ cup brown sugar.

John Berg

Best Carrot Cake Ever

Serves 12

2 cups flour
2 cups sugar
1½ cups salad oil
4 eggs, well beaten
2 teaspoons baking soda
2 teaspoons baking powder
2 teaspoons cinnamon
1 teaspoon salt
1 cup chopped pecans
3 cups grated, raw carrots (1 pound)

FROSTING
8-ounce package cream cheese
½ cup chopped pecans
¼ cup butter
1 box confectioners sugar
2 teaspoons vanilla

Mix together sugar and salad oil. Add well-beaten eggs and mix. Combine dry ingredients and add egg-oil mixture. Stir until smooth. Add chopped nuts and grated carrots. Bake in 3 greased, 9-inch, layer pans at 325° for about 30 minutes. For 2 pans, bake a few minutes longer.

FROSTING

Combine cream cheese with butter and sugar. Add nuts and vanilla. Mix well. Frosts a 3-layer cake.

Sybil Amitay
Jane Stein
Anne Wesson

Cap's Cake

Serves 12 to 15

Serve very thin slices to very thin people!

CAKE
- ¼ pound butter, softened
- 1 cup sugar
- ½ cup milk
- 1⅔ cups cake flour
- 2 teaspoons baking powder
- 2 egg whites
- 1 teaspoon vanilla

CHOCOLATE FILLING
- 2 squares bitter chocolate, melted
- ¼ pound butter
- Pinch salt
- 2 tablespoons Kahlua or brandy
- ½ cup light cream
- 2 egg yolks
- 5 cups confectioners sugar

SEMI-SWEET CHOCOLATE ICING
- 3 squares bitter chocolate
- 1 teaspoon vanilla
- ¼ cup boiling water
- 2 tablespoons butter
- 1 cup confectioners sugar
- Blanched almonds, for garnish

CAKE

Combine butter, sugar, milk, flour, baking powder, egg whites, and vanilla in a large mixing bowl; beat at low speed, scraping often, until smooth and well blended. Increase speed to high and beat for 3 minutes. Pour into 2 greased, 9-inch, round pans and bake for about 20 to 25 minutes at 350°. Cool slightly and turn out onto cake rack. When cakes are cooled, split each into 2 layers.

CHOCOLATE FILLING

In mixing bowl cream butter, salt, and yolks. Add cream mixture to cooled chocolate. Beat well. Continue beating while adding sugar, a little at a time. Add brandy or Kahlua and beat at high speed until thoroughly creamed and light.

CHOCOLATE ICING

Melt chocolate and butter. Add water and vanilla and beat in confectioners sugar to make glossy, smooth icing.

TO ASSEMBLE

Place one split cake layer on plate, top with filling and repeat, ending with last cake layer. Frost top and sides with icing and decorate with blanched almonds.

Jane Weinberger

Pumpkin Cheesecake

Serves 10 to 12

CRUST
1½ cups graham cracker
   crumbs
3 tablespoons butter,
   melted
3 tablespoons sugar

TOPPING
1 cup sour cream
2 tablespoons sugar
½ teaspoon vanilla

FILLING
2 8-ounce packages
   cream cheese
1 cup heavy or light
   cream
1 cup pumpkin
¾ cup sugar
4 eggs, separated
3 tablespoons flour
1 teaspoon vanilla
1 teaspoon cinnamon
½ teaspoon ginger
½ teaspoon nutmeg
¼ teaspoon salt

For crust, combine ingredients and press into spring-form pan. Bake at 325° for about 15 minutes.

For filling, combine all ingredients except egg whites and blend well. Beat egg whites and fold into cheesecake mixture. Pour into springform pan and bake at 325° for 1 hour.

For topping, combine ingredients and pour evenly over baked cake. Return cake to 325° oven for 5 more minutes.

Debra Finlayson

Cellist's Cheesecake

Serves 16

This looming 6-inch high dessert, baked in an angelfood cakepan, was used in the NSO/WGMS Radiothon March 1983.

CRUST
16 Zwieback crackers,
   crumbled
¼ cup sugar
   Dash of cinnamon
¼ cup melted butter

FILLING
6 eggs
2¼ cups sugar
¼ cup flour plus 2
   tablespoons
1 teaspoon salt
   Juice of 1 lemon
1 teaspoon vanilla
3 pounds cream cheese
1½ cups light cream

Combine Zwieback crumbs, sugar, cinnamon, and butter. Press into bottom of a 10-inch tube pan that has a removable bottom.

Beat eggs for 5 minutes, adding sugar gradually. Add flour, salt, lemon, and vanilla.

In another bowl, beat softened cream cheese with cream until smooth adding cream gradually after cheese is fluffy. Add egg mixture to cheese and keep beating.

Pour batter into crust and bake at 325° for 1 hour. Open oven door after that, and let cake stand in oven until cool (overnight is fine).

Refrigerate at least 8 hours before serving.

Yvonne Caruthers
NSO Member

Praline Cheesecake

Serves 10 to 12

CRUST
1 cup graham cracker crumbs
3 tablespoons sugar
3 tablespoons butter, melted

FILLING
3 8-ounce packages cream cheese
1¼ cups packed dark brown sugar
2 tablespoons flour
3 eggs
1½ teaspoons vanilla
½ cup finely chopped pecans
8 pecan halves
¼ cup maple syrup

CRUST

Combine crumbs, sugar, and butter; press onto bottom of 9-inch springform pan. Bake at 350° for 10 minutes.

FILLING

Combine softened cream cheese, sugar, and flour. Mix at medium speed until blended well. Add eggs one at a time, beating well after each addition. Blend in vanilla and chopped nuts. Pour mixture over crumbs. Bake at 350° for 50 to 55 minutes. Loosen springform ring but cool cake completely before removing it. Chill. Brush top with maple syrup and top with pecan halves.

Susan M. Carlson

Chocaholic Bourbon Cake

Serves 16 to 18

2 cups butter
1 cup granulated sugar
1 cup confectioners sugar
4 ounces unsweetened chocolate, melted
12 eggs, separated
1 teaspoon vanilla
1 cup chopped pecans
18 double ladyfingers
48 macaroons, broken and soaked in
½–⅔ cup bourbon
1 cup heavy cream, whipped

This cake was made especially for the March 1983 NSO/WGMS Radiothon.

Cream butter, ½ cup granulated sugar and all confectioners sugar until light and fluffy. Beat egg yolks until light; blend into butter mixture. Beat in chocolate. Add vanilla and pecans.

Beat egg whites until fluffy; add remaining granulated sugar and beat until stiff but not dry. Fold into chocolate mixture.

Line sides and bottom of a 10-inch springform pan with split ladyfingers.

Soak macaroons in bourbon. Alternate layers of macaroons and chocolate mixture over ladyfingers in pan. Chill overnight.

Remove sides of pan and cover cake with whipped cream. This cake freezes well. Ice with whipped cream *after defrosting* however.

James D. Kraft
NSO Member

Chocolate Cake

Serves 6

¾ cup sugar
¼ pound unsalted butter
5 eggs, separated
1 cup chocolate chips
1 teaspoon rum

Cream sugar, butter, and egg yolks. Melt chocolate chips in double boiler or over simmering water. Stir in rum. Add to creamed mixture. Beat egg whites until stiff but not dry. Fold chocolate-rum mixture into beaten egg whites. Pour into buttered, 9-inch square, pyrex dish. Bake at 350° for 15 to 20 minutes. Cut into squares and dust with powdered sugar.

Narciso Yepes

CAKES & TORTES   **239**

Chocolate Concord Cake

Serves 4 to 6

MERINGUE
8 egg whites
8 ounces superfine sugar
2 ounces cocoa powder
8 ounces confectioners
    sugar

MOUSSE FILLING
½ quart heavy cream
4 egg yolks
2 tablespoons rum
3 ounces semi-sweet
    chocolate, melted

MERINGUE

Beat egg whites and superfine sugar together until fluffy. Set aside. Sift together cocoa powder and confectioners sugar; fold into egg whites. Pipe mixture through a round #2 pastry tube onto an ungreased cookie sheet, making 3, 8-inch solid, concentric circles. On a separate cookie sheet, pipe remainder of mixture into long, thin strips. Bake circles at 200° for 1 hour. Bake strips at 200° for 40 minutes. Cool.

MOUSSE FILLING

Beat egg yolks and rum in a double boiler until just warm. Quickly mix melted chocolate into mixture. In a mixing bowl, whip cream to medium consistency. Fold in egg-rum-chocolate mixture. Refrigerate for 1 hour.

TO ASSEMBLE

Place 1 meringue circle on cake plate and cover with small amount of mousse. Repeat with 2 more layers of meringue and mousse. Cover sides and top with remaining mousse mixture. Break up meringue strips and use to decorate cake. Best when served the same day.

The Roof Terrace Restaurant at the Kennedy Center
Restaurant Associates

Chocolate Mousse Cake 1789

Serves 8 to 10

PASTRY CREAM
6   egg yolks
¾   cup granulated sugar
6   tablespoons flour
2⅓ cups milk
1   teaspoon vanilla

CHANTILLY CREAM
1   cup cold heavy cream
3   tablespoons
    confectioners sugar

CHOCOLATE COUVERTURE
5   ounces semi-sweet
    chocolate

RUM SYRUP
⅓   cup water
2   tablespoons
    granulated sugar
3   tablespoons rum

CHOCOLATE GENOISE
½   cup flour
½   cup sugar
½   cup cocoa powder
5   eggs
1   teaspoon vanilla

PASTRY CREAM

In a bowl, mix egg yolks with sugar and flour. Bring milk to a boil in a saucepan. Gradually stir boiling milk into egg yolk mixture. Pour hot milk mixture back into saucepan and place over low heat, stirring constantly until it thickens. Do not allow mixture to boil. Stir in vanilla. Pour thickened mixture into bowl and chill.

CHANTILLY CREAM

Whip cream with chilled beaters until doubled in volume. Add sugar and beat until soft peaks form. Refrigerate.

CHOCOLATE COUVERTURE

Place chocolate in top of double boiler and melt over low heat. Remove from heat. Set aside.

RUM SYRUP

In a small saucepan over high heat dissolve sugar in water. Bring to boil, remove from heat, and stir in rum.

CHOCOLATE GENOISE

Butter a 9-inch cake pan (3-inch deep). Line bottom of pan with a wax paper round; butter paper, and dust with flour. In a small bowl beat eggs and sugar at slow, medium, then high speed for 4 or 5 minutes. Reduce mixing speed and gradually beat in flour and cocoa. Pour into prepared pan and bake at 350° for 25 minutes or until a toothpick inserted comes out clean. Cool in pan for 10 minutes, unmold, and remove wax paper. Freeze 1 hour, then slice into 3 layers.

TO ASSEMBLE

Fold together pastry cream, Chantilly cream, and

chocolate couverture in large bowl to make mousse filling. Refrigerate for at least 3 to 4 hours.

Place bottom layer of cake, cut side up, on cake plate and brush with rum syrup. Spread mousse in thick layer, add second cake layer and repeat process. Top with third layer and brush with remaining rum syrup. Ice top and sides of cake with remaining mousse. Chill a few hours.

Chef Pierre Dupont
1789 Restaurant

Helene Berman's Best Devil's Food Cake

Serves 12 to 14

CAKE
¼ pound butter
2 scant cups superfine sugar
2 eggs
1 scant teaspoon salt
1 teaspoon baking powder
3 full cups cake flour
2 cups buttermilk
2 scant teaspoons baking soda
2 squares semi-sweet baking chocolate
1 teaspoon vanilla

ICING
1 cup water
1 teaspoon butter
2 squares semi-sweet baking chocolate
½ cup superfine sugar
1 heaping tablespoon cornstarch
1 teaspoon vanilla

CAKE

Cream butter and gradually add sugar. Add eggs, one at a time. Sift flour 3 times; then add salt and baking powder. Melt chocolate. Sift baking soda into buttermilk and stir. Add melted chocolate to creamed mixture; then add vanilla. Add flour and buttermilk to creamed mixture alternately, beginning and ending with flour. Beat at low speed.

Grease a $13 \times 9 \times 2$-inch pan and line with wax paper. Pour batter into pan and bake at 350° for 45 to 50 minutes, or until a toothpick inserted in center comes out dry. Cool on rack for 15 minutes, turn out on tray and remove wax paper.

ICING

Melt butter and chocolate in water over low heat. Mix cornstarch into sugar. Add gradually to butter-chocolate mixture, stirring until it thickens like chocolate pudding and comes to a boil. Remove from heat and add vanilla. Stir until smooth. Frost cake when cool.

Helene Berman

Date Cake

Serves 10 to 12

½ cup butter
1 cup sugar
1 egg
1 cup cake flour
1 teaspoon vanilla
1 cup chopped dates
1 cup boiling water
1 teaspoon baking soda
½ cup chopped pecans
1 teaspoon cinnamon

Cream butter, sugar, and egg. Beat in flour, vanilla, and cinnamon. Set aside.

In another bowl, mix dates, boiling water, and soda. Let stand for 10 minutes. Add to creamed mixture. Stir in nuts.

Pour into well-greased, 8-inch square pan and bake at 375° for 30 minutes.

Delicious and moist. Serve warm with dollop of whipped cream.

JoAnn Mason

Garrity's Dark and Spicy Fruitcake

Makes 10 cakes

This is a 30 year old recipe. Cakes can be frozen for up to 1 year.

1 pint Cointreau or bourbon
2 pounds golden raisins
3 pounds candied, mixed fruit
¼ pound candied cherries, unsliced for top of cakes
¼ pound candied pineapple, unsliced for top of cakes
1 pound almonds
1 pound walnuts
1 pound pecans
1 pound figs
7 cups flour
3 cups honey
1½ cups molasses

1 pound dark brown sugar
2 tablespoons almond extract
2 tablespoons vanilla
2 tablespoons lemon extract
2 teaspoons baking soda
1½ cups buttermilk
16 eggs
1 pound butter
2 teaspoons allspice
2 teaspoons cloves
2 teaspoons mace
2 teaspoons cinammon
2 teaspoons nutmeg

Procedures begin on opposite page.

DAY ONE

Combine fruit, raisins, freshly-shelled nuts, and cut-up figs and dates in large container. Pour 1 pint Cointreau or bourbon and honey over fruit and nut mixture. Stir, cover, and let sit overnight at room temperature, stirring occasionally.

DAY TWO

Grease sides and bottom of 10, 1-pound coffee cans and line bottom and sides with brown paper, using a double thickness on bottom. This prevents excessive browning. Let brown paper stick 2 inches above top of can.

Cream butter and sugar in electric mixer. Set aside. Sift flour, baking soda, and spices together 3 times. Make sure spices are blended well. Stir one third of flour mixture into fruit and nut mixture. Use hands to mix well. Set other two thirds flour aside.

Add eggs, molasses, extracts, and buttermilk to creamed mixture. Using electric mixer, combine all ingredients and beat at medium speed for 1 to 2 minutes. Add remaining flour mixture and combine. Handle this mixture as little as possible. Pour batter over fruit-nut mixture and mix with hands from bottom up until batter is evenly distributed.

Fill coffee cans an inch or so from top. Place in 300° oven and bake for 2½ hours or until broom straw comes out clean. *DO NOT OVERBAKE.* Let cool in can for 1 hour. Remove from can and take off brown paper. Wrap cakes in bourbon-soaked cheesecloth. Wrap in aluminum foil and place in plastic airtight bag; let cakes sit for 3 weeks.

M. Henry Garrity

Susan Porter's Party Genoise

Serves 12 to 15

CAKE
6 large eggs at room
   temperature
1 cup superfine sugar
1 teaspoon vanilla
1 cup cake flour, sifted
3 ounces unsalted butter,
   clarified and melted,
   at room temperature

FRENCH BUTTERCREAM
 10 egg yolks
⅔–¾ cup water
1½ cups sugar
    Pinch cream of
    tartar
  5 ounces bittersweet
    chocolate
4½ sticks unsalted
    butter, softened
  4 tablespoons dark rum
 ¾ cup pecans

JAM
1 cup apricot jam,
   cooked and cooled

GANACHE
¾ pound semi-sweet
   chocolate, cut into
   pieces
1 cup crème frâiche or
   whipping cream

CAKE

Preheat oven to 350°. Butter 2, 8-inch cake tins and place a wax paper round in bottom of each. Butter and flour paper. In bowl of an electric mixer beat eggs and sugar slowly. Add vanilla and beat slowly for 15 minutes; eggs should hold their shape. Using a slotted spoon, add flour very gently to egg-sugar mixture. Add butter by spoonfuls, then by dribbles and combine.

Place 3 large spoonfuls into each cake tin to evenly distribute batter. Bake until cake shrinks from sides of tin and springs back when pressed, about 28 minutes. When cool, cut each cake in half slightly above halfway point. Place wax paper between cake layers and refrigerate. Place cake in plastic bag. Cake can be frozen at this point.

BUTTERCREAM

Beat egg yolks for 15 minutes with electric mixer. Place water, sugar, and cream of tartar in saucepan. Bring to boil without stirring, shaking pan gently from time to time. Wash down crystals with a pastry brush dipped in cold water. Heat to 238° on a candy thermometer. In a slow stream, add bubbling sugar syrup to egg yolks by letting it run down sides of bowl while continuing to beat eggs. Cool.

Melt chocolate in a double boiler. Add 4½ sticks of butter to egg mixture. Divide cream into separate bowls, one third and two thirds. Add chocolate to two thirds of mixture and stir in 1½ teaspoons rum. Add nuts and remaining rum to remaining one third of cream.

GANACHE

Place chocolate in a bowl. Bring cream to a boil and pour over chocolate. Let sit for 3 minutes. Blend with a wire whisk until smooth and shiny. Cool. May be refrigerated and brought to room temperature when ready to use.

TO ASSEMBLE

Place a layer of cake on a serving plate. Spread with ganache. Top with cake layer. Spread apricot jam forced through a sieve and top with cake layer. Spread with chocolate buttercream and top with final layer. Spread top and sides of cake with nut buttercream. Refrigerate. Can be frozen for 2 weeks. To serve, defrost in refrigerator overnight.

Susan Porter

Grand Marnier Cake

Serves 8 to 12

CAKE

1 cup butter, at room temperature
1 cup sugar
3 eggs, separated
1 tablespoon Grand Marnier
2 cups sifted flour
¾ teaspoon baking powder
¾ teaspoon baking soda
1 cup sour cream
½ teaspoon grated orange rind
½ cup ground walnuts

SYRUP

¼ cup fresh orange juice
½ cup sugar
⅓ cup Grand Marnier
⅓ cup slivered, toasted almonds

Cream butter with sugar until light and fluffy. Add 3 egg yolks, one at a time, beating after each addition. Mix in Grand Marnier.

Sift flour, baking powder, and baking soda. Add to butter mixture alternately with sour cream, using one third of dry ingredients and one half of sour cream each time. Stir in orange rind and nuts.

Beat egg whites until stiff but not dry. Fold mixture gently into egg whites.

Place in lightly buttered, 9-inch, tube pan and bake 50 to 55 minutes at 350 degrees.

SYRUP

Combine orange juice, sugar, and Grand Marnier. Spoon over hot cake and let cake cool in pan before removing it. Stud top of cake with toasted, slivered almonds standing upright.

Gwen Holmes
Barbara Phillips

Mennonite Oatmeal Cake

Serves 10 to 12

½ cup flour
1 teaspoon baking soda
1 teaspoon cinnamon
1 teaspoon ground
   cloves
½ teaspoon salt
1 cup boiling water
2 cups rolled oats
¾ cup butter

2 cups brown sugar
2 eggs
1½ cups finely chopped
   dates
1½ cups chopped
   walnuts

Sift together flour, baking soda, cinnamon, cloves, and salt.

Pour boiling water over rolled oats and mix well. Cool slightly. Blend in butter, brown sugar, eggs, chopped dates, and chopped walnuts.

Pour mixture into dry ingredients and mix well. Bake in buttered and floured 8-inch square pan for 45 minutes at 350°.

Makes a nice tea cake.

Sally Wile

Grandmother's Orange Raisin Cake

Serves 12 to 15

1 orange
½ cup sour milk
1 cup raisins
½ cup butter
1 cup white sugar
2 eggs
2 cups flour
1½ teaspoons baking
   powder
½ teaspoon baking
   soda
½ teaspoon salt

Squeeze orange and add juice to sour milk. Put orange peels and raisins through a chopper. Reserve 2 tablespoons of raisins and peels for frosting.

Cream butter, gradually adding sugar. Add eggs and beat well. Sift together dry ingredients and add to creamed mixture alternately with milk and orange juice. Fold in raisin and orange mixture. Place in a 9 × 9-inch, greased pan and bake at 350° 40 to 45 minutes.

Frost with a buttercream frosting to which reserved raisins and orange peel have been added.

Maureen Forrester

Pineapple Macadamia Cake

Makes 2 large or
3 small loaves

CANDIED PINEAPPLE

- 3 20-ounce cans pineapple chunks, undrained
- 3 cups sugar
- 1½ cups light corn syrup
- 2 tablespoons butter

CAKE

- ¾ cup butter
- 1½ cups sugar
- 5 large eggs
- 2 cups flour
- 2 tablespoons milk
- 1 teaspoon vanilla
- 1½ cups chopped macadamia nuts
- 1 cup flaked coconut

CANDIED PINEAPPLE

Combine all ingredients except butter in saucepan and boil gently for 50 minutes. Add butter and cook 10 minutes longer. Remove pineapple with slotted spoon to rack or wax paper. Cool several hours or overnight. Makes about 5 cups candied pineapple.

CAKE

Using electric mixer, cream butter and sugar at low speed. Add eggs, one at a time. Add 1¾ cups flour to creamed mixture alternately with milk to which vanilla has been added.

Coat nuts, coconut, and 4 cups candied pineapple with ¼ cup flour. Add to mixture.

Pour into 2 large or 3 small pans lined with wax paper. Press remaining pineapple into top of batter. Bake at 300° for 1¼ to 1½ hours, until toothpick comes out clean from center of cake. Cool in pan on rack for 15 minutes, then turn onto rack and cool completely.

Save the pineapple syrup for ice cream or pancakes.

Frances L. Fentress

East Texas Pound Cake

Serves 12 to 20

CAKE
½ pound butter
1¾ cups sugar
5–6 eggs
2 cups sifted flour
1 teaspoon vanilla

RUM GLAZE
½ cup sugar
¼ cup water
1 ounce dark rum or
1 tablespoon rum
    extract

CAKE

The pound cake that sold so well at the FANS Auction.

Preheat oven to 325°. Grease and flour tube pan or 2 standard loaf pans.

Cream together sugar and butter in bowl of an electric mixer. Add eggs, one at a time, beating well. Add flour slowly, again beating well. Add vanilla.

Bake at 325° for about 1½ hours in middle of oven. Check after 1 hour. Cake is done when it leaves sides of pan. Cool in pan for 5 to 10 minutes; then turn out onto a rack. Cooking time should be shortened if using loaf pans; check after 45 minutes.

RUM GLAZE

Combine sugar and water in saucepan and bring to a bubbling boil. Boil for 3 seconds, remove from heat, and add rum. Drizzle over cake while both are still warm.

The ideal working person's cake. Put out eggs and butter before leaving in the morning, combine ingredients in the evening and bake while eating supper!

Gus S. Morris

"Ton" Cake

Serves 12 to 16

½ pound butter
8 ounces cream cheese
2 cups sugar
2 teaspoons vanilla
2 teaspoons lemon
    juice, or to taste
5 eggs, slightly beaten
2 cups self-rising flour

Cream together cream cheese and sugar. Mix with remaining ingredients for 3 minutes.

Bake at 350° for 1 hour in a tube pan. This is a very rich and heavy cake.

Pamela Powers

Bourbon Pound Cake

Serves 12 to 20

1 pound butter
3 cups sugar
8 eggs, separated
¼ teaspoon salt
3 cups all-purpose flour, sifted before measuring
½ cup chopped pecans
1½ tablespoons bourbon
2 teaspoons vanilla
2 teaspoons almond extract

Cream butter and sugar. Add egg yolks, one at a time, beating after each addition. Add flour gradually.

Beat egg whites until stiff. Fold into creamed mixture. Add bourbon, vanilla, almond extract, and salt.

Line bottom of a large tube pan with wax paper. Cover bottom of pan with chopped pecans and pour batter over them. Bake in preheated 325° oven for 1½ hours. Turn off oven and let cake stand for 5 minutes. Remove to a cake cooling rack. When pan is cool to touch, remove cake and wax paper. Do not open oven door until a few minutes before 1½ hours is up.

Linda Taylor

Pumpkin Cake

Serves 12 to 20

4 cups unbleached flour
1 teaspoon salt
2 rounded teaspoons baking powder
2 rounded teaspoons baking soda
4 teaspoons cinnamon
½ teaspoon powdered ginger
¼ teaspoon powdered cloves
¼ teaspoon nutmeg
¼ teaspoon allspice
1½ cups raisins
2 cups walnuts, chopped
2 cups plain, canned pumpkin
2¼ cups sugar
1¼ cups sunflower oil
7 large eggs, at room temperature

Good as breakfast bread.

Preheat oven to 350°. Grease 12-cup bundt pan.

Sift together first 4 ingredients; stir in spices.

In large bowl of electric mixer place pumpkin, sugar, and oil. Beat at medium speed until smooth. Add eggs, one at a time, beating after each addition. Beat mixture at medium speed until bubbles form.

Fold in flour-spice mixture. Fold in raisins and nuts. Pour into prepared pan and level off with spatula.

Bake for 1 hour or until done. Do not open oven door until cake has baked at least 45 minutes. Cool upright for 10 minutes, then invert onto rack.

Lewis Lipnick
NSO Member

Renaissance Cake

Serves 8

1 cup butter
¾ cup honey
2 eggs, lightly beaten
1 cup flour
½ cup chopped dates or
   figs
⅛ cup pine nuts,
   coarsely chopped

Place room-temperature butter and honey in large bowl and cream together. Add eggs and flour, a little at a time, to make smooth batter. Add dates and pine nuts and mix. Place in 9-inch pie plate or 8 × 8-inch baking dish. Bake at 375° for 40 minutes.

Richard Skinner

Almond Orange Torte

Serves 10 to 12

2 navel oranges
1½ cups ground
   blanched almonds
6 eggs
⅛ teaspoon salt
1 teaspoon baking
   powder
1 cup granulated sugar
1 cup whipping cream
1 tablespoon Amaretto

Place unpeeled oranges in saucepan with enough water to cover. Simmer for 1½ hours or until very soft. Drain and cool. Remove navel and any seeds. Purée oranges in food processor.

Butter and flour a 9-inch springform pan.

Beat eggs until light. Add to eggs salt, baking powder, sugar, orange purée, and almonds. Pour batter into prepared pan. Bake at 400° for 1 hour, until a toothpick inserted in center comes clean. Cool in pan. Remove and top with whipped cream flavored with Amaretto.

Cake can be made ahead and frozen without topping.

Noelle Vitt

Strawberry Shortcake Torte

Serves 12

9 egg whites
1½ cups sugar
¾ cup blanched almonds, finely chopped or ground
1 teaspoon vanilla
1 quart strawberries, cut and sugared

1 pint heavy cream, whipped

In large bowl, at room temperature, beat egg whites until stiff and dry. Add sugar gradually and continue beating. Add vanilla and fold in almonds. Spread evenly in 2 buttered and floured cake pans; bake at 325° for 25 to 30 minutes.

When cool, split layers; put strawberries and whipped cream between layers and on top. Garnish cake with whole strawberries and whipped cream. Refrigerate. Best made day of serving.

Mrs. Max Rudolf

Walnut Torte

Serves 8 to 10

TORTE
3 extra large egg whites
1 cup sugar
½ teaspoon cream of tartar
20 Ritz crackers, rolled fine
¾ cup chopped walnuts
1 teaspoon vanilla extract

TOPPING
½ pint whipping cream
¼ cup dark brown sugar
¼ cup chopped walnuts
Walnut halves

TORTE

Beat egg whites until almost stiff. Gradually beat in sugar and cream of tartar. Continue beating until very stiff and peaks form. Fold in crackers, nuts, and vanilla. Pour into well-greased, 10-inch, pie plate. Bake at 350° for 25 to 30 minutes. Cool completely.

TOPPING

Make while torte is cooling.

Whip cream until it begins to thicken, then add brown sugar and continue to whip until very thick. Add nuts. Cover torte with topping and decorate with walnut halves.

Ann Woollatt

Laura's Raspberry Walnut Torte

Serves 8

TORTE
1 cup flour
⅓ cup superfine sugar
½ cup butter
1 package frozen
   raspberries, thawed
¾ cup chopped walnuts

FILLING
2 eggs
1 cup sugar
¼ cup flour
½ teaspoon baking
   powder
½ teaspoon salt
1 teaspoon vanilla

SAUCE
½ cup sugar
2 tablespoons
   cornstarch
½ cup water
   Raspberry juice
1 tablespoon lemon
   juice

For torte combine flour, sugar, and butter. Press into ungreased 9-inch pan. Bake at 350° for 15 minutes and cool. Drain raspberries, reserving liquid for sauce. Spread berries over crust; add walnuts.

For filling mix ingredients. Pour into crust.

Bake at 350°, 30 to 35 minutes. Cool and cut in squares. Serve with sauce and whipped cream.

For sauce combine all ingredients except lemon juice in a small saucepan. Cook until clear. Stir in lemon juice.

Gerry Englund

Grape Torte

Serves 6 to 8

PASTRY
⅓ cup hazelnuts,
   ground fine
⅓ cup sugar
9 tablespoons butter
1 cup flour
2–3 tablespoons milk

FILLING
2 tablespoons apricot
   jam
1 cup grated walnuts
½ cup sugar
4 tablespoons milk
3 tablespoons brandy
¼ pound grapes
   Pastry glaze

For pastry, cream butter and ⅓ cup sugar. Add hazelnuts, flour, and milk. Press dough in any type of pyrex or cake pan; size can vary. Bake at 350° for 20 minutes.

For filling, mix grated walnuts, ½ cup sugar, milk, and brandy.

Spread top of cake with apricot jam. Spread filling over jam. Stand grapes into creamy filling. Top with clear instant pastry glaze.

Walter Klien

Gateau Diane

Serves 8

CAKE

2 large egg whites
4½ ounces superfine
      sugar

FILLING

1 large egg white
2 ounces confectioners
      sugar
4 ounces butter
2 ounces semi-sweet
      baking chocolate
   Chopped, browned
      almonds
   Confectioners sugar

CAKE

Whip 2 egg whites until stiff. Beat in 1 tablespoon sugar and fold in rest. Do not overfold.

On a buttered and floured baking sheet, spread mixture into 2 rounds about ¼ inch thick. Bake in very slow oven (225° to 250°) until firm, approximately 1½ hours. Turn oven off. Very carefully turn rounds over and dry in cool oven.

FILLING

Melt chocolate in a dish placed over water. Heat gently. Cool. Cream butter well.

Whip egg white with confectioners sugar over gentle heat until thick. Then beat until cool. Beat this meringue mixture into creamed butter by degrees. Add cooled chocolate.

TO ASSEMBLE

Sandwich cake rounds with chocolate cream filling. Spread cream over sides and top, and cover sides and top with chopped almonds.

Cut 3 strips of wax paper about 1½ inchs wide. Lay them across cake diagonally and dust with confectioners sugar. Remove wax paper.

Freezes well. Can be made a day ahead as well.

Cookbook Committee

Apricot Hearts

Makes about 2 dozen hearts

1 cup sifted flour
   Pinch of salt
½ cup butter
4 ounces cream cheese
   Apricot jam
1 egg

Into a bowl, sift flour and salt. Add butter and cheese. With pastry blender, cut butter and cheese into flour mixture until well blended. (Food processor does this beautifully.)

Lightly shape into ball, wrap dough in wax paper, and refrigerate until well chilled; otherwise, dough will get soft and sticky.

Heat oven to 400°. Lightly grease 2 cookie sheets. On a floured board, roll out dough fairly thin. Cut into hearts.

Place 1 teaspoon of jam on half of hearts. Brush edges with beaten egg. Cover with another heart and press edges together.

Arrange on cookie sheets. Brush tops with beaten egg. Sprinkle with sugar and bake approximately 10 to 12 minutes.

Mrs. Eugene Ormandy

Crispy Cookies

Makes 3 dozen

¼ pound softened butter
4 ounces softened cream
     cheese
½ cup sugar
1 cup sifted flour
     Ground walnuts for
       sprinkling on top

Place all ingredients in bowl and mix well.

Drop by teaspoons onto ungreased cookie sheet, flatten very thin and sprinkle with ground walnuts.

Bake for 10 to 12 minutes in a 350° oven. Edges should be brown. Remove at once with spatula to cool. Cookies keep well in tightly covered container and will remain very crispy.

Peter Lindemann
NSO Member

Crunchy Lace Cookies

Makes approximately
4 dozen

1 cup oatmeal
¾ cup sugar
3 tablespoons flour
½ teaspoon vanilla,
     lemon, or almond
       extract
¼ teaspoon salt
½ teaspoon baking
       powder
1 stick butter
1 egg

Melt butter and pour over oatmeal, sugar, flour, extract flavoring, salt, and baking powder. Add egg and mix well.

Drop by half teaspoons on foil about 3 to 4 inches apart (they will spread). Bake at 350° for 7 to 9 minutes, or until light brown. Leave on foil to cool.

Marilyn Erickson

Armenian Butter Cookies

Makes 4 to 5 dozen

2 cups sifted flour
8 tablespoons sugar
½ pound butter
1 teaspoon vanilla
  Cinnamon-sugar
    mixture

Mix together all ingredients.
Divide pastry into 2 or 3 rolls. Wrap each roll in wax paper and refrigerate.
Slice into ¼-inch slices and place them onto cookie sheet. Sprinkle with a mixture of cinnamon and sugar. Bake at 350° for about 10 minutes or until lightly brown.

JoAnn Mason

Almond Cookies

Makes at least 6 dozen

6 cups flour
1½ teaspoons baking
    soda
1 teaspoon salt
2 cups sugar
2½ cups shortening
2 eggs
2–3 teaspoons almond
    extract

"They may not be authentic cookies from Luxembourg, but I do promise they have become the favorite cookies of the Luxembourg Embassy since my marriage."

Cream together sugar and shortening. Add eggs one at a time. Add sifted flour, soda, and salt. Add almond extract.
Roll dough into balls and press with thumb to make a hole in the middle.
Bake at 350° for 20 minutes or until done (very light brown).

*Candace Johnson Meisch
Wife of the Ambassador of Luxembourg*

Quick Almond Cookies

Makes 3 dozen

½ cup shortening (not
      butter)
1 cup sugar
1 egg
1 teaspoon almond
      extract
¼–½ cup crushed
      almonds
1½ cups Bisquick

Mix all ingredients. Drop by teaspoons onto greased cookie sheet.

Bake at 350° for 5 to 10 minutes. Cool on rack. Store in an airtight container until ready to serve.

Mrs. Roger Mudd

Auntie I's Mandelbrot

Makes 3 dozen

1½ cups flour
2 teaspoons baking
      powder
2 teaspoons almond
      extract
4 beaten eggs
1 cup sugar
¾ cup corn oil
1 cup coarsely chopped
      walnuts or pecans

Preheat oven to 350°. Grease and flour 3 metal ice cube trays.

Mix all ingredients together. Divide batter into 3 parts and fill trays.

Bake until browned, about 20 to 30 minutes. Turn out tins on cutting board to cool. Cut the individual squares of pastry with a sharp knife.

Place slices on cookie sheet and return to a 350° oven to crisp and brown on both sides. Freezes and stores well.

Mrs. Joseph Weinstein

"Good" Cookies

Makes 3 dozen

½ cup butter
½ cup margarine
1 cup brown sugar
2 eggs
1¼ cups wheat germ
2 teaspoons vanilla
1 teaspoon almond extract
1½ cups whole wheat flour
3 tablespoons white flour
⅔ cup non-instant powdered milk (buy in health food store)
1 tablespoon double acting baking powder
½ teaspoon salt
1 6-ounce package chocolate chips
1 cup chopped walnuts
1 cup sunflower seeds, optional

Cream together butter, margarine, and brown sugar. Add and mix well the eggs, wheat germ, vanilla and almond extracts.

Sift wheat flour, white flour, powdered milk, baking powder, and salt. Add and mix well with batter (batter will be stiff). Add chocolate chips, nuts and seeds.

Form dough into a long 2 to 2½-inch diameter roll. Wrap in foil. Freeze until hard.

Preheat oven at 350°. Grease cookie sheets. Slice dough into ¼-inch pieces. Bake for 12 to 15 minutes. Allow cookies to cool a few minutes before removing from cookie sheet.

Marisa Ryan

Brownies for Thin People Only!

Makes approximately
30 brownies

4 eggs
2 cups sugar
1 cup butter
4 ounces unsweetened
   chocolate
1 cup sifted flour
   6-ounce package
   chocolate chips

Beat eggs and sugar together until thick and light.
Melt butter and chocolate together; add to eggs.
   Mix in flour; add chocolate chips. Pour into greased
and floured 7 × 11-inch pan.
   Bake in preheated 350° oven for 20 to 30 minutes. Cool
in pan and cut into squares.

Martha Goodman

Val's Brownies

Makes 36 small squares

½ pound butter
4 ounces unsweetened
   chocolate
3 eggs
2 cups sugar
1–2 teaspoons vanilla
   (almond or mint can
   be substituted for
   second teaspoon
   vanilla)
1 cup flour

Melt butter and chocolate (do not boil).
   Beat eggs with sugar; add flavoring and melted butter-
chocolate mixture.
   Gradually add flour. Do not over beat.
   Preheat oven to 350°. Grease 9 × 9-inch pan. Pour
batter into pan. Bake for 45 minutes.

Valerie Lapcinski

Chocolate Nut Bars

Makes 4 dozen

½ cup butter
1 cup brown sugar
1 cup white sugar
2 eggs
2 teaspoons vanilla
2 cups flour
½ teaspoon soda
½ teaspoon salt
1 cup semi-sweet
   chocolate chips
1 cup chopped nuts,
   optional

Cream butter and sugar. Add egg and vanilla. Beat well.

Sift together flour, salt, and soda. Add to creamy mixture. Stir in chocolate chips and nuts.

Spread batter into 2, greased, 11×7×2-inch pans. Push down; batter will rise. Bake 20 to 25 minutes at 375°.

Cut into squares while warm.

Norma Dugger

Raisin Bars

Makes approximately
5 dozen squares

1 cup seedless raisins
1⅛ cups water
½ cup butter
1 cup sugar
1 teaspoon salt
1 teaspoon baking
   soda
1 egg
1¾ cups flour

½ teaspoon cinnamon
½ teaspoon nutmeg
¼ teaspoon mace
¼ teaspoon cloves
½ cup chopped nuts
1 lemon, juiced and
   rind grated
Confectioners sugar

Boil raisins in water in large, covered saucepan for 4 or 5 minutes until raisins are plump and soft.

Add butter, stirring until melted. Add sugar, salt, and baking soda. Cool slightly.

Beat in egg. Sift dry ingredients and add to mixture. Add nuts.

Bake in 10×15-inch pan for 20 minutes at 375°. Remove when done and cool.

To make frosting, mix lemon juice, grated rind, and confectioners sugar to desired consistency. Frost and cut into squares.

Virginia Harpham
NSO Member

Apricot Squares

Makes about 2 or 3 dozen

1 cup sugar
2 cups flour
¾ cup butter
1¼ cups coconut
½ cup chopped nuts
  12-ounce jar apricot
  jam (or raspberry)

Mix all ingredients except jam.

Spread ½ of batter into a 9 × 9-inch ungreased baking pan and pat down. Cover with jam. Add remaining batter and pat down.

Bake at 350° for approximately 30 to 35 minutes. Remove when done; cool slightly and cut into squares.

Pat Byram

Raisin- Filled Cookies

Makes 2 to 2½ dozen

1 cup white sugar
1 cup brown sugar
1 cup butter
5 cups flour
3 eggs
1 teaspoon baking
  powder
½ teaspoon salt
½ teaspoon cinnamon
1 teaspoon baking soda
1 tablespoon sour milk
2 teaspoons vanilla
1 cup raisins
¾ cup sugar
1 cup water

1 heaping tablespoon
  cornstarch
1 teaspoon vanilla
  Lemon juice to taste
1 cup nuts

Cream sugars and butter together; then add eggs. Sift dry ingredients and blend well with creamy mixture.

Dissolve baking soda in sour milk. Mix with vanilla and add to batter.

Roll onto a floured board to about ⅛-inch thickness. Set aside in cool place while preparing filling.

To make filling, cook raisins, sugar, water, cornstarch, vanilla, lemon juice and nuts until thickened. Cool.

Cut rolled dough with cookie cutter (doughnut size), leaving cutter on dough. Place a teaspoon of filling in cutter; top with another round of cookie dough; then press top and bottom together.

Bake for 10 to 12 minutes at 375°.

Sally Hedrick

Orange Cookies

Makes 4 to 5 dozen

2 cups white sugar
1 cup butter
2 eggs
4 cups flour
1 teaspoon baking
    powder
1 cup sour cream
    Juice and grated rind
    of 2 oranges and
    1 lemon
1 teaspoon baking soda
    Confectioners sugar
½ stick butter
    Orange and lemon
    juices enough for
    preferred consistency

Cream together sugar and butter; add eggs. Sift dry ingredients, adding alternately with sour cream and juice mixture. Add flour last.

Drop by teaspoons onto a greased cookie sheet. Bake at 375° for 12 to 15 minutes.

After removing from oven, let cool. Frost with topping of confectioners sugar, butter and juice mixed until preferred consistency.

Sally Hedrick

Beth's Frosted Shortbread

Makes 2 dozen

1 cup soft butter
½ cup light brown sugar
2 cups flour
2 teaspoons vanilla
6 ounces semi-sweet
    chocolate
½ cup chopped nuts

Cream butter 10 minutes. Add sugar and beat an additional 10 minutes. Slowly add flour and beat 5 minutes more. Add vanilla.

Press dough into 11 × 15-inch jelly roll pan. Bake in preheated 325° oven for 25 to 30 minutes until golden brown.

Melt chocolate; cool slightly and spread over warm cookies. Sprinkle with nuts. Cut into squares in the pan and remove.

Wonderful right out of the freezer.

Mrs. Edward J. Leonard

Scotch Shortbread

Serves 8 to 10

2 cups flour
1 cup butter
½ cup sugar

Cream sugar and butter together. Add flour gradually.

Press out smoothly onto an ungreased cookie sheet, keeping dough a generous ¼-inch in thickness. Sprinkle evenly with granulated sugar and prick freely with a fork.

Bake in a preheated 300° oven for about 45 minutes or until light brown. Cut into squares and cool on cookie sheet.

Holly Bodman

Butter Crunch Ice Cream Topping

Makes about 2 to 2½ cups

½ cup butter
¼ cup brown sugar
1 cup sifted flour
½ cup chopped pecans
     or walnuts

Cream together butter and sugar. Add flour and nuts and mix thoroughly.

Spread mixture into a 9 × 12-inch pan. Bake in preheated 400° oven for 15 minutes.

Remove from oven; cool. Break up with a fork. Can be stored in a well-sealed container in refrigerator indefinitely.

Gloria Hamilton

Peanut Brittle

Makes 3½ pounds

3 cups granulated sugar
1½ cups water
1 cup white corn syrup
3 cups raw peanuts
2 tablespoons baking soda
½ stick butter
1 teaspoon vanilla

Boil sugar, water, and syrup until it spins thread; add peanuts. After adding peanuts, stir continually until syrup turns golden brown.

Remove from heat and add remaining ingredients. Stir until butter melts.

Pour quickly onto 2 cookie sheets with sides. As mixture begins to harden around the edges, pull until thin.

The Jimmy Carter Family

Chocolate Peanut Butter Cups

Makes about 4 dozen small candies

⅓ cup creamy or super chunk peanut butter
⅓ cup butter, softened
1⅔ cups sifted confectioners sugar
12-ounce package semi-sweet or milk chocolate pieces, melted

Place miniature muffin cups on tray.

In medium bowl stir together peanut butter and butter until blended. Gradually stir in confectioners sugar.

Turn onto board. Knead until smooth. Press with hands or roll out to ½-inch thickness. Cut into ½-inch circles with small cookie cutter.

Spoon some chocolate into paper cups to cover bottom generously. Place one peanut butter circle on top of chocolate in each cup. Gently push down to coat sides. Spread additional chocolate over top, making sure sides are completely coated.

Chill until firm. Store in refrigerator.

Gene A. Burns

Molded Mints

Makes about 60 mints

3 ounces cream cheese
16 ounces confectioners sugar
Mint flavorings
Superfine sugar, for dipping
Food coloring, if desired
Small rubber molds

Mix cream cheese with confectioners sugar until completely smooth. Add flavoring (peppermint, wintergreen, etc.) and mix. Then add desired food coloring.

Take enough mixture to put into small rubber mold that has been dipped into superfine sugar. Press into mold and turn mold over. Release mint onto waxed paper.

I mix the colors to make prettier designs or flowers, etc. (example: green stem, white flower, yellow center). These are time consuming to make, but worth it. Can be frozen or refrigerated.

Gwen Holmes

Mint Squares

Makes many squares depending on how large you slice them

1 cup sugar
1 cup butter
4 eggs
1 cup flour
½ teaspoon salt
1 teaspoon vanilla
16-ounce can chocolate syrup
2 cups confectioners sugar
½ cup butter
4 tablespoons crème de menthe
6-ounce package chocolate chips
6 tablespoons butter

"A little goes a long way."

Cream together sugar and butter. Add eggs, flour, salt, vanilla, and chocolate syrup.

Bake in 9 × 13-inch greased pan for 30 to 40 minutes at 350°. Cool.

Mix together confectioners sugar, butter, and crème de menthe. Spread over cooled cake and refrigerate until top layer stiffens.

Melt chocolate chips and butter. Cool slightly and dribble on as frosting. Store in refrigerator. Tends to melt if kept out of refrigerator very long.

Julie Smith

Swiss Kiss

Makes 20 to 40 kisses, depending on size

FILLING
3 ounces soft butter, unsalted
2 ounces confectioners sugar, sifted
4 ounces semi-sweet chocolate, melted
½ to 1 ounce of kirsch, rum or Grand Marnier

CHOCOLATE FOR DIPPING
1 pound of chocolate, tempered (see directions)

In a mixing bowl (1 to 2 quarts), place butter. Mix with a mixer on medium-high speed to thoroughly cream butter. It should be light and fluffy.

Add confectioners sugar and mix well. Add melted chocolate and mix well. Add kirsch and mix well. Place bowl in a cool place.

Temper chocolate (directions follow).

Place a sheet of wax paper on a cookie sheet. Make a piping bag out of wax paper. Fill with about 1 ounce of tempered chocolate. Make a small hole at tip of piping bag to pipe chocolate through.

Pipe 20 to 30 small dots onto wax paper, using between ¼ and ⅛ teaspoon of chocolate for each dot. (You may need to refill bag.) Then bang cookie sheet down on work surface very hard to spread out dots to about size of a quarter. Place cookie sheet containing chocolate dots in refrigerator to harden.

Fill a pastry bag (use a #6 star tube) with Swiss candy filling and pipe stars on chocolate dots. Filling should be in shape of a hershey kiss and about that size.

Remove candies one at a time from wax paper onto a chocolate dipping fork and dip into tempered chocolate. Allow to cool and harden on a wire rack. Do not refrigerate. When hard, place in paper candy cups and refrigerate in tin for up to 2 weeks.

TEMPERED CHOCOLATE

Chocolate needs to be tempered when using for decoration or for dipping candies and fruit. The cocoa, cocoa butter, and other ingredients are blended together so they do not separate when cooling.

Use a *couveture* such as Krön or Carma brand.

Cut chocolate into small pieces, about 1-inch squares.

Place hot water in bottom pan of double boiler. Place over low heat. Water should never boil. Place top pan of double boiler over hot water, making sure it does not touch water.

Continued

Swiss Kiss

Add pieces of chocolate. Stir chocolate well while it is melting. As soon as most of chocolate is melted, remove from heat.

Use a bowl that is large enough to hold top pan of double boiler. Fill it with ice and some water (about 1 cup water to 2 trays of ice cubes).

Place pan with chocolate over ice. Stir chocolate constantly to cool down. It will become very thick. Do not cool it down so much that chocolate hardens again. Place double boiler back over low heat to warm chocolate gently to consistency desired.

To test if chocolate is tempered, place end of a kitchen knife in chocolate about ¾ inch, at room temperature (no higher than 68°). The chocolate, when hardened, should be shiny with no white streaks in it. If it is dull or has streaks in it, you must begin tempering process all over again.

Julia M. Logue-Riordan

P A S T R I E S
P I E S
&
F R U I T   D E S S E R T S

Chocolate Ice Box Dessert

Serves 8 to 10

1 angel food cake
6 eggs
12 ounces chocolate chips
4 tablespoons sugar
6 tablespoons water
2 teaspoons vanilla
1 teaspoon salt
2 cups whipping cream

Line a flat 9×9-inch cake pan with wax paper. Slice angel food cake and place a layer of cake in pan. (Angel food cake slices better when frozen.)

Separate eggs; beat egg yolks.

Melt chocolate chips in a double boiler, add sugar and water, mix well, and be sure sugar melts.

Remove from heat and stir hot chocolate mixture gradually into beaten egg yolks and beat until smooth. Cool chocolate mixture completely. Add vanilla and salt and mix. Beat egg whites until stiff; whip cream. Fold egg whites into cooled chocolate mixture. Fold in whipped cream. Place a layer of chocolate mixture on sliced angel food cake, then another layer of cake, then a layer of chocolate.

Place in refrigerator and chill overnight. This may be frozen and used later. Be sure to chill overnight before freezing.

Mrs. Gerald Ford

Baklava
à la Grecque

Makes about 25 large pieces
or 50 small ones

1½ packages (about 26 ounces) phyllo, (available in Greek and other specialty stores)
2 cups grated walnuts (do not crush or pulp nuts)
5 ounces white bread crumbs
1½ cups sweet butter
Cinnamon, cloves

SYRUP
5 cups sugar
3½ cups water
Lemon peel

Make syrup by mixing water, sugar, and lemon peel in a saucepan. Boil, stirring with a wooden spoon, for about 10 minutes. Remove from heat and allow to cool. Then add syrup to walnuts and bread crumbs, with cinnamon to taste. Blend well.

Melt butter and brush bottom and sides of a baking pan measuring about 22 × 15 × 2 inches. Place 6 sheets of phyllo on bottom of pan, brushing each sheet with melted butter. Care should be taken to keep unused phyllo sheets covered with a slightly damp towel while preparing pastry. Spread top sheet with syrup and nut mixture; then continue adding sheets of pastry until only 7 sheets are left, buttering each sheet and spreading each thinly but evenly with mixture. Make sure mixture reaches all corners evenly. Put some melted butter around corners. Finish off with last 7 buttered sheets placed on top of each other without any syrup mixture.

Cut into pieces of desired size; place a single clove on each piece and bake at 280° for 3 hours. Remove from oven and pour over remaining syrup which should be cold or lukewarm.

The pastry should not be eaten for at least 12 hours. It keeps well, without refrigeration, for about 3 weeks.

For cocktail parties, serve baklava in bite-size pieces placed in paper cups. Each piece should have its own clove.

Embassy of Greece

Napoleon Nut Roll à la Crème Chantilly

Serves 8 to 10

4 eggs, separated
½ cup sugar
½ cup English walnuts
½ cup regular walnuts
¾ teaspoon baking
    powder
1½ cups whipping cream
2 tablespoons
    confectioners sugar
    Your favorite liqueur

Bring egg yolks and egg whites to room temperature. Finely grind English walnuts and regular walnuts. You should have 1 cup of ground walnuts.

Beat egg yolks and sugar together. Mix ground nuts with baking powder and add to yolk mixture.

Beat egg whites (not too stiff) then fold lightly (do not stir) into yolk and nut mixture.

Carefully grease a 10 × 15 × 1½-inch cookie sheet. Cover bottom with wax paper that has been lightly greased. Pour mixture onto cookie sheet and spread lightly over entire pan. Place in a preheated 350° oven and bake 15 to 20 minutes. (Do not overbake or it will not roll.)

Remove from oven and cover with a damp tea towel. Refrigerate until cold.

Dust with confectioners sugar. Turn nut roll onto sheet of wax paper and slowly peel off wax paper on back. With a spoon, lightly sprinkle surface with your favorite liqueur. Spread surface with whipped cream to which 1 tablespoon of confectioners sugar has been added.

Roll into a log using wax paper on which it is resting. Decorate top with remaining whipped cream and garnish with nuts, sprinkles, or jimmies.

Serve sliced on an angle. You can bake roll ahead, but whipped cream filling has to be done the day you serve it.

Mrs. Sarah G. Epstein

Pashka

Traditional Easter Dessert of Old Russia

Serves 16 to 18

4 8-ounce packages cream cheese
1 cup butter
3 egg yolks
2 cups confectioners sugar
2 teaspoons vanilla
¾ cup chopped, candied citron
¾ cup toasted, slivered almonds
Strawberries

Let cream cheese, butter, and egg yolks stand at room temperature at least 2 hours before making pashka. Place cream cheese in a mixing bowl and beat with a wooden spoon. If an electric mixer is used, blend on low speed. Add butter and continue beating or blending on low speed. When well blended, add sugar, then egg yolks, 1 at a time. Add vanilla. Fold in citron and almonds.

Wash well and dry inside of a 2-quart clay or plastic flowerpot. There should be holes in bottom of pot for drainage. Line pot with a double thickness of cheesecloth, wrung out in cold water. Spoon cheese mixture into pot, filling it to brim. Cover with clear plastic wrap and refrigerate several hours or overnight.

To unmold, trim around and discard top of cheesecloth. Place a dessert plate over flowerpot and invert quickly. Gently lift off pot, tugging at a bit of cheesecloth lining, if necessary. When pot is clear, gently remove cheesecloth.

Garnish base of pashka with whole strawberries and strawberry halves. Serve with additional, crushed, sweetened strawberries made into a sauce.

Dorothy Stahl
NSO Member

Apfelkuchen
Apple Tart
Serves 8

PASTRY DOUGH
1½ sticks butter
1½ cups all-purpose
flour
3 tablespoons cold
water
Dash of salt

LAYER
2 pounds apples
3 tablespoons apricot
marmalade
3 tablespoons Calvados
Roasted almonds for
decoration

Stir together flour and salt; cut in butter until pieces are size of small peas. Sprinkle with water and mix together rapidly. Dough should be pliable (neither dry nor sticky). Wrap in plastic and refrigerate for 12 hours.

Roll chilled dough thinly, about ¹⁄₁₆ inch, into rectangle and place on a cookie sheet.

Core and peel apples; cut into thin, long slices and cover dough. Place in preheated oven and bake for 20 minutes at 450°. Lower temperature to 400° and bake for 10 to 15 minutes.

While Apfelkuchen is baking, heat apricot marmalade with Calvados. Strain sauce, and glaze warm cake and decorate with roasted almonds. Serve warm.

Embassy of Austria

Apple-Cranberry Pie
Serves 6 to 8

9-inch double crust
pastry
¾ cup sugar
2 tablespoons corn-
starch
1 teaspoon cinnamon

2 pounds apples, peeled,
cored, and sliced
(about 6 cups)
1 cup cranberries,
chopped
1 tablespoon butter

Line a 9-inch pie plate with pastry rolled to ⅛ to ½ inch thick, allowing a 1-inch overhang.

In a large bowl stir together sugar, cornstarch, and cinnamon. Toss with apple slices and cranberries until well coated. Turn into pie plate. Dot with butter.

Roll remaining pastry to 12-inch circle. Cut into 10, ½-inch strips with pastry wheel or knife. Place 5 of strips across filling. Weave lattice crust with remaining strips by folding back alternate strips as each cross strip is added. Fold trimmed edge of lower crusts over ends of strips. Seal and flute.

Sprinkle top of pastry lightly with sugar before baking. Bake in 400° oven 15 minutes. Reduce heat to 350° and bake 45 minutes longer or until bubbly and apples are tender.

The cranberries are a tasty and tart addition to this pie.

Gene A. Burns

Sour Cream Apple Pie

Serves 6 to 8

FILLING

2 eggs
½ cup sugar
1 cup sour cream
1½ tablespoons flour
½ teaspoon vanilla
¼ teaspoon salt
4–5 medium to large tart apples, peeled, cored, and thinly sliced

TOPPING

6 tablespoons brown sugar
½ cup flour
3 tablespoons butter, softened

9-inch unbaked pie shell

Preheat oven to 400°. In a medium bowl, beat eggs lightly. Add sugar, sour cream, flour, vanilla, and salt, mixing well. Add apples, tossing until slices are thoroughly coated with mixture. Turn into unbaked pie shell and bake 30 minutes.

For topping, combine in a small bowl sugar, flour, and butter, mixing until crumbly. After 30 minutes remove pie from oven, and lower oven temperature to 350°. Sprinkle topping evenly over pie and return to oven for 15 minutes. Cool 20 minutes and serve while still warm.

John Baird

Avocado Pie

Serves 8

1 prepared crust (butter, chocolate, or graham cracker)
14-ounce can condensed milk
1 avocado, peeled and sliced
⅓ cup lemon juice

2 kiwi fruit or 1 pint strawberries sliced
8 ounces sour cream
2 tablespoons sugar, or to taste
Vanilla

Purée condensed milk, lemon juice, and avocado in blender. Pour into crust.

Mix sour cream with sugar and add vanilla to taste. Let stand until congealed. Spread mixture on top of filling.

Decorate with kiwi or strawberries.

Ruth Sturgis

Banana Cognac Pie

Serves 6 to 10

5   egg yolks
¾   cup sugar
1   envelope unflavored
    gelatin
¼   cup water
½   cup Cognac or
    unflavored brandy

1½ cups heavy cream
2   bananas
1   ounce semi-sweet
    chocolate
10-inch or 2 smaller-
    size graham cracker
    pie shells

Beat egg yolks until thick and lemon colored. Gradually beat in sugar.

In top of a double boiler, soften gelatin in ¼ cup water and ¼ cup Cognac. Heat over boiling water until gelatin dissolves. Pour gelatin mixture into egg yolk and sugar combination, stirring briskly. Stir in remaining ¼ cup Cognac.

Whip 1 cup of cream and fold it into mixture. Cut one of bananas into thin slices and place in a layer in pie shell. Pour filling mixture into pie shell over banana slices.

Chill in refrigerator until set. After filling is set and just before serving, whip remaining ½ cup of cream, slice other banana, and grate chocolate. Decorate pie with cream, banana, and chocolate shavings.

Milt Stevens
NSO Member

Butterscotch Pie

Serves 8

2   eggs, separated
1   cup dark brown
    sugar
½   teaspoon salt
4   tablespoons flour
1½ cups milk
4   tablespoons butter

1   teaspoon vanilla
4   tablespoons sugar for
    meringue
1   cup pecans, optional
1   cup coconut, optional
1   large pre-baked pie
    shell

Separate eggs and reserve whites for meringue.

Combine beaten egg yolks, brown sugar, salt, flour, milk, and butter. Cook over water *on low* heat, stirring constantly until thick. This takes time.

Add vanilla and nuts (and coconut if desired) and pour into baked pie shell. Cool filling completely before topping with meringue, made from egg whites and 4 tablespoons sugar. Bake meringue at 425° until golden brown, as in Baked Alaska.

Mrs. Juanita Grubbs

Italian Cheese Pie

Serves 6 to 8

CRUST
10–12 graham crackers
 4 tablespoons butter, softened

PIE
 8 ounces ricotta cheese
 8 ounces cream cheese
 2 tablespoons sour cream
 2 eggs
 ¾ cup sugar
 1 cup chocolate chips, chopped
 ½ cup toasted almonds, slivered or sliced
 2 tablespoons lemon juice
 1 teaspoon vanilla

TOPPING
 ½ pint sour cream
 1 tablespoon lemon juice
 2 tablespoons sugar
 1 teaspoon vanilla
 Cinnamon sugar

Crush graham crackers and mix with butter. Use mixture to line a 10-inch pie plate.

Mix ricotta and cream cheese. Add eggs, sugar, sour cream, vanilla, and lemon juice. Mix well and fold in chocolate chips and almonds. Pour into crust and place in a 375° oven for 20 minutes.

While pie is baking, make topping. Mix sour cream, sugar, vanilla, and lemon juice.

Remove pie from oven and set oven at 450°. Pour topping over pie and sprinkle with cinnamon sugar. After oven reaches 450°, return pie to oven for another 4 minutes.

Cool and refrigerate

David Bragunier
NSO member

Chocolate Pie Harbison

Serves 8 to 12

This is not a cream pie but rather similar to a pecan pie in texture, with a "crust" on top.

3 cups brown sugar, lightly packed
½ cup butter
3 eggs
1 teaspoon vanilla
½ cup light cream or evaporated milk
1 square chocolate (unsweetened), melted
1 unbaked 9- or 10-inch pie shell

Cream butter and sugar. Add eggs and vanilla; beat. Add cream and mix. Add chocolate. Pour into shell.
Bake at 350° for 30 minutes, then at 250° for 50 minutes. Serve chilled with whipped cream.

*Kenneth Harbison, NSO Member &
Marie Harbison*

Grandmother's Lemon Pie

Serves 12

CRUST
¼ pound butter
3-ounce package cream cheese
1 cup flour

FILLING
8 eggs, separated
Pinch of salt
Juice of 4 lemons
¾ cup sugar
Rind of 2 lemons
1 tablespoon flour
½ cup superfine sugar
½ teaspoon baking powder
Small lump of butter

PIE CRUST

Mix ingredients together; roll out to fit a 10-inch pie plate; line and bake in a 425° oven for about 12 to 15 minutes or until golden brown. If crust starts to burn around edges, turn heat down to 375° to 350°.

FILLING

Beat egg yolks until thick and light. Add salt, sugar, flour, juice, rind of lemons and small lump of butter. Place in top of a double boiler. Cook until very, very thick and mixture coats a spoon. Let it cool.
While mixture is cooling, beat egg whites until stiff but not dry; add superfine sugar and baking powder. Fold ½ of egg-white mixture into cooled, lemon filling; put into crust. Put balance of egg white mixture on top of pie; cover all crust. Bake in a hot (450°) oven until golden brown.

Mrs. Theodore L. Kaye

Mincemeat Pie

Serves 6 to 8

4 small or 3 large
  apples, cored and
  diced (not peeled)
1½ cups raisins or
  currants
4 ounces candied
  citron
1 lemon, grated peel
  and juice
⅓ cup apple juice

⅓ cup brown sugar
½ cup ground beef
¼ teaspoon each salt,
  cloves, ginger,
  allspice
½ teaspoon each
  cinnamon, nutmeg
¼ cup each rum and
  brandy, or to taste
Pie dough for 9-inch
  double shell

Combine all ingredients except rum and brandy. Simmer for 1 hour, adding water if necessary. Add spirits during last 15 minutes.

Chill in refrigerator for at least 1 day. Pour into 9-inch unbaked pie shell, add top crust and bake in a 400° oven for 30 to 40 minutes.

David Whaley
NSO Member

Peach Pie with Mint

Serves 6

Pastry for 9-inch
  double crust pie
4 cups sliced, peeled,
  ripe peaches
1 tablespoon Amaretto
1 tablespoon lemon
  juice
¼ cup sugar
2 tablespoons
  cornstarch
2 teaspoons chopped,
  fresh mint
1 egg, separated

Combine peaches, Amaretto, and lemon juice. Mix 3 tablespoons sugar, cornstarch, and mint in food processor. Mix mint-mixture with peaches.

Brush bottom crust with egg white. Fill pie with peaches. Use lattice top. Brush with beaten egg yolk. Sprinkle 1 tablespoon sugar over pie.

Bake at 350° for 45 minutes until golden brown and bubbly.

Cookbook Committee

Pineapple Whip Pie

Serves 8

1 graham cracker crust
1 can (20 ounces) crushed
   pineapple, drained
1 cup heavy cream,
   whipped
1 can sweetened
   condensed milk
5 tablespoons lemon
   juice

Mix pineapple, whipped cream, condensed milk, and lemon juice together. Pour into pie crust. Refrigerate for several hours before serving.

For variety, substitute one package of frozen raspberries, drained, for pineapple.

Excellent as a warm weather dessert.

Kit Ryan

Strawberry–Rhubarb Pie

Serves 6 to 8

Pastry for 9-inch
   double crust pie
3 cups sliced rhubarb
1 cup fresh, sliced
   strawberries
1 cup sugar
3 tablespoons flour

Line a 9-inch pie pan with pastry. Combine rhubarb, strawberries, sugar and flour. Pour into pie pan. Cover with top crust, making several slits for steam to escape. Bake at 350° in preheated oven for 35 to 40 minutes.

Howard B. Mitchell,
NSO Music Director
(1949–1969)

Apricot Tart

Serves 6 to 8

DOUGH
¼ pound butter
¼ cup sugar
⅓ cup light brown
sugar
1½ cups flour
¼ teaspoon salt
½ teaspoon baking
powder
1 egg yolk
2 tablespoons milk
1 teaspoon grated
lemon rind

FILLING
(for 2, 9-inch tarts)
6-ounce package dried
apricots
17-ounce can apricot
halves
½ cup sugar
Juice of half a lemon

Put dried apricots in small saucepan. Cover with water until fruit is just covered. Bring to a boil; then simmer 20 minutes or until tender. Add sugar and stir 5 minutes.

Blend canned and cooked apricots just until smooth. Do not use all canned juice at once; filling should not be runny. Add lemon juice.

Cream butter and sugars. Add yolk and milk, plus lemon rind. Fold in flour mixture. Rest dough for 30 minutes in refrigerator.

Roll two thirds of dough to about ⅛-inch thickness.

Fit into greased and lightly floured tart pan. Fill with half of above filling.

Roll out remaining dough on well-floured surface. Cut into strips. Lay them on top of filling in lattice fashion. Brush with egg yolk thinned with 1 tablespoon cream. Sprinkle with granulated sugar.

Bake in a 350° oven for about 30 minutes.

Tart can be prepared fully for 2 to 3 days before baking. Keep it well covered, refrigerated. Brush with egg and sugar just before baking.

Mia Rojas

Fresh Blueberry Tart

Serves 10 to 12

10–12-inch partially-baked, sweet, short pastry shell
8 ounces cream cheese, softened
½ cup sugar
2 eggs
½ cup chopped pecans
1 teaspoon vanilla
2 pints blueberries
10-ounce jar blackberry jelly
1 tablespoon water
Whipped cream

PASTRY SHELL
2 cups sifted, all-purpose flour
2 tablespoons sugar
⅛ teaspoon salt
8 tablespoons chilled butter
3 tablespoons vegetable shortening
5–6 tablespoons cold water

Prepare and pre-bake pastry.

Blend cream cheese and sugar; add eggs and beat well. Add nuts and vanilla. Pour into partially-baked crust and bake at 350° for 10 minutes or until lightly browned around edges. Cool.

Spread blueberries over cheese layer and cover with glaze made of combining jelly and water and melting over low heat. Chill tart. Top with dollops of whipped cream before serving.

PASTRY

Make pastry in a food processor; mix dry ingredients first, then cut butter into flour, and lastly, add water. Chill dough 1 hour in freezer or 2 hours in refrigerator. Mold in false-bottom tart pan.

Once you are ready to bake dough, line pastry with light-weight foil. Weight it with a handful of dry beans to keep sides of pastry shell from collapsing and bottom from puffing up. Preheat oven to 400°.

Bake at middle level of oven for about 9 minutes until pastry is set. Remove foil and beans. Fill with cream cheese mixture and bake as instructed.

Jacqueline Anderson
NSO Member

Hazelnut Fruit Tart

Serves 8

2 cups flour
2 tablespoons sugar
¼ teaspoon salt
4 ounces unsalted butter
1 large egg
1 tablespoon cold water
4 ounces ground,
    toasted hazelnuts
1 tablespoon egg white
2 tablespoons sugar
12 ounces cream cheese
⅔ cup sugar
1 teaspoon vanilla
    Seasonal fruits, as
    needed
¾ cup apple jelly,
    melted
¼ cup ground, toasted
    hazelnuts

Preheat oven to 400°. Combine flour, 2 tablespoons sugar, and salt. Crumble butter into flour mixture. Stir in egg and water. Blend in 4 ounces hazelnuts and refrigerate 1 hour.

Roll out dough and pat into 14-inch tart pan. Brush with egg white and sprinkle with sugar. Bake at 400° for 20 minutes. Let cool; flip shell out of pan.

For filling, beat cream cheese, ⅔ cup sugar and vanilla until smooth and no lumps remain. Place filling on fruit tart shell and spread to edges. Place fruit in concentric circles on top of cream cheese. Brush melted apple jelly over fruits as glaze. Cover circle edge of tart with ¼ cup hazelnuts.

Refrigerate for at least 30 minutes before serving.

The Pleasant Peasant Restaurant

Plum Tart with Almond Cream Base

Serves 8

1½–2 pounds Italian prunes (plums)
1½ cups flour
¼ teaspoon baking powder
½ cup butter, frozen, if using food processor
1 egg
⅓ cup sugar
Dash salt
¼ cup cinnamon-sugar
Peel of 1 orange or lemon, grated, optional

ALMOND CREAM
¾ cup blanched almonds, pulverized
⅓ cup sugar
1 egg
2 tablespoons butter
¼ teaspoon almond extract

Sift flour and baking powder together; blend in butter. Beat egg separately; then add sugar, salt and beat. Add this to flour and make dough. Dough may be refrigerated for later use or it can be spread immediately into a 10-inch false-bottom tart pan.

Blend almond cream ingredients in food processor. Spread evenly into unbaked tart shell. Place plums circularly over almond cream and then sprinkle top with about ¼ cup cinnamon sugar. You may also want to add lemon peel.

Bake tart at 400° for 15 minutes; lower temperature to 350° and bake 40 minutes longer. Cool. When pastry shrinks from sides of pan, lift out. Serve at room temperature; refrigerate otherwise.

Tart may be made without almond base. If so, add ½ cup cinnamon-sugar on top to offset tartness of plums. May be served with sweetened whipped cream.

Cookbook Committee

Crepia aux Pommes

Serves 6

8 apples
6 whole eggs
1 cup milk
¼ cup sugar
2 tablespoons flour
6 tablespoons butter
Apple jack liqueur

Peel, core and slice apples very thin. Sauté rapidly in butter.

In a bowl, mix together flour, sugar, and milk. Add eggs and blend to an even consistency.

Pour a thin layer of flour mixture into a hot, buttered crêpe pan. Next lay apples over flour mixture in pan as if on a tarte. Cover apples with another thin layer of mixture.

Place pan in a preheated 450° oven for 5 minutes.

Remove from oven and slide on to plate. Flambé with apple jack.

Chef Garard Vettraino
Jean-Pierre Restaurant

Palacsinta
Apricot Pancakes

Serves 6

3 eggs
1 cup milk
⅓ cup club soda, freshly opened
1 cup sifted flour
3 tablespoons granulated sugar
¼ teaspoon salt
1 teaspoon vanilla
4 tablespoons butter
¾ cup apricot jam
1 cup ground walnuts or filberts
Confectioners sugar

Beat eggs lightly with milk in a large mixing bowl. Combine with club soda. With a wooden spoon, stir in flour and sugar; then add salt and vanilla. Continue to stir until batter is smooth.

Melt 1 teaspoon butter in an 8-inch skillet until hot. Ladle in enough batter to cover bottom of skillet thickly and tilt skillet from side to side to spread batter evenly. Cook until lightly browned on one side; then turn and brown lightly on other.

Spread 2 teaspoons of jam over pancake and roll it up loosely. Put it in a baking dish in a 200° oven to keep warm until all pancakes are rolled up. Serve warm as a dessert, sprinkled with nuts and confectioners sugar.

Bèla Màrtay
Former NSO Member

Pumpkin Strudel

Makes 3 strudels

14 ounces phyllo
1 cup oil
1½ pounds grated
   pumpkin
1 cup sugar mixed with
   cinnamon

1 cup bread crumbs
Confectioners sugar
Vanilla

Using 6 sheets of phyllo, place first sheet on a small tablecloth or tea towel and brush lightly with oil. Repeat this process until all 6 pastry sheets have been placed on top of each other. Then sprinkle grated pumpkin, some cinnamon-sugar, and bread crumbs on top.

Roll and place in a well-greased baking pan. Repeat this process until all pastry leaves and ingredients are used. Bake in a 375° oven for 35 to 45 minutes, or until golden brown.

Cut into individual, bite-size pieces. Dust with confectioners sugar and vanilla.

Mrs. Janja Loncar
Wife of the Ambassador of Yugoslavia

Fresh Strawberry or Raspberry Sherbet

Serves 4 to 6

1 quart fresh
   strawberries or
   raspberries
2 egg whites
½ cup superfine sugar
¼ cup lemon juice

Clean berries and purée in blender or food mill. Beat egg whites until they form soft peaks.

Beat sugar and lemon juice into berries and beat several seconds to dissolve sugar completely. Whip in beaten egg whites and freeze, covered with plastic wrap, in a bowl or in ice cube trays.

Freeze for 1 to 2 hours until partially set, scrape into a mixing bowl and beat with an electric mixer to increase volume. Cover and freeze again for about 1 hour; then beat again. Cover and freeze again for several hours before serving.

This can be made days ahead of serving; however, allow mixture to soften to a nice consistency in the bottom of the refrigerator, about ½ hour, before serving.

This is very nice to fill cookie cups and garnish each with a fresh berry.

Mrs. Harry E. Gould, Jr.

Grapefruit Sherbert

Serves 8 to 10

2 cups sugar
4 cups water
2 cups fresh grapefruit
   juice (about 3–4
   grapefruits)
Zest of 2 grapefruits
Vodka or Crème de
   Cassis (optional)

Heat sugar and water to dissolve sugar. Add grapefruit juice and zest. Pour into a metal bowl and freeze. Process the frozen mixture in a food processor and either serve or refreeze. This should always be reprocessed right before serving or it is too hard.

Serve in sherbert glasses with a tablespoon of vodka or Crème de Cassis over each serving.

This may be made with lemons, limes (12 to 16 of each), or with oranges (10).

If used as an Intermezzo, cut down on amount of sugar.

Serve with slices of kiwi fruit as alternate to vodka or Crème de Cassis.

Cookbook Committee

Green Grape Delight

Serves 6 to 8

2 pounds fresh,
   seedless, green
   grapes
1 cup sour cream
2–3 tablespoons dark
   brown sugar

Wash and drain grapes. Stir in sour cream. Top with brown sugar.

VARIATION

This can be made with strawberries, blueberries, or any fresh fruit. It is easy and refreshing.

Anne Keiser

Florida Favorite Dessert

Serves 8

1½ pounds green
         seedless grapes
1 cup brandy
1 cup honey
1½ teaspoons lemon
         juice
3 tablespoons
         confectioners sugar
1 cup sour cream

Wash, stem, and dry grapes. Place in deep bowl. Mix brandy, honey, lemon juice, and sugar. Pour over grapes. Chill at least 5 hours. Serve in small bowls, juice and all, with a dollop of sour cream.

Marie P. Hombs

Spiced Amber Apples

Serves 6 to 8

2 pounds eating apples
1 cup water
1 cup sugar
1 teaspoon grated
         lemon peel
1½ teaspoons cinnamon
         Juice of ½ lemon
2 cloves, crushed
         Whipped cream
1 tablespoon sugar
1 teaspoon cinnamon
         or 1 tablespoon rum

Peel and slice apples; combine all ingredients in a heavy saucepan. Bring to a boil, cover, and simmer for 1¼ to 1½ hours until apples are amber-colored and transparent.

Pour into a round mold and leave to set in refrigerator for at least 3 hours (overnight is better).

Dip mold in very hot water. Turn out apple pudding and cover with whipped cream sweetened with 1 tablespoon sugar and flavored with cinnamon *or* rum.

Jeananne Petrus

Pêches au Vin de Bordeaux

Serves 4 to 6

6 large, ripe peaches
4 cups red Bordeaux
1 pound granulated sugar
4 tablespoons Cognac

Boil enough water to cover peaches. Drop peaches in boiling water for 1 minute. Drain, cool, and peel.

Boil red Bordeaux and sugar for 5 minutes in a deep saucepan. Drop peaches in this red wine syrup. Simmer for 5 minutes or until tender. Remove fruits. Put them in a jar. Heat syrup to 230° and cool thoroughly. To each cup of syrup add 1 tablespoon Cognac. Fill jar to top until fruits are well covered.

Place jar in refrigerator. Serve peaches chilled and in syrup or garnished with whipped cream or scoops of vanilla ice cream.

Peaches will taste much better if they macerate in their syrup for about a week in the refrigerator.

Embassy of France

Apricot Mold

Serves 8 to 10

1 large or 2 small packages apricot jello
1¼ cups boiling water
2 1-pound cans peeled apricots (1 extra can for garnish)
½ pint sour cream
1 pint vanilla ice cream

Dissolve jello in 1¼ cups hot water. Add liquid from 1 can of apricots to jello. Refrigerate about ½ hour.

Drain apricots. Purée half of apricots in a blender with sour cream and ice cream. Add mixture to jello.

Place remaining apricot halves in a 6½-cup mold which has been greased with oil. Pour in mixture and refrigerate until set.

Unmold and garnish with additional apricot halves (and parsley if using as a salad).

Jane Lehrman

Crema Española
Spanish Cream
Egg Custard

Serves 4

1 quart plus ¼ cup fresh whole milk
½ cup sugar
2 cinnamon sticks
3 inches vanilla bean, cut lengthwise
4–6 egg yolks
½ teaspoon lemon rind
3 heaping tablespoons corn starch
½ teaspoon powdered cinnamon

In a heavy 2-quart saucepan heat 1 quart milk, sugar, cinnamon sticks, vanilla bean, egg yolks and lemon rind.

In a small bowl mix starch and ¼ cup milk until smooth and free of lumps. Pour starch mixture very slowly into heating milk while stirring. Continue to stir over medium-high heat until custard begins to thicken. Reduce heat and continue stirring (until about consistency of condensed milk).

Remove from heat. Let stand uncovered for about ½ hour before placing in refrigerator to chill (3 hours). Sprinkle powdered cinnamon over custard. Serve with pirouettes or vanilla wafers.

Clemencia Sanchez

Chestnut Mousse

Serves 6 to 8

15½-ounce can
  unsweetened chestnut
  purée
2 cups milk
8 tablespoons sugar
1 envelope unflavored
  gelatin, softened
1 teaspoon vanilla
6 egg yolks
3 tablespoons Grand
  Marnier
1 cup heavy cream
2 cups Crème Anglais

In blender blend chestnut purée with milk. Add sugar. Put mixture in pot. Beat with a wire whisk until smooth. Add gelatin, bring to a boil and stir in vanilla.

Beat egg yolks in a mixing bowl and beat in a little of hot sauce. Take pan off stove and add egg yolk mixture to hot sauce, stirring rapidly. Return pan to low heat and stir until mixture thickens slightly. Do not boil. Stir in liqueur.

Strain mixture through a sieve into mixing bowl and let cool but not set. Whip cream and fold into mousse mixture. Pour into lightly oiled 1½-quart mold and refrigerate several hours or overnight. Serve with Crème Anglais, found in most cook books, or whipped cream on the side.

Michael Phillips

Mousseline au Chocolat

Serves 6 to 8

6 ounces semi-sweet baking chocolate (1 cup chocolate chips)
4 tablespoons strong coffee
4 egg yolks
¾ cup superfine sugar
¼ cup orange liqueur, rum, Benedictine, or strong coffee
6 ounces softened, unsalted butter
4 egg whites
Pinch of salt
2 tablespoons finely granulated sugar

Stir chocolate and coffee in a small saucepan over hot water. When partially melted, set chocolate aside in its pan of water, stirring occasionally.

Beat egg yolks and sugar until they are thick, pale, and form a ribbon. Beat in liqueur or coffee. Set bowl over pan of simmering water and beat until foamy and almost too hot for your finger. Set bowl over cold water and continue beating until mixture is cool and again forms ribbons. It should be consistency of mayonnaise.

Stir chocolate again until perfectly smooth. Gradually beat in softened butter. Beat chocolate and butter into egg yolk mixture. Beat egg whites and salt until soft peaks form; sprinkle on sugar and beat until stiff peaks form. Stir one quarter of beaten egg whites into chocolate mixture; delicately fold in rest of egg whites.

Turn into a bowl, or individual serving cups. Chill several hours or overnight.

Mrs. David R. Williams, Jr.

Mme. Depagne's Bittersweet Chocolate Mousse

Serves 8

"This recipe comes from my landlady in Paris where I was a student. It can be made with sweeter chocolate, if desired."

¼ pound sweet butter
6 large eggs
6 ounces bittersweet chocolate

Melt butter and chocolate on top of double boiler. Separate eggs. Beat egg whites until peaks form. Set aside. Add egg yolks to melted butter and chocolate. Mix well. Fold chocolate mixture into egg whites. Spoon into dessert dishes and chill. May be topped with whipped cream.

Alice Kogan Weinreb
NSO Member

White Chocolate Mousse

Serves 12 to 16

This is a recipe for the experienced cook!

3 ounces (⅓ cup) skinned, toasted hazelnuts
⅓ cup skinned, toasted almonds
½ cup sugar
5 egg whites
   Pinch of salt
3 ounces (⅓ cup) sugar
1 pound white chocolate
1 quart heavy cream
1 drop vanilla

To make praline, crush coarsely hazelnuts and almonds. Caramelize ⅓ cup sugar and combine with nuts. Pour onto oiled marble slab. Wait 1 hour and then crush praline coarsely.

Grate chocolate.

Whip egg whites and pinch of salt until firm. Immediately add second ⅓ cup sugar (that has been cooked to hard crack stage) to egg whites. Keep beating (don't worry if it deflates). Add chocolate and put bowl over boiling water to melt chocolate.

Whip cream with vanilla until thick. Pour egg white mixture over cream and fold with rubber spatula. When blended, add crushed praline. Pour into serving bowl and refrigerate 6 hours before serving.

Chef Yannick Cam
Le Pavillon Restaurant

Easy Lemon Mousse

Serves 4 to 6

5 eggs
2 lemons
1 teaspoon lemon rind, grated
½ cup sugar
1 cup whipping cream

Separate eggs; beat yolks with sugar until fluffy. Add juice of 2 lemons and 1 teaspoon grated rind to yolks. Heat over hot water (double boiler). Stir until thick. Cool.

Beat egg whites. Beat whipped cream separately. Fold egg mixture into whipped cream. Fold egg whites into all of above. Chill 4 hours.

Kathy Butler Phelan

Mousse de Pruneau à l'Armagnac

Makes 2 quarts of ice cream

1 pound dried prunes,
   preferably sour
2 cups milk
1 vanilla bean split
   down middle or 1
   teaspoon vanilla
   extract
12 egg yolks
⅓ cup granulated sugar
⅔ cup light corn syrup
2 cups heavy cream
   Armagnac

Marinate prunes in Armagnac to cover for at least 2 weeks, adding more Armagnac as required.

Prepare ice cream one day in advance of serving. In a small saucepan, heat milk with vanilla bean; remove from heat. Lift out vanilla bean; scrape seeds into milk, discard shell and set vanilla-flavored hot milk aside, covered.

In heavy-bottomed, 3-quart saucepan, whisk together egg yolks, sugar and a pinch of salt until pale yellow and creamy. Gradually add hot milk in a steady stream, whisking constantly. Add corn syrup; slowly heat, stirring with a wooden spoon, until mixture thickens sufficiently, registering about 175°. Do not allow to boil. Remove from heat; strain through fine sieve into chilled mixing bowl to stop cooking. Cool. Stir in heavy cream. Cover with plastic wrap and chill about 2 hours.

Pour mixture into container of an electric or hand-operated ice cream churner and freeze until mush, operating machine according to manufacturer's directions.

Remove prunes from Armagnac and pit them; reserve Armagnac. In work bowl of a food processor fitted with the metal blade, process prunes for 10 seconds, or until well chopped. When ice cream is half frozen, add chopped prunes and ¼ cup of Armagnac. (The remaining Armagnac will be used as a syrup to be served with ice cream.)

Pack ice cream into a 2-quart ice cream mold and freeze until hard, preferably overnight.

One-half hour before serving, transfer ice cream to refrigerator compartment to soften slightly. Invert onto a serving plate. To help loosen ice cream, soak a kitchen cloth in hot water, wring out and wrap around mold. If necessary, tap mold lightly with your fingers and shake it to loosen. If surface needs a little patching up, smooth it with a spatula dipped in hot water. Return ice cream to freezer for 5 minutes to firm up. Serve each portion with a drizzle of remaining Armagnac.

Albert J. Beveridge, III

Maple Syrup Mousse

Serves 6 to 8

1 envelope plus 2 teaspoons unflavored gelatin
½ cup water
1 cup pure maple syrup
4 egg yolks
½ cup dark brown sugar
4 egg whites
2 cups chilled heavy cream (60% butterfat, optional)

OPTIONAL
¼ cup kahlua and
¼ cup water for
½ cup water

This mousse is not as sweet as you may think, and it tastes like coffee mousse!

Sprinkle gelatin into ½ cup of cold water. Let it soften for about 5 minutes. Set cup in a shallow pan of simmering water and stir until gelatin has dissolved and is clear. Combine with maple syrup. In a large mixing bowl, beat egg yolks with a whisk or beater for 2 or 3 minutes until thick and lemon yellow.

Beat into yolks maple syrup mixture and pour into a small saucepan. Cook over moderate heat, stirring constantly, until mixture thickens enough to coat spoon heavily. Do not let it boil or eggs will curdle. Remove from heat, stir in brown sugar and mix thoroughly. Transfer to a large bowl and cool to room temperature.

Meanwhile, beat egg whites until they form firm peaks. In another bowl, whip chilled cream until it holds its shape softly. With a rubber spatula, fold cream gently but thoroughly into maple syrup mixture; then fold in egg whites, folding until streaks of white no longer show.

Rinse a 1½-quart mold, preferably a charlotte mold, in cold water. Shake out excess water and pour in mousse mixture. Chill in refrigerator for at least 4 hours, or until firm.

To unmold, run a knife around inside edge of mold, dip bottom briefly in hot water and wipe it dry. Place a chilled platter on top of mold, invert and rap it on the table. Chill until ready to serve. Decorate with whipped cream and chocolate curls, if desired.

Barry E. Huber

Pudding de Noël
Christmas Pudding

Serves 10

1½ cups currants
1½ cups seedless white raisins
Fresh white breadcrumbs, using 3 slices bread
½ generous cup flour, sifted
½ cup brown sugar
1 medium carrot, grated
½ scant cup walnuts, chopped
⅓ cup candied orange peel, diced
⅓ cup candied lemon peel, diced
1 teaspoon bitter almonds, chopped (or regular almonds may be used)
½ teaspoon salt
Mixed spices: ginger, cinnamon, cloves, nutmeg (¼ teaspoon each)
2½ ounces beef suet
2 eggs, lightly beaten
Scant ½ pint beer
Scant ½ pint brandy

Plum puddings should be prepared well in advance. In the old days they were prepared almost a year ahead.

Thoroughly mix all dry ingredients. Add beef suet, eggs, beer and brandy. Cover bowl and let it stand in a cool place for 2 days.

Mix again and pour into a buttered pudding mold. Cover with a piece of greaseproof paper or foil. Tie a large cloth over this, laying cloth flat over top of basin, tying it around rim with string, and then tying ends over top in a knot. Boil or steam pudding in a large covered pan of boiling water for 6 hours.

Remove and allow to cool. When pudding is completely cold, wrap mold in foil. Keep in a cool place until needed.

Before serving, boil or steam for another 3 hours. Unmold onto a deep heated dish. Heat ⅓ pint brandy, pour it over pudding and set alight before serving.

At Christmas, place a sprig of holly in the center of the pudding. The chef also puts holly round the dish and this increases the flames around the pudding. We serve the pudding with brandy butter at Christmas time and with vanilla ice cream added to a cold pudding in the summer.

Lady Henderson
Wife of the Ambassador of Great Britain

Ballinaclough Pudding and Sauce

Serves 6

PUDDING
- 1-pound jar mincement
- 2 eggs
- A little milk
- Scant ½ cup coarsely ground bread crumbs
- Scant 1 cup self-rising flour

SAUCE
- 2 tablespoons flour
- 1 tablespoon butter
- 1 cup milk
- 2 teaspoons sugar
- 1 tablespoon Irish (or Scotch) whiskey

PUDDING

Mix all pudding ingredients together to a soft consistency. Pour into a greased bowl about ⅔ full; cover with lid or foil. Stand on rack in an inch of boiling water in a pot with a tight lid. Steam 2 hours, adding more boiling water if necessary.

SAUCE

Heat butter, add flour and cook, stirring well until mixture is dry and sandy. Do not brown. Remove from heat and gradually stir in milk and sugar. Return to heat. Bring to a boil, stirring all the time and boil for 5 minutes. Flavor with whiskey.

Serve sauce over the steamed pudding.

Carol O'Colmain

Green Pawpaw Pudding

Papaya Pudding

Serves 6

3 tablespoons self-rising flour
2 tablespoons sugar
1 tablespoon butter
1 tablespoon oil
1 egg, beaten until it is thick
⅓ cup milk
Rind of ½ lemon, grated
Ground cinnamon, to taste

GREEN PAPAYA FILLING
1 medium size green papaya (apples may be substituted)
Juice of 1 lemon
Sugar to taste
A few cloves
1 stick cinnamon

Beat sugar, butter and oil. Add beaten egg little by little, then flour, mixing alternately with milk and lemon rind. Cover base of pie dish or loaf pan with green papaya filling (see directions below). Sprinkle filling with a little cinnamon, sugar and a few small pieces of butter. Bake at 350° for 20 minutes, or until firm and nicely browned. Serve with fresh cream or custard.

GREEN PAPAYA FILLING

Peel and cut papaya into small pieces. Boil with cloves and cinnamon and a small piece of lemon peel until soft enough to break with a fork, but not soft enough to be mashed. Remove remaining water, break papaya with a fork. Add lemon juice first, then papaya with a fork and then sugar to taste. Let papaya filling simmer for a while. Keep in a cool place and use as required. May be kept in freezer.

Mrs. C. Melamu
Wife of the Ambassador of Botswana

Soufflé-Orange and Chocolate

Serves 4

PASTRY CREAM
- 2 cups milk
- 3 eggs
- 1 egg yolk
- ½ cup sugar
- ¾ cup flour

SOUFFLE
- 2 cups pastry cream
- 3 egg yolks
- 5 egg whites

FOR CHOCOLATE SOUFFLE

Vanilla Sauce
- 1 cup milk
- 1 vanilla bean
- 4 egg yolks
- ¼ cup sugar

Chocolate
- 5 tablespoons melted chocolate

FOR ORANGE SOUFFLE

- 2 tablespoons candied orange rind
- 3 tablespoons Cointreau
  Orange sections

Apricot liqueur
Cognac
Confectioners sugar

PASTRY CREAM

Bring milk to boil. Mix eggs and sugar until smooth. Add flour and mix until smooth. Pour boiling milk into mixture. While mixing put back on stove and boil again, stirring constantly.

Souffle

Add egg yolks to pastry cream and heat. Whip egg whites until stiff and add 2 tablespoons sugar. For orange soufflé add orange rind and Cointreau to pastry cream. For chocolate soufflé add melted chocolate to pastry cream. Add one quarter of egg white and mix well. Fold in rest of egg whites. Butter and coat your soufflé dish with sugar. Pour soufflé into dish (for orange, add fresh orange section). Fill to top and smooth with a spatula. Bake in a 375° oven for 20 minutes.

FOR CHOCOLATE SOUFFLE

Boil milk with vanilla bean. Mix egg yolks and sugar. Pour boiling milk over mixture. Mix well, put back on stove and cook until it thickens without boiling. Add 2 tablespoons Cognac.

FOR ORANGE SOUFFLE

Sprinkle with confectioners sugar. For decoration place a few orange sections and candied orange rinds around. Flambé with Cointreau and serve.

For apricot sauce, whip cream mixed with apricot glaze and apricot liqueur.

Chef Jean-Pierre Goyenvalle
Le Lion d'Or Restaurant

Orange Marmalade Soufflé

Serves 4 to 5

4 egg whites
4 tablespoons sugar
4 tablespoons orange marmalade
4 egg yolks
½ cup confectioners sugar
1 jigger rum (2 ounces)
1 cup whipped cream

Beat egg whites until stiff. Add sugar. Fold marmalade into mixture. Generously butter top of a 2-quart double boiler and sprinkle with sugar. Put mixture in pan when water is boiling rapidly. Do not let water touch bottom of pan or evaporate completely. Put lid on pan. Simmer gently 1 hour. Do not remove lid. Turn onto a platter when done.

SAUCE

Beat yolks well. Add sugar, rum, and whipped cream. Pour a little sauce on top of unmolded soufflé. Serve rest in a sauce bowl. Sauce can be prepared a few hours before and refrigerated.

Juliet P. Hart

Prepare-Ahead Chocolate Soufflé

Serves 8

5 egg yolks
¾ cup sugar
4 drops vanilla
1 cup unbleached flour
2 cups milk
2 ounces unsweetened
     chocolate, melted
8 egg whites
   Confectioners sugar
½ pint heavy cream,
     whipped

In a bowl beat yolks with ½ cup sugar and vanilla until light and fluffy. Gradually beat in flour until a paste is formed.

Meanwhile, bring milk to boil. Add egg mixture all at once and bring again to boil, beating vigorously with wire whisk until paste is smooth. Continue stirring with wooden spoon until mixture is thick, like a pasty cream. Add melted chocolate and stir until blended. Cool.

Beat egg whites until soft peaks form; gradually beat in remaining ¼ cup sugar until stiff peaks form. Fold egg whites into batter. Cover bowl lightly and allow to sit at room temperature for up to 4 hours before serving.

To serve, spoon into 8, greased, individual, 2-inch, soufflé dishes and bake at 350° for 20 minutes. Dust with confectioners sugar and serve with whipped cream on the side.

Marian Burros

Chocolate Soufflé with Crème de Cacao

Serves 8 to 10

2 envelopes unflavored gelatin	8 egg yolks
½ cup water	8 egg whites
⅔ cup Crème de Cacao	½ teaspoon salt
1¼ cups brown sugar	2 cups heavy cream, whipped
12-ounce package chocolate chips, chopped fine	½ cup chopped pecans or almonds

In a saucepan mix gelatin, water, ½ cup sugar and Crème de Cacao. Place over low heat. Stir constantly until all is well dissolved and mixed. Add chocolate chips and stir until they melt. Remove from heat and stir in egg yolks one at a time, beating after each addition. Cool.

Beat egg whites with a pinch of salt until stiff peaks form. Gradually beat in remaining brown sugar until very stiff. Fold egg whites into gelatin mixture with a spatula or wire whisk. Fold in whipped cream.

Add a 2-inch paper collar to your 2-quart soufflé dish by tying it on with string. Pile mixture into dish and slightly mound top. Chill for several hours or overnight. Sprinkle with chopped nuts and serve. If desired, whipped cream can be piped through a pastry bag fitted with a star tube as added decoration.

Linda Taylor

Blintz Soufflé

Serves 4 to 6

12 uncooked blintzes
½ cup melted butter
6 eggs
2 cups sour cream
2 teaspoons vanilla
4 tablespoons orange juice
2 tablespoons sugar
½ teaspoon salt

Place blintzes in casserole. Pour butter on top. Combine remaining ingredients one at a time with wire whisk. Pour over blintzes. Bake 1 hour at 350° uncovered.

Louise Cohen

Mohr im Hemd
Austrian Steamed Pudding

Serves 4

½ cup butter, room
  temperature
4 ounces baking
  chocolate
½ cup sugar
1 cup finely chopped
  almonds
¾ cup white bread
  crumbs
¼ cup all-purpose flour
4 eggs, separated

CHOCOLATE SAUCE
2 ounces unsweetened
  chocolate
6 tablespoons water
½ cup sugar
  Dash salt
3 tablespoons unsalted
  butter
¼ teaspoon vanilla

Melt chocolate in double boiler. Add chocolate to butter and sugar; blend until fluffy. Add egg yolks, one at a time, beating 1 minute after each addition. Add almonds, bread crumbs, and flour. The mixture will be fairly stiff. Beat egg whites until stiff and shiny. Fold gently into chocolate mixture.

Place batter in greased and sugared cake pan or pudding form and cover with foil. Place pan in a larger pan filled with water. Bake in preheated oven at 350° for about 1 hour. Pudding is done when straw comes out clean. Unmold, decorate with warm chocolate sauce, and serve with whipped cream.

CHOCOLATE SAUCE

Melt chocolate with water over low heat, stirring until smooth. Add sugar and salt; cook until smooth and slightly thickened, stirring constantly. Add butter and vanilla. Stir until blended. Serve warm.

Mrs. Annerose Clausen
Embassy of Austria

Salzburger Nockerl

Serves 6 to 8

6 egg whites
6 tablespoons sugar
  A drop or 2 of vanilla
  or lemon extract,
  optional

4–5 tablespoons flour
3 egg yolks
  Sugar
  Grand Marnier

Beat egg whites until fairly stiff. Add sugar gradually. Add flavoring. Add yolks unbeaten one at a time, folding in thoroughly. Fold in flour. Mix delicately; place in 6 or 8 mounds on buttered, oven-proof platter.

Bake at 400° about 5 minutes until golden. Sprinkle with sugar or slosh with Grand Marnier or similar liqueur. Serve warm.

Paula Jeffries

Chocolate Paxton

Serves 8

2½ packages ladyfingers
1½ cups superfine,
       granulated sugar
½ pound butter.
3 ounces melted bitter
       (unsweetened)
       chocolate
6 egg whites

6 egg yolks
2 teaspoons vanilla
1 cup cream, whipped
1 cup heavy cream,
       whipped and
       sweetened to taste
    Semi-sweet chocolate
       shavings (optional)

Line bottom and sides of a bowl with ladyfingers. (They should extend an inch above sides to create a "crown" appearance.)

Cream sugar with butter. Add melted chocolate and mix well. Beat in egg yolks and vanilla. Gently fold in unsweetened whipped cream and then whipped egg whites.

Pour half of mixture into bowl. Add layer of ladyfingers and then semi-sweet chocolate shavings. Carefully pour remaining mixture over middle layers. Add a topping layer of sweetened whipped cream. Sprinkle with semi-sweet chocolate shavings.

Best if refrigerated 8 hours before serving.

Mrs. Frank Paxton

Wine Jelly Dessert

Serves 6 to 8

1 bottle claret (any
       inexpensive but
       decent red wine)
    Juice and rind of
       1 lemon
1 cup red currant jelly
1 small wine glass of
       brandy
½ pound sugar
1 package unflavored
       gelatin

Boil all ingredients together (except gelatin) for 5 minutes, making sure red currant jelly dissolves completely.

Stir melted gelatin (in a minimum amount of water) into hot mixture and strain into a decorative mold. Chill mold in refrigerator until ready to unmold and serve.

Serve with Crème Chantilly (flavored whipped cream)

Raymond Leppard

Mocha Chip Ice Cream

Makes ½ gallon ice cream

1 pint heavy cream
1 pint light cream (or half-and-half to make it less rich)
1 cup sugar
1 teaspoon vanilla extract
Pinch of salt
4 tablespoons instant coffee (regular or decaffinated)

6 tablespoons cocoa
8 ounces chocolate chips or semi-sweet chocolate cut into small chunks

Refrain from eating it all at once.

Following directions for ice cream maker, combine cream, ¾ cup sugar, vanilla, and salt in canister. Combine coffee, cocoa, and ¼ cup sugar with just enough hot water to make a dissolved paste. Add to ingredients and mix well.

Make ice cream according to directions. Before freezing add chocolate chips or chunks.

Can be served with Kahlua or coffee brandy.

Robert Stein

Fine Chocolate Sauce

Makes 1 cup

5 ounces semi-sweet baking chocolate
1 ounce bitter baking chocolate
4 ounces sweet butter
½ cup finely chopped, freshly shelled walnuts
Vanilla ice cream

Simmer, but do not boil water in bottom of a double boiler. In top half, slowly melt semi-sweet baking chocolate, bitter chocolate and sweet butter; stir gently to blend thoroughly. Do not cover double boiler! Condensation will form on lid, and if it should spill into chocolate, mixture will stiffen and then turn rigid. Stir as you may, the result will be a small chocolate cannonball.

Having avoided catastrophe, you now add walnuts. Stir to blend, and all is ready for pouring over bombes of the finest vanilla ice cream you can lay your hands on.

You can prepare this in the afternoon and serve it, at dinner, over a warming candle.

William A. Marsano

MENUS

BOARD OF DIRECTORS DINNER FOR SIXTEEN

DONATED FOR AN NSO/WGMS RADIOTHON

Fresh Spring Asparagus Vinaigrette

*Soufflé de Poisson a la Florentine, Sauce Mousseline

Filet de Boeuf en Croute

Sauce Madère

*Mousse de Pruneau a l'Armagnac

*Recipe appears in cookbook

FUND RAISING DINNER

PRESENTED BY THE 1789 RESTAURANT

*Agnolotti a la Crema

Bibb, Mushroom, and Endive Salad

Chicken with Leeks or Sole Grenobloise

Vegetable du Jour

*Chocolate Mousse Cake 1789

*Recipe appears in Cookbook

LIGHT SUPPER

BEFORE OR AFTER THE SYMPHONY

*WALNUT BRIE WHEEL

*PUFFED CHICKEN POCKETS

*WILD RICE WITH ALMONDS AND WATERCHESTNUTS

*WATERCRESS, ENDIVE, AND ORANGE SALAD

LEMON MOUSSE

FLORENTINES

*Recipe appears in cookbook

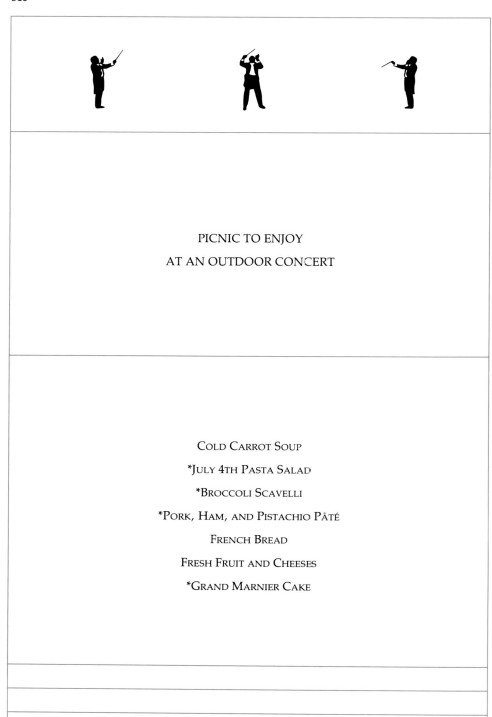

PICNIC TO ENJOY

AT AN OUTDOOR CONCERT

COLD CARROT SOUP

*JULY 4TH PASTA SALAD

*BROCCOLI SCAVELLI

*PORK, HAM, AND PISTACHIO PÂTÉ

FRENCH BREAD

FRESH FRUIT AND CHEESES

*GRAND MARNIER CAKE

*Recipe appears in cookbook

INDEX

I N D E X

(Asterisks in Index mean one-dish meal)

COLOPHON

The National Symphony Orchestra Cookbook is published by FANS—Friends Assisting the National Symphony. Address correspondence to: FANS, The John F. Kennedy Center for the Performing Arts, Washington, D.C. 20566.

Typefaces:
Palatino Semibold, 18, 9 & 8 point
Palatino, 9 point
Palatino Italic, 9 & 8 point
All rules ½ point

Typesetter:
Automated Graphic Systems, Inc.

Paper:
King James Cast Coat, C1S, 18 point & Lustro Gloss, 70 lb.
Ink:
Black & silver

Printer:
Automated Graphic Systems, Inc.

Please send me _____ copies of
THE NATIONAL SYMPHONY ORCHESTRA COOKBOOK
at $11.95 each plus $1.75 handling and postage per copy.

Enclosed is my check or money order for $_____ made payable to
FANS/NSO Cookbook. District of Columbia residents please add 6% sales tax.

NAME: _____

STREET ADDRESS: _____

CITY: _____ STATE: _____ ZIP CODE: _____

MAIL TO: FANS/NSO COOKBOOK
          John F. Kennedy Center for the Performing Arts
          Washington, D.C. 20566

- -

Please send me _____ copies of
THE NATIONAL SYMPHONY ORCHESTRA COOKBOOK
at $11.95 each plus $1.75 handling and postage per copy.

Enclosed is my check or money order for $_____ made payable to
FANS/NSO Cookbook. District of Columbia residents please add 6% sales tax.

NAME: _____

STREET ADDRESS: _____

CITY: _____ STATE: _____ ZIP CODE: _____

MAIL TO: FANS/NSO COOKBOOK
          John F. Kennedy Center for the Performing Arts
          Washington, D.C. 20566

SUGGESTED MERCHANTS WHO MIGHT WANT TO SELL
THE NATIONAL SYMPHONY ORCHESTRA COOKBOOK

NAME: _____
STREET ADDRESS: _____
CITY: _____ STATE: _____ ZIP CODE: _____
AREA CODE: _____ PHONE NUMBER _____

NAME: _____
STREET ADDRESS: _____
CITY: _____ STATE: _____ ZIP CODE: _____
AREA CODE: _____ PHONE NUMBER _____

MAIL TO: FANS/NSO COOKBOOK
          John F. Kennedy Center for the Performing Arts
          Washington, D.C. 20566